My Sad Is All Gone

A Family's Triumph over Violent Autism

Thelma Wheatley

Lucky Press

Lucky Press, LLC
126 S. Maple St.
Lancaster, Ohio 43130
United States
www.luckypress.com

First Edition

Library of Congress Cataloging-in-Publication Data

Wheatley, Thelma.
  My sad is all gone : a family's triumph over violent autism / Thelma Wheatley.--
1st ed.
    p. cm.
  ISBN 0-9760576-0-3 (pbk. : alk. paper)
  1. Orchard, Julian--Mental health. 2. Autistic children--Canada--Biography.
3. Violence in children. I. Title.
RJ506.A9O738 2004
362.198'9285882'0092--dc22

2004020001

Book design: Janice M. Phelps (www.janicephelps.com)
Cover illustration: "The Cat" by Julian Orchard
Author's photo: Taken by Mandy Alexander
Disclaimer:
The information in this book is provided as an insight into the particular challenges, needs, and improvements of one young man and his family. While details regarding therapy and drug treatment are described, this information should not be taken as medical advice, directly or indirectly, nor should it be a substitute for the medical advice of a physician. Readers interested in the medications discussed in this book are advised to talk directly with a physician experienced in these specialties. Neither the publisher nor the author will be held responsible for the results of any path, therapy, or treatment undertaken as a result of reading this book.

The publisher disclaims any warranty of any kind, whether expressed or implied, as to any matter whatsoever relating to this book, including without limitation its merchantability or fitness for any particular purpose. In no event shall the publisher be liable for any direct or indirect, special, incidental or consequential damages arising out of the use or inability to use the materials and information in this book.

Confidentiality: The names of individuals have been changed in this book, with the exception of Julian and the author, and the following: Dr. Joseph Huggins, Dr. Soula Homatidis, Dr. Mary Konstantareas, Paul Madaule, Paul Lauzon, Rolph Schellenberg and Temple Grandin, who kindly gave permission.

Book sales: Contact the publisher at 740-689-2950 or via e-mail at books@luckypress.com

For Julian,
and all his friends

Acknowledgments

The author thanks the following family members and friends for their ongoing support and tireless proofreading of the manuscript over the last five years:

Angus Orchard, Mandy Alexander, Robert Graham, Sherry MacEachern, Bernice Lever, the author's first mentor, Eleanor West, Louise Auclair, Rozalyn Werner of the Roeher Institute, and Temple Grandin for her timely advice.

Special thanks to Dr. Joe Huggins, to whom my husband, son Julian, and I will be ever indebted, and to my editor and publisher, Janice Phelps, whose faith in this book made it possible.

Last, but not least, many thanks to the coffee shops and McDonald's of Port Credit, where this entire book was written.

"And a little prayer is also not out of the question."
–Dr. Joseph Huggins

Part One

Julian Orchard at age 3: "retarded and autistic"

One

D r. Rakka leaned forward, her stethoscope glinting. This was one of the most famous hospitals for children in Toronto, in the world, and Dr. Adelina Rakka, M.D., F.R.C.P. (C), F.A.A.P., was one of its most famous diagnosticians. Short and stout, with iron-grey hair and not unkindly eyes, she had diagnosed over three thousand children so far she said, without mistake.

"I'm sorry, Mr. and Mrs. Orchard."

Alec was sobbing. I gripped my purse. So this was what it had all come down to. Surely there must be some mistake, but developmental pediatricians like Dr. Rakka did not make mistakes. We did not know the word *autistic*, but it had a dread sound to it like the tolling of a bell deep under the sea. You knew then without being told it meant all Julian's oddities and strangeness. It was what was wrong with him.

We could see him through the observation window playing in the dollhouse with his eight-year-old sister, his long dark curls fringing his eyes. But whereas Polly peeked through the latticed windows calling out and waving "Hi Mommy! Hi Daddy!" Julian sat still, uninvolved, staring through space in that familiar, vacant, distant way, that *retarded* way. Oh, Jules!

Dr. Rakka raised her arms with the hapless motion of one who can say terrible things to parents because it was her job and not her fault. After all, nothing had been hidden from us: we had been present throughout the testing. I myself had sat next to Julian with Dr. Rakka — he had been sandwiched between us at the little wooden table; I'd observed how poorly he had done on the Dolch word-box alone. We had both been there for the physical. Dr. Rakka had slid her hand down deftly inside his little under-shorts to cup his testicles. "Normal," she had sighed. She had meant normal physically. Normal *looking*.

She had watched from behind a two-way window as we'd struggled to get Julian undressed. He'd resisted furiously biting and screaming at having his clothes removed in the middle of the day. How could he understand the word "examine"? We'd ended up practically tearing the shirt off his back, standing breathless, over-excited ourselves. Dr. Rakka had emerged quietly smiling from the next room.

"Receptive language at a two-year level; expressive language, eighteen months," had been the final conclusion.

"But he knows over fifty words, Dr. Rakka!" I had fumbled through my purse, eagerly drawing out the list of words I had been compiling for months: *eggy, da-da, no! bye-bye's, Ganma, Plly, dum-dum* (he still sucked a soother), *cuckie, wawa , chipsies, fishies, wavies, liby* (library) . . . *Juyan* . . . *train*. His latest were "liberary" and "pasgetti" (spaghetti).

"He can say all these words, I can vouch for it, Dr. Rakka!" I was foolishly eager with my fifty-plus word count, "I counted them myself!" The classic mother who could not "face" it. Dr. Rakka's lips had curled with bemusement. Did I not know a mere baby of thirteen months comprehended fifty words and the average *three* year old had a working vocabulary of thousands, yes, thousands, Mrs. Orchard. It was stunning. Unconsciously, effortlessly, without even thinking about it, three year olds joyfully, greedily, absorbing language, acquiring words, and not just words, whole phrases, sentences.

It wasn't just a question of the number of words, Dr. Rakka had pursued. It was Julian's lack of spontaneous speech altogether. He was not *using* language. He was not asking questions. There was no eye contact. Julian sitting between us, sorrowful in his chair, not looking at us. Not giving this all-important eye contact everyone talked about, that one so took for granted.

"But he does know those fifty words, Dr. Rakka! If he knows fifty, he could learn more, surely?"

I just could not let go of those words, of his achievement at least in this, small though it be.

Dr. Rakka's eyelids had lowered like scales. She had large dark yellowish eyes, heavy-lidded, iridescent. There was something sphinx-like about Dr. Rakka, subtle. She had handled him so beautifully during the testing, it had been a shock, how instinctively Jules had gravitated towards her, secure. I'd seen it, undeniable. I'd envied her. Her bosom had grazed his cheek as she bent down and guided his shoulders to the table, her firm hands holding him, and he had allowed it.

"Now sit here, Jul-ee-an, next to me." And he had. He had sat for Dr. Rakka, obeyed, his silken lashes brushing his cheek.

"Dog," he'd whispered, letting her body touch his. So why didn't he for me, his mother, the one who wanted to be close to him the most, loved him so much? He was the dearest little boy. *Sit close to me, Juli!* But he had fretted and stiffened and edged away. Had she noticed? Of course she had; Dr. Rakka saw everything.

Alec was still sobbing, *his son, his son.*

"Come, now, Mr. Orchard, this cannot be such a shock," said Dr. Rakka sharply. After all, Julian was well over four, she pointed out. We must have had *some* inkling of the truth; Dr. Geene must have broached it with us.

There was the speech pathologist Dr. Geene had recommended when Julian had been three. Mr. Carson had said Julian was "a year behind," I mumbled. That was all. No indication of anything this serious, of retardation. Though a year behind was a year behind. Which was why we were here with her, I pointed out, sensing the invisible circle we somehow seemed to have been moving in. It was obvious now much more had been "wrong" with Julian than just a year behind. Dr. Rakka's lips pursed.

She moved on quickly, there were other clients waiting. Autism was a life-long developmental disorder with serious language, behavioral and social impairments. Julian would need to be placed in a residential treatment center. Fortunately there was an immediate opening in the autistic unit at Thistletown Regional Centre, in Etobicoke, part of the Greater Toronto Area. We could count ourselves lucky, most parents usually had a long wait, she frowned. Permission forms were available. We only had to sign in triplicate, if agreeable. She motioned, as if why wouldn't we be.

Dr. Rakka was brusque now: best thing for him, get proper treatment, training, and discipline round-the-clock. We had ourselves to think of — our own lives — never cope — still young. We had Polly to think of too, her future — her chance of marriage — not throw away our lives on him. She had seen it, and we both teachers. *He would never amount to anything.*

But to leave a little boy, *my* little boy, merely four, in such a place. How would I be able to keep up daily visits? It was a long drive to Thistletown, longer in winter.

"You won't *be* visiting, Mrs. Orchard." Dr. Rakka paused, as if trying to get a patently obvious message across. What was the point of parents placing a child in a treatment center only to be constantly visiting and interfering with the programming? We would want what was best for him, surely. And what was best was residential placement for life.

Long light swept down University Avenue as we stepped outside. Everything seemed as before, except that now we had a retarded, autistic child whom we were deemed less capable of raising than trained workers – though we seemed to have done all right so far without any help. The streets of Toronto burned bright and hard, stretching forever. Jules and Polly skipped between us holding hands.

Dr. Rakka was known in the field for her bluntness, I was to learn later from other parents who had sought out her expertise. But Alec and I had a grudging respect for that. At least she had told us the truth, we reasoned. Wasn't ruthless honesty better than all the placebos, innuendoes, half-truths and evasions we seemed to have been fed over the past four years?

In the terrible days and weeks that followed it seemed that everyone around us suddenly had known about Julian all along but hadn't wanted to say.

"It's good you can finally face it, Thelma," purred even Lainey next door.

"You mean you knew . . . ?"

"Oh, well, it was pretty obvious. I mean, the way he didn't talk, or look at you, and the funny things he does with his fingers, and he never plays like other kids . . . "

I was stunned. Lainey, my next-door neighbor, was inadvertently reeling off the cardinal symptoms of autism as if she were Dr. Rakka. "So why didn't you tell me?'

"You weren't ready, dear."

When was a mother *ready?* I felt unaccountable anguish that quickly moved into self-recrimination. I hadn't heeded the many warnings and signals, the little telltale signs and symptoms that now in retrospect I understood so clearly. I hadn't figured it out, faced it — that most of all. For I *had* known, hadn't I? I thought over the past four years, looking for the evidence that had led us to this moment, starting with that early summer morning in 1977. . .

Two

I was sitting in the Donut Man in Port Credit with my twin sister, Elsie, and her baby boy, Brett, as was our usual Sunday morning ritual. I had with me my young daughter, Polly, and six-month-old Julian.

"There's something wrong with him . . . " Elsie said. She peered at Julian with that odd, discerning frown on her face. She flicked her cigarette and blew out a trail of smoke. "Definitely."

"What do you mean?"

I knew to keep my voice calm and steady, carefully maintaining that smooth nonchalance I'd developed concerning any talk about Julian. Yet fear had clutched at me like a premonition. It was not the first time Elsie had given hints. I could no longer dismiss it as sibling rivalry. Her own baby had been born only months before Jules. The two cousins were virtually the same age and the implication was they should be at the same level of development.

"Oh, I dunno. Just *look* at him, Thel. The way he is compared with Brett."

We both glanced at Julian — so pensive and quiet, still as a doll. His large black eyes, curved and lustrous, inherited from Alec's side of the family, stared into the distance as though we weren't there. His cousin Brett, on the other hand, sat up urgently in Elsie's lap, gurgling with delight through wisps of smoke at the sight of Julian's five-year-old sister, Polly. He seemed to know Pollywogs with her thick fair curls and delicate face. He just couldn't keep still, his little face flushed with recognition, alive and sparkling with the sheer joy of living.

He squirmed with delight when Polly squeezed his cheek and said "Bwett! Bwett!" She didn't attempt to tease her baby brother the same way, having long discovered there would be no response, just a blank stare – no fun. Brett, on the other hand, tried to reach for her hair, take her donut, hug her, grab her Sprite. "P-p-p," he went. He wanted attention, love, reciprocation and warmth, just as Polly had when she was a baby.

"But Dr. Geene hasn't noticed anything wrong, nor Dr. Vikram," I protested. Surely Dr. Geene would have noticed, said something by now in the well-baby visits.

If he had, he'd kept it to himself. Dr. Geene was our pediatrician and Dr. Vikram had assisted at the cesarian section delivery. He had not given me the usual baby APGAR rating after Julian's birth – Polly had been a ten, as had Brett – and I had not insisted. I'd been only too glad to get out of that hospital. My delivery day fell on Christmas and the maternity wing was understaffed. With the shortage of nurses and Christmas holiday short cuts, everything had been frantic and stressful. I'd been excited, exhausted, and strung-out with the thrill of producing a boy for the family. The only obvious problem with Julian had been his refusal to nurse. Dr. Geene finally diagnosed lactose intolerance after Julian dropped below his birth weight. He was put on Prosobie, a revolting greyish soybean formula which he loved, and from that moment on he'd thrived, put on weight, and seemed content.

I shifted my gaze to the scene outside: the Credit River in early June, unseasonably grey. Port Credit is on the shore of Lake Ontario, at the southernmost tip of a large suburban region, a sort of "dormitory" of the Greater Toronto Area. Unexpected rain buffeted the boats. The widening estuary spread grimly into the lake and a wrecked tanker lay anchored at the headland. Gulls swooped over the masts, and a limp line of flags trailed in the wind.

Elsie had once said, "If I suddenly die tomorrow, Thel, promise me, don't throw my ashes into Lake Ontario. Anywhere but there!" We'd laughed. I knew what she meant: that vast anonymous stretch of water flat as a board was so different from the sheltered little bay of our childhood home on the Welsh coast.

I made a point of meeting Elsie each Sunday. I had been the first to come to Canada to take up a teaching post. Elsie had followed later, eager for adventure like one of the heroines in the romance novels she favored. Now she was a single parent. Her small pert face was topped with a twist of little curls irrepressibly bubbly, at the moment blond. I was the darker one in looks and temperament, I'd had a scholarship to study for a master's in English, and now I was a teacher.

I rocked my baby anxiously. We always tried to get the window-seats, overloaded as we were with our strollers; tote-bags bursting with diapers, bottles, dummies, rattles, Elsie's cigs and knitting, my journal, and Elsie's latest romance, *Passionate Embers* by Rosamunde Hartley, to take the edge off her problems.

"He just doesn't seem to *notice* us," Elsie frowned.

"You're just used to the way Polly was. Julian's different — he's the quiet type. I'm not complaining!" I forced a laugh, almost convincing her.

"Yeah . . . well, I s'pose so." Elsie nodded grudgingly, grinding out her cigarette butt.

I tried to forget Elsie's words — a sort of mental subterfuge. But then there was another incident, nothing too big, but disturbing all the same.

We lived in a vast new subdivision just outside Toronto. Row upon row of freshly built houses with white plastic siding stretched neatly along the horizon like so many dollhouses, square on their carved lots. They were occupied mainly by newly married couples either expecting children or with two young children each. Two of my neighbors, Darlene and Jane, had babies about the same age as Julian, so it was natural to compare. Since Jules was a winter baby, I had kept him indoors for the first few months, so it wasn't until early summer that we were able to meet outside with our children.

We sat on Darlene's red brick patio facing a stretch of fresh sod and fifty feet of cedar fencing backed by an enormous sky. The babies lay at our feet on a blanket scattered with the usual assortment of baby toys — rattles, balls, rubber duckies, mobiles that swung and chimed from a pole near our chairs to keep them amused.

We sipped iced tea and watched as Darlene's and Jane's baby girls rolled about, clutching at the rubber duckies, shaking rattles, cooing and gurgling at their mums, trying to make the usual one-syllable attempts at words. The girls stretched out chubby little hands with pleasure, sharing every moment with their mums and demanding responses, like Brett. But all the while, Julian lay like a plastic doll, unmoving, seemingly unaware of anyone's presence, least of all mine, and ignored the babies next to him. He just stared at the sky. I caught a subtle look pass between the women that seemed to say, "What's wrong with him?"

"Amazing, isn't it," said Jane sweetly, "what difference three months can make in a baby?" Their girls were three and four months older than Julian; I seized the "out."

"Yeah," I laughed, trying to sound casual. "Before you know it, Julian will be a little terror the way Polly was. But right now he needs his nap, otherwise he gets grouchy, just like his father!"

I picked up Julian with a careful, regretful sigh as if I had to put him to bed right then. Everyone laughed and relaxed, and the incident passed off.

Why had I deliberately lied? Julian didn't need a nap, he wasn't even sleepy. In fact, he had just had a short sleep after lunch and, if anything, he needed to be outside to play in the sun. He should have been bursting with energy, with baby eagerness to explore everything going on around him, including people – myself most of all.

"Anxiously I lifted him to my face: *Look at me, Jules, I am your Mommy.* I kissed his cheeks – he was so beautiful, so sweet, my little Jules. While he didn't object to my kisses he also didn't respond. There was only that placid vague expression on his face again as if he were putting up with me. I felt tears well.

I took care never to expose Julian too closely to Jane and Darlene and their babies again. I did it almost subconsciously. I was out if they came knocking on the door. I was always "just about to feed him" or "put him down" if I saw Darlene across the fence. I took him to parks the other end of the subdivision to meet and mix with other toddlers, except he did not seem interested in them. Instead, he preferred to trickle grains of sand through his fingers over and over for what seemed like hours. If I walked away he did not raise his head or seem to notice I was gone – he *did not miss me.* But Jane and Darlene would not witness that.

Gradually the importance of that afternoon dimmed. Jane and Darlene had probably put it out of mind long ago. In fact, Darlene seemed envious of our tightly knit family. Whenever she saw the four of us setting out on our evening walk, she'd coo, "You're always doing things together." Alec wanted to be an involved father, and we wanted to do things with our children whenever possible. We expected Jules to respond happily.

So what was it then? It was hard to put a finger on. As Alec tossed Jules playfully into the air going "Whooo" while Polly hid behind the orange chair, her lion cave, it struck me again that as amiably as Julian looked down at his father, he did not try to grab at his beard or pull his glasses off his nose as I'd seen Darlene's baby do with Rolph, or as Polly had done at that age. There was no real interaction somehow; what were we doing wrong?

When I mentioned Elsie's remarks Alec dismissed them.

"She's just jealous, sibling rivalry. You having a boy took the limelight away from Brett, and her nose is out of joint a bit. Besides, Julian is ahead in some things for his age, look at his teeth."

"Well, Brett's just late teething."

"Precisely."

Despite some peculiarities in Julian's behaviors, he showed many signs of normal, if not advanced, development. One day, at nine months of age, as if to verify his father's faith in him, Jules amazingly *got up and walked!*

Elsie had come over with Brett to celebrate Brett's first birthday. I had a chocolate cake and one curly blue candle and presents ready. Elsie insisted on taking the children outside. She loved chatting with the neighbors and sharing baby stories with other young mothers, and she loved showing Brett off. She soon drew Darlene and Jane into comparison talk over the fence, sharing their babies' latest displays of prowess. At once I felt uncomfortable, pushed to think of some achievement of Jules other than his teeth. When I looked away, Jules struggled against the wall, pushed himself to his feet and half-ran, half-tottered, arms outstretched for balance, right towards me.

"He's *walking!*" cried Darlene and Jane, their jaws dropping with amazement. Neither of their one-year-old daughters were ambulatory yet. They'd just been recounting how cleverly the girls were pulling themselves upright against chairs.

"Oh, well, Polly walked at nine months, too," I said nonchalantly, hoping the implication would not be lost. But I was thrilled. Waves of joy and relief for Jules swept through me. He was exonerated. *Normal.*

"Early for his age," remarked Dr. Geene at the well-baby check-up, as Julian toddled into the room. "Some walk at nine months, some much later. Even two is all within the range, like talking."

Elsie was quiet after that, but she added pointedly, "Actually, a long period crawling, they've proved, stimulates speech, Thelma. Don't ask me why, but it does. Early walking doesn't mean anything intellectually."

Something about that remark struck me, the fact that Polly had continued crawling for well over a year after she first walked, combining them both, and was verbally advanced. She already had been designated gifted at school. And Brett, who was already attempting words like "Ma-ma," "c'ckie," "Plly," still crawled. Julian now stopped crawling. He tottered everywhere determinedly, and made no attempt at baby-babble.

Over the next weeks, Elsie's remark continued to niggle at me. I decided to mention it casually to my mother-in-law. She was a counsellor at Surrey Place, a diagnostic center in Toronto for retarded, emotionally disturbed and learning-delayed children and adolescents. If anyone should recognize anything "wrong" with Julian, it would surely be she.

Alec and I sat in the old familiar kitchen of her bungalow in Willowdale, which was still a lovely neighborhood north of Toronto with shady old tree-lined streets. Alec's family had lived there since they had arrived in Toronto from Ceylon, now Sri Lanka, in the mid-'50s.

Sun had slanted through the kitchen window. Clematis frilled mauve up the rickety trellis outside, the garden was an orchard filled with delight. Frisky, one of the cats, nothing like his name, sprawled across the step; Blackie was hiding as usual under one of the beds, and Tabby, my father-in-law's favorite, lay at Granpa's feet alternately purring and spitting at anyone who passed too close.

Everything was comfortable inside. The rooms, shaded by the cedar hedge outside, were filled with worn carpets, heavy old chesterfields and deep comfy armchairs. On one wall was a picture of Kandy Lake and the Buddhist temple in Sri Lanka and on another wall plaques with sayings like *"Blessed Be All Who Enter Here."*

Mother-in-Law — Ma — was rocking Julian gently in her arms, her dark skin brushing his golden cheek, cooing something in Singhalese, *"Amah, amah."*

"Elsie says there's something wrong with Julian, he's not normal."

My words hit a silence. I waited for her to say "Oh! Why would she say that? There's absolutely nothing wrong with him."

"Well, he's just a bit . . . well . . . *slow,*" she said, cautiously.

Alec and I put down our cups of tea. The baby stared blankly at his granma with that curious, vague, troubled look that was becoming more familiar.

"Slow?" we echoed in disbelief.

"Just give him lots of love and attention!" Ma continued.

What kind of answer was that? The words were enigmatic.

"But we do!"

The students Alec taught in the inner city of Toronto were also identified as "slow." Brockley High School was streamed for low academic achievers learning at a basic level. Alec was familiar with their learning disabilities. Surely, I thought, he would have recognized if his son were slow. The thought nagged at me: Why hadn't Mother-in-Law brought it up before if she had noticed something wrong, which she obviously had.

"Ah, it's nothing serious. Babies develop at different stages, some just take longer than others. He'll be fine."

This did not sound particularly reassuring, but we had respect for her opinion, especially since she worked at Surrey Place. Ma's job was hands-on, helping to feed, dress, and toilet-train the children in residence. She was dedicated, hard working, and knowledgeable.

Ma had once recognized that Petrie, a little boy at the center, was not retarded. His behaviors were due to blindness, she'd insisted to her superior. When he was tested, it had turned out Ma had been correct. Petrie was re-assessed and transferred to the School for the Blind where he'd gone on to learn Braille and then finish high school and college. Petrie had even come to the bungalow to thank Mother-in-Law for saving his life.

Early in our marriage, I'd paid a visit to Surrey Place, curious about Ma's work. The building had once been the Toronto Asylum, an assessment center for female felons. It was a dark, gloomy place; you wondered how it could be seen as suitable for children even for short periods of time. Alec's mother and I clattered down long gloomy halls. There was a certain hush, broken by occasional children's wails or agitated yells from somewhere.

Ma had arranged for me to watch snack-time and play period. Most of the children had been very young and needed assistants to help them eat. At playtime the children were either listless and unmotivated, or frustrated and restless, biting at each other and squealing. One small girl slapped my face when I bent to say hello. My cheek burned. Ma quickly assured me that it was not personal, the child was just acting out. I tried not to look too closely at some of the children's features, and a certain look they wore on their faces.

Julian surely bore no resemblance to those children, I reminded myself, with his beautiful, high intelligent forehead. He was strange, that was all, strange and beautiful. As Ma had said, babies developed at their own pace. Yet I thought of the rattles unrattled on his playmat, the Touch 'n' Tell left untouched, the squeaky-squeegies never squeezed.

Oh, what was his pace?

Three

Over the next few years, Julian continued to demonstrate a complex mix of normal development with odd quirks to his personality that though sometimes disturbing were not necessarily too out of kilter. In some things he was advanced for his age. He had immense stamina that far-outstripped Brett's. Not only had he been walking since he was nine months old, but at eighteen months he could climb and balance precariously at the top of the Jungle Jim at the park. He also had an uncanny ability to form a mental road map in his head of our routes round the Toronto area. He protested whenever we diverged from the usual route on a visit to Willowdale or he'd scream if we took the Don Valley Parkway for a change.

Dr. Geene had not seemed to note anything untoward in the well-baby visits. When I mentioned once I was concerned that Julian still sucked a soother, Dr. Geene had brushed it off humorously: "I've never yet sent a kid to college with a soother! Relax."

Around this time we sold the model home in suburbia and moved into a lovely old English-style cottage with a large garden in Port Credit. Eighteen-month-old Julian reacted vehemently, even given that most toddlers have difficulty with change. He screamed continuously day and night showing distress in every room of the house, including his own bedroom, a pleasant room at the back overlooking the garden. Nothing could pacify him. We tried bringing him into our room at night, but he sat up in his cot frantically beating his head against the bars. I put it down to the strangeness of the move, unfamiliar surroundings, even though Elsie had also moved to a new neighborhood and a new apartment with little protest from Brett. He had quickly settled in and adapted.

But at least Polly had a new little friend, Charlotte. They played happily in the playhouse at the bottom of the garden, and gradually Julian toddled around after them not actually playing, but lingering nearby.

I had to go back to teaching that fall. I was lucky to get a half-time job a five-minute drive from home. There was a daycare center called Little Bo Peep nearby for Julian. It was in a cozy converted old house, a more homey atmosphere than the usual daycare centers in high-rise buildings. It would be good for Julian, I told myself. *Up the Years from One to Six*, the baby book my mother-in-law had given me, assured that mixing with other children encouraged a child to talk and socialize.

"And what does Julian like to do, Mrs. Orchard?" smiled Miss Carruthers, the director of the preschool. Alec and I were sitting in her office after a tour of the center. It was a standard question for a first meeting, but the question stalled me.

What *did* Julian like to do? I fudged about, confused. I explained that Julian did not play much, adding quickly that his language and play were not developing as we had hoped because he had not mixed much with children his own age, which was why we were trying daycare. It sounded reasonable, and in a sense, it was true. I ignored the fact that we hadn't felt the same need to send Polly to daycare when she was Julian's age."Well, there'll be plenty of stimulation here!" Miss Carruthers smiled "He'll soon be chattering away!"

May Carruthers was an Englishwoman. While the atmosphere at the center seemed busy and friendly, there was an undercurrent of good old British discipline. Children were punished for misdemeanors by being made to sit alone out on the stairs, and sobbing was resolutely ignored. I wasn't sure I liked the sound of this, but there had to be some sort of follow-up for misbehavior with forty children to deal with.

"So you're a teacher," Miss Carruthers continued warmly, giving me a look of approbation. I had the feeling she believed that my toddler, then, would be automatically intelligent, well-adjusted, and just fine.

But Julian never seemed to settle in. Worse, he screamed whenever we passed by Little Bo Peep Daycare in the car, obviously afraid we were going to drop him off. For the first three months he stayed in the bathroom during playtime, showing great distress when coaxed to come out. Alec and I agreed with the teachers that the best thing was not to force him, but to give him time to adjust.

Colleen and Shea, his capable young teachers, tried taking toys into the bathroom to meet Julian on his own terms, where he was comfortable. He became attached to a train, and held onto it all day. This attachment later extended to a Fisher-Price cassette player upon which he played *Twinkle, Twinkle, Little Star* over and over. Colleen was puzzled that he never tired of it.

"Does he play with the others yet?" I'd always ask when I picked him up. He had been at the center for nearly three months. I couldn't help noticing the happy, noisy little groups of toddlers and children chattering to each other, sometimes arguing, while Julian sat cross-legged, mournful and silent, watching at the edge of the playground, or standing with his back pressed fearfully against the fence. How I longed to arrive and not be able to spot him instantly. He always stared, dazed, as I swept him into my arms.

The two young teachers hesitated to answer. "We-ell, he doesn't make eye contact, Mrs. Orchard," frowned Colleen. "But, you know I feel he is aware of everything going on."

That term, "eye-contact," had a strange sense to it. It sounded more like clinical terminology than a nursery school assistant's comment on the fun a toddler was supposed to be having with his friends. But Julian had no friends. He didn't play with children and they didn't play with him, and that was the truth.

"And another odd thing," Shea hesitated. "He doesn't seem to mind being punished . . . " Marg Carruthers let every parent know right from the beginning, that any child's sobs, no matter how desperate and lonely they sounded, were to be firmly ignored. Most parents liked the sound of this firm approach and were only too eager to cooperate.

But the teachers didn't know what to do when it came to Julian. He didn't sob or call out "I'm weady to come ba-ack, Miss Cawuthers" when placed on the stairs and told not to move until he was ready to eat what had been put in front of him. He didn't move. "We could leave him there for hours," echoed Colleen. He actually seemed to forget why he was there.

Also, Jules did not seem to recognize me when I picked him up. It was as if he'd forgotten who I was for a moment, as if disconnected from the morning drop-off. He looked lost and passively resigned, as I wheeled him home to make Polly's lunch.

Polly loved watching cartoons on TV while eating her sandwiches, laughing gleefully, and Julian would clamber up on the sofa as if watching, too. At such times they looked like any other little sister and baby brother together. I checked out *Up the Years from One to Six* again. "Try to free your mind of worry and stress," it advised. "Take an easy-going view of his slowness in talking and you may never have to take any other step." *Nothing was wrong.* I was overreacting again.

But once Polly went back to school I was lost. I didn't know what to *do* with Julian — a problem I'd never had with Polly. All he wanted to do was to play with the same red train over and over, pushing it back and forth saying "train train train" in a monotone or play *Twinkle, Twinkle, Little Star* again and again for hours. He never got bored with this; even I was getting mesmerised.

I knew Julian was intelligent. One rainy day I put on Mozart's clarinet concerto. Jules was sitting on the carpet pushing the train back and forth again. As the clarinet came in with its long, sad notes Julian suddenly joined in humming in perfect tune with the clarinet. When the clarinet stopped, Julian stopped; when the clarinet came in again, Jules, without looking up or pausing, sang again, silvery, sweet.

His musical sensibility seemed remarkable for a child barely two. I began to test him in small ways. I laid out stacking cups and put them in order from small to biggest inside each other. At once, without speaking or looking at me, Jules did the same in seconds. This task was rated at a one-and-a-half to three-year-old level.

Next, I put the wooden inlaid puzzle of a teddy bear on the coffee table. Again Julian put the pieces together quickly, even though the puzzle was facing him upside down — he wasn't doing it by following the picture, but solely by contour of the shapes, which seemed odd. Didn't most children and adults instinctively look at the picture on the cover for help? But the actual picture seemed irrelevant to Julian.

"Teddy," I urged, pointing to the picture. "See, you made a teddy bear, Julian." He tipped the puzzle over and did it again — sideways!

But it was the way he had played with the cash register that piqued my interest most. He didn't play imaginatively with it, pretending he was a store clerk ringing up items, but what he did seemed to demonstrate intelligence nonetheless. I made note of it in my journal:

Watched Jules play with the cash register today. He was not one bit interested in dropping the big plastic coins in the slot and watching them come out like most kids. Instead he examined the drawer below, peering into it, poking his finger inside right to the back, then pushed a penny to the back to see how far it would go. Then he threw the penny hard into the drawer and put his ear down listening — testing? Then he lifted up the whole register and shook it, as if testing it again for something. Then held it upside down and peered through every available hole and chink examining, exploring. Shook it violently again, poked his finger into the holes and drawers and tested it again. Then he suddenly left it.

Four

If only people wouldn't ask. *Was it so obvious, then?* Of course it was. Julian was well past three years of age and still did not talk. Myra, our neighbor, said I should get him "assessed."

But I was always too intimidated by Dr. Geene to approach him on the subject. Small, wiry, high-strung and brilliant, with crazy flyaway tendrils of hair, he often snapped at parents. I accepted it because he was the best and everyone knew it. There were waiting lists to get into his practice. It never occurred to me to resent or protest his manner. The British class system had been too well instilled into me to presume to question the authority of a doctor, even if I was right. I'd been brought up to believe that doctors were superior in intelligence, spent years in medical school, lived in the best houses with wrought-iron gates, and were never ever to have their time wasted.

"Ugh-huh!" went Elsie, who didn't share my hesitation to question the status quo. Elsie had once gone to a great podiatrist in London to have her bunions removed. The famous doctor had taken one look at Elsie's short, splayed, bulbous feet twisted from years of fashionable shoes and said, "My God, you've got the ugliest feet in the United Kingdom!"

Elsie had retorted: "Look, I haven't come here for compliments. Get on with your job, Dr. Poona." She now looked at me exasperated.

"You've got to make him check out Julian, it's what he's paid for, Thelma. It's a wonder he hasn't noticed anything long before now if he's such a hotshot," my sister snorted.

But I hadn't needed to ask, as it turned out. Something about the way three-and-a-half-year-old Julian had sat on the table so still, so passive, so *uninvolved,* while Dr. Geene had pressed a stethoscope to his chest, seemed to strike Dr. Geene for the first time. "Is he always like this?" he'd said sharply.

"You mean quiet?" I was nervous.

"It's up here," he said, and tapped his own forehead.

Dr. Geene clearly looked uncomfortable, and I was alarmed. I was hesitant to pursue this oblique statement, but the moment had presented itself, and I seized it. Cautiously I asked if he could recommend someone to test Julian's language skills.

Dr. Geene quickly said that the first step was to send Julian to an audiologist for testing to rule out deafness, then to a speech pathologist, and then we'd see.

The audiologist was a big jovial man. His presence filled the arid little room as soon as he stepped in. His hair flared backwards like the wind.

"Where's the little fella then?"

Julian darted out from under the bed, tossed aside his pacifier and ran excitedly round the room touching every instrument with delight. He jiggled and tested the apparatus clamped to the wall; smelled instruments, pressing them to his lips; opened and shut the many shallow steel drawers in cabinets. I had never seen him so vibrant, interested, curious, excited or radiant. He ignored Dr. Saul and me — we were not there for him. It was so noticeable. I went to intervene, encouraging Julian to look at Dr. Saul.

"No!" whispered Dr. Saul, restraining my arm. "Just watch . . .

"This is an active intelligence!" he mused, fascinated by Julian. A half-hour later he emerged from the testing room and confirmed there was nothing wrong with Julian's hearing. I said Julian was supposed to be "slow." Sadness filled me to say such a word about my lovely little boy. Dr. Saul shook his head vehemently.

"This is not a slow child. This is an intelligent child! A bright child!"

A week later in the same hospital, the speech pathologist, Mr. Corsen, pronounced Julian slow. "At least a year behind, Mrs. Orchard. Specifically, 3.6 years of age functioning at 1.9. years."

I told this young man as honestly and simply as possible our concerns about Julian's behaviors, which were getting increasingly strange and difficult to deal with: his obsessions with the buttons of his shirt done up in a certain order, and his addiction to certain shoes and particular tunes. But my main concern was that Jules did not talk, at least not the way my nephew did. A normal child like Brett would have tackled the little tasks Mr. Corsen had given Julian with zest, chatting away, if only to please Mommy.

"You have valid cause for concern," agreed Mr. Corsen.

I felt a thudding sensation. Yet what was a year behind, really? I seized at it eagerly. I knew as a teacher that many children had to repeat a year in school, which made them fall a year behind their peers, without disastrous outcome. Philip, Alec's younger brother, had been a year behind when he'd arrived in Toronto from Sri Lanka at age seven. He'd been put back a grade; progress had been slow at first, but he'd ended up with a master's degree in urban geography and now had a good position as an environmentalist with the federal government. Julian could surely catch up a year, I reasoned.

Mr. Corsen looked uncomfortable. He had not been able to fully assess Julian or administer any actual tests due to Julian's behavior.

I sensed that the speech pathologist was the one who had not related well to Julian. I saw only a cool detached clinical attitude in Mr. Corsen, a relatively young man. Yet I respected him as a trained professional in the field and therefore didn't say anything.

Mr. Corsen advised that it would be helpful if Julian could go to a playgroup or attend nursery school to stimulate his language. But he fell silent when I said Julian already attended Little Bo Peep.

"I think maybe then a child and family clinic might offer the kind of help you need," he said slowly. "I'll be in touch with Dr. Geene. We'll see you in September."

It was May. It couldn't be that urgent if he did not want to see Julian for another four months. Jules could change, improve. Anything could happen by the fall.

When Dr. Geene suggested we visit The Creche in our follow-up meeting a few weeks later, it was obvious he had been in touch with Mr. Corsen. When we questioned him about Mr. Corsen's diagnosis and any report, Dr. Geene simply repeated that Julian was more than a year behind in language development and what more did we need to know? Action was what was important, intimated Dr. Geene, and The Creche would direct us towards some likely strategy. It was more of an answer than we'd had yet.

Miss Cicely Nugent, the director of The Creche, was a solid, middle-aged woman dressed in a stern grey business suit. She had been in the field of special education for decades. She was the third professional we'd faced so far "in the field." Alec and I met her and a social worker at Burnaby Public School where The Creche ran a small class of its own. Julian was not alone in the region, then, as it seemed many pre-school children were a year or so "behind."

"As we sat in her office, Julian was jumping up and down on the sofa, scrambling at my hair, my face, anything to stop me from talking! We were as shocked as Miss Nugent. Julian was glaring at her.

"You realize, Mrs. Orchard, if we take him on we won't be putting up with misbehavior like this. We'll have to break his will. Oh, I know that sounds upsetting to parents," Miss Nugent smiled waving her hand through the air as if brushing off any protest, "But it's essential he understand right from the start who's boss. Otherwise, he can't learn."

"He isn't usually like this," I began when Julian slapped my face.

Miss Nugent's lips tightened.

"Oh, he understands already!" smiled the social worker. "Look how he's looking at you, Cicely."

I burrowed in my purse for Julian's pacifier and gave it to him to help settle him. I guessed Miss Nugent would be aghast, and she was.

"That will have to go right off!"

"He needs it," I said defensively.

"Or *you* need it," Miss Nugent and the social worker chorused.

"Did you breastfeed Julian, Mrs. Orchard?"

I wondered what that had to do with anything. I was yet to learn that many professionals felt they could probe parents at will. I admitted I'd had difficulty nursing; failed at the outset. My husband was more direct.

"Do you have one program for breast-fed babies and another for bottle-fed babies?" asked Alec.

Miss Nugent frowned. "No . . . well . . . we just like to have the general background of the child."

"You know, I was breast-fed until I was three years old," chuckled Alec.

Miss Nugent looked startled and the social worker's pencil poised mid-air.

I was still feeling distracted by Julian's behavior, as he continued to whine and pull at my clothes. We were so used to Julian's behavior that seeing it from an outsider's viewpoint raised the question: why did I put up with behavior I would not have accepted from Polly at the same age? Because it was not normal, I intuited. How long had I known *that?* I realized I was longing for some help and expertise.

Miss Nugent took us to see their classroom.

Six children sat on the floor in a circle round their teacher; an aide sat to the side as if in readiness. I was concerned about the unnatural quietness of the children. Surely, the room should be alive with noise, busy with little hands exploring materials, learning through doing – I had never seen such absolute passivity. One or two of the children reminded me of the retarded children I'd seen at Surrey Place. Miss Nugent explained that "each child was working at his or her own level."

A small wooden chair stood outside the door, in the hall." Miss Nugent pointed at it. One of their methods of behavior modification was separating an uncooperative child from his peers, she explained. This idea was not unlike May Carruthers' measure of making little ones sit out on the stairs at Little Bo Peep Daycare. But she didn't call it "behavior modification" – just plain old punishment.

"Well," I hesitated, "Julian wouldn't much care about being removed from his peers. It won't have any effect on him. In fact he'd like it," I challenged.

"Oh no he wouldn't," snapped Miss Nugent. "He'd have to *sit!*"

After the tour, Miss Nugent suggested we take home a questionnaire to fill out. I was eager to comply. It turned out to be a mini-book of questions about our backgrounds, our marital relationship, and other intimate facts I had never considered such as whether I had ever had syphilis or gonnorhea, or any other venereal infections; whether there was anyone in the family with schizophrenia or mood disorders.

I had to remind myself at this point that this was for Jules' sake, to get him help he needed. I wanted to cooperate, to keep The

Creche open as an option since it was the only tangible help we'd been offered so far. Yet I felt dazed at the nature of the questions, which seemed to point to us as the cause of Julian's dysfunction. Suddenly every quirk in my character seemed magnified, every disatisfaction Alec and I had ever felt with each other was exposed, even ordinary petty irritations we normally wouldn't give a second thought to – such as the time Alec and I had argued crazily over a pot of potatoes I'd let boil over on the stove. What would Miss Nugent think?

Yet even as I labored with the questions, which took weeks to complete, Father's Day came and went and Polly shyly presented Alec with a poem, "My Dad," which ended, "My dad is the best because he is the best person I know."

"There!" said Alec beaming. "Put that in Miss Nugent's questionnaire!"

I finished the monolithic task and sent it off in the mail. Then I began to pack for our upcoming visit to Wales.

"Longing to see Julian for the first time ever! Mother."

Five

I expected Jules to be difficult on this three-week holiday knowing how hard change was for him, but he loved Wales. He settled in from the start as if he'd always lived in a Tudor house by the sea. The furniture was old in style and heavy, especially the carved dresser, a gnarled old sideboard the likes of which he'd never seen before. Julian soon learned to pry open the many fascinating little drawers with brass handles, sucking on the old silverware and odds and ends jammed inside.

He loved the long, straggly flower garden that July, the stone walls fronting the properties down to the seashore. The walls had been there forever, bleached with sun, drenched by rain and storm. Jules ran along the tops, never losing his footing, fearless, intense, just as I had done as a child. I'd never seen him so happy, even though he still did not smile or talk.

I missed my father who had died earlier. I'd been hoping Papa would be a role model for Jules while we were there. Alec had stayed back in Toronto — he couldn't stand the rain!

Julian got to sleep in the big, front bedroom with Polly, sharing the huge double feather bed, which was fun. Yet it was Polly who whispered tearfully in that big old bed at night, "I miss Daddy, Mommy. I want my daddy!" But I had the uncanny feeling that if we were to stay in Wales forever, Julian wouldn't mind.

Throughout our visit, Mother still did not seem to notice anything wrong with Julian. "Hell, you worry about that kid too much, he's just a three year old! For God's sakes have a sherry!"

I hadn't told her anything up to this point. She actually thought Julian intelligent. I was surprised — how closely was she looking?

"But Ma, he doesn't talk."

It was time to have it out – she may as well know. "Haven't you noticed? Actually, they think he's a year behind in speech and language development, and that he's . . slow."

I well knew the galvanizing effect of that word. I told her about the speech pathologist and The Creche, and our worries.

"Codswallop!" said Mother. "They don't know anything about kids in North America. Besides, he does talk. He's talking all the time. Just listen to him."

"But you can't tell what he's saying. If he does speak, it's only single words."

Mother pointed out she had not understood a word my brother's twins had said until they were seven. I tried to sense the tone of this, reassure myself that she wasn't trying to placate me. I so wanted to believe that "Jueegagabaoneggypliss," meant something intelligible. Ever since our visit to the speech pathologist, I was constantly trying to stimulate Julian's language like a running commentary. I spoke in an artificial way, feeling I had to emphasise every little action and object: "Oh you're putting SEASHELLS in your BUCKET, Jules!"

"Wawachipsies!" cried Julian, watching Mother prepare fish out in the kitchen. The chips were deep-fried in dripping, thick fat – luscious, soggy chips Julian loved. Jules looked like Alec, with his olive complexion and deep black eyes slightly curved, but his taste buds were obviously "British."

"Yes, you know what's good for you, don't you, old boy?" Mother ladled the chips onto his plate.

"O' boy," echoed Julian.

"See," Mother said, looking in my direction, "you're just being melodramatic."

To Mother, Jules was simply a sensitive child with his own quirks and oddities that he was entitled to, picking up negative and positive vibrations around him like most children, only in his case more so. It was obvious: I was relaxed and happy here, and so he was.

The last day of the holiday we went out for lunch to The Mariner's Arms in the new Swansea Marina. While waiting in line, I inadvertently let go of Julian's hand while searching for money in my purse. He disappeared in a flash, just like that. I pushed my way through the throng to Mother who was coming out of the ladies' room, but Julian hadn't gone to her. I crouched to his eye-level and looked around the legs of others in line. No, Julian. Frantic, I ran to the door, then outside, looking anxiously up and down the road, but he was nowhere in sight. I began to sob.

"Stay calm," said Mother, lighting a cigarette. "It's no good panicking, he'll come back."

"But he won't!" I cried in anguish. At once, Welsh-fashion, women gathered round us on the kerb.

"There, there, dear, don't cry, he'll soon be back looking for his mammy."

"No, no he won't," I sobbed again. *He won't come back looking for me, his mother!* flashed through me with despairing certitude, but how to explain that.

"Look, love, you stay right here with your mother; don't move, so he can see you." said one woman. "How old was he?" she asked gently. "What was his name? What was he wearing? Where had we been?" Best thing was to retrace our steps; he might have gone back to where we'd been.

"We — we went to Fortino's ice cream parlor and the Dylan Thomas Centre."

"Bet he's in the ice cream parlor. Bessie, you go to Fortino's. Mr. Matthias, you go to the Centre. Mr. Pritchard, you better go with him, two eyes is better than one. His name's Julian, he's three and a half, and he's wearing a red T-shirt and blue shorts. You'll know him, he'll be sobbing his little heart out."

But he wasn't at Fortino's or at the Dylan Thomas Literary Centre. He wasn't anywhere, and time was going by. I couldn't stop sobbing. Mother's face was drawn.

I leaned against the window — the reality of the situation was devastating. Double-deckers began rolling round the corner. Beyond the station was the road to the marina and boats, and a sheer drop over the edge to the murky water below where he might have been drawn, quite unaware of danger. I hurried across the square, weaving in and out of swaying buses and people waiting in line, when I saw him. Two young mothers were walking along chatting, one pushing a pram, and the other carrying Julian and trying to hold onto a toddler of her own.

"That's my son!"

I staggered across, sobbing again with relief.

"Oh here's his mother, thank God. We were just about to take him to the police station."

The women took one look at my tear-stained face and handed him over sympathetically. "Bet you're glad to get him back."

Julian didn't reach his arms out to me, or cry "Mommy" or show any recognition of me. He just looked at the boats.

"He can't talk yet much, he has problems," I heard myself blurt as if some explanation were due.

"There's a shame, and him such a beautiful little boy. We tried to get him to give us his name and where he lived, but he said nothing . . . "

I dreaded asking the next question but had to:

"Was he crying?" *For me, for his Mommy.*

"Well, no-o, he wasn't. He was marching along straight as a pin – that was what drew our attention. We were afraid he'd walk under a bus."

Now anger gripped me. Anger – and despair. I held him tight in my arms as Mother appeared, flustered and relieved. "I told you, Thel . . . " Julian looked wonderingly at my swollen face. He'd been gone an hour. He didn't understand. Of course there were explanations: he was only three and a half, still young; he had no sense of time, or his thoughts had been centered elsewhere, on the boats perhaps, familiar from Port Credit Harbor. Yet when Elsie had lost Brett once in Zellers she hadn't really had to search for him, though she'd been sick with dread. She'd just had to stand still and listen.

Brett's sobs and wails could be heard from one end of the store to the other: "Mommy, Mommy . . . where is you?"

Six

U pon our return to Canada, Julian showed no special emotion at seeing Alec again, whereas Polly threw herself into his arms at the airport, "Daddy, Daddy! Oh, Daddy!" nuzzling her face into his beard. Julian was indifferent — as if he'd forgotten him and was more interested in twirling the string of his jacket.

Nevertheless he came to life at McDonald's, where we'd decided to stop for a fast snack. He seemed to enjoy the familiarity: the same ordered hamburger, the same predictable surroundings, the shining arborite tables and long aisles always in the same configuration, the hypnotic soothing background music and a certain casual ambience as we settled at our table like so many other families with kids around us.

"Pop!" cried Jules eagerly. He grabbed at the orange drink as soon as Alec put down the tray.

"Julian can talk now, Daddy," shared Polly.

Yes, Jules had a funny little singsong voice that made me scrunch up inside with joy. At last we were hearing it.

One day some time much later, after the children had spent a weekend with my mother-in-law, I heard Polly playing a tape of herself in the bedroom. Ma had given her a tape recorder to play with one rainy Sunday afternoon. Polly's voice prattled on delightfully with a story she was making up as she went along, sprinkled with bedtime songs. But there was another high whining singsong sound going on in the background; it was Julian attempting to keep up with Polly. He was struggling with phrases, but more than that he was shaping singsong sentences of gibberish in the flow of her sentences. He was absorbing conversation even though he wasn't yet able to keep up with the speed of individual words that formed her sentence! It was a real advance. I was sure he'd start speaking soon.

Encouraging though this was, I couldn't help but notice Brett's language. Elsie and I were in the Donut Man on our weekly visit, and Brett and Polly were playing with Brett's action figures. I was struck by how imaginative, how full of allusions and metaphors, Brett's language was for a four year old while I was getting excited over Julian saying "Juice please."

"Aunty Fely, me and Polly doin' this play." Brett turned to me. "I'se gonna be Lukes Skywalker and Polly be Pwincess Leia wiv hair of gold, an' I touch her wiv my mashic wand [a wooden stir stick] and she will be my pwincess forever. But first I gotta slay Darf Vader."

Julian never played imaginatively. He never pretended to be someone else.

"Play with Julian, too. Include him," I said sharply, and instantly regretted it at the look of anguish on Polly's eager face.

"But Julian won't play wiv me, Mommy," she said sadly.

"Yes, I know, Poll. I'm sorry, it's not your fault." I wondered if Brett's ebullient personality overwhelmed Julian; he certainly played with Polly when they were alone together. "Look maybe Jules could be Leia's bodyguard," I said gently, "He has a magic dummy that has powers to slay Darth Vader every time he puts it in his mouth."

"Cripes! How the hell do you expect him to talk with that thing stuck forever in his mouth?" Elsie snorted.

Julian had scrabbled in my purse for his dummy and was sucking vigorously.

"When he's ready he'll throw it away of his own accord," I said firmly, really believing it.

I kept up repeating words and phrases to Julian slowly in conjunction with solid objects whenever possible; he really seemed to be grasping the idea. His conversation was now full of directives like "Egg please," limited to nouns and verbs, but I didn't mind as long as he was talking. But no sooner was I feeling enthused than another problem emerged as Julian expected you to fill in the gaps between his words. This led to inevitable bursts of frustration as I struggled by osmosis to figure out what one explosive word might really signify.

There followed intense episodes full of anger and sorrow, and always over the oddest things. New shoes hurled tempestuously across the room. Was it because they were new, or red? He even took to hurling his breakfast across the table at times, even food I knew he liked, as he fought to get out a word he obviously wanted to express. Had I misunderstood his words and given him "scrambled" eggs instead of "fried" by mistake? It seemed to be change he resisted, however unimportant it might seem to us.

"Sounds like the terrible twos, two years too late," said Else.

I pulled my journal out of my purse and looked through the pages for clues to my son's behaviors. I'd started keeping notes of these outbursts as well as of his new words since they often went together. One entry said "Hell."

"Hell"

J. wanted to go out on the swings in the garden, but the grass was soaking wet. Boots, boots, he cried when I got out his new Wellingtons. Yelled, screamed, kicked them & refused to put them on. I insisted. He threw the Wellingtons against the closet door. Then no swings I cried. No boots, no swings. Polly found hers and put them on in kitchen. Now she had to take them off again grumbling she'd never wanted to go outside anyway. Julian crying bitterly by now over the new yellow (?) Wellingtons. Is it his old brown winter boots he wants? But I'd thrown them away to make him wear the new yellow ones. I pick him up in my arms & take him outside on the deck to show him the wet grass after the rain, but he pushed my face & thumped me struggling to get down. Went inside again. He took off upstairs saying "pants." "Oh, you want to wear your pants," I said.

"But it's hot, Jules, it's still summer." But now I understood. At last! Boots are always worn with long pants and he was wearing shorts. But we wear pants in winter, Jules. It's hot out, very very hot. Julian pulled on pants AND new Wellingtons & off he went happily. I'm exhausted. I'm left weak & trembling & miserable. Sink into wicker chair in sunroom. It's only 9:30 & I've already gone through all this. Why? Why? Why can't he act normal? Think how sorry Mother would be for me if she knew & cry all the more! No wonder I've got allergies.

Julian was in his second year at Little Bo Peep Daycare. One day when I was picking him up, May Carruthers asked me to join her in her office. Her tone was serious. She told me that earlier in the day one of the assistants had made Julian enter the toilet cubicle, something he always refused to do. He had got extremely upset, to the point of hysteria. May hesitated, looking uncomfortable. I sensed there was more to the story.

"You know," she began nervously, "We're more than glad to keep Julian on next year, half-day, when he starts kindergarten, but you might find ABC Nursery School uptown more suited to his needs. They have a smaller ratio of children to assistants. They can give the one-on-one attention Julian needs, which we just can't afford, Mrs. Orchard."

May was looking hard at my face. Did I understand, her look seemed to ask, that Julian *needed* this "one-on-one"? I felt a sense of warning. I did not want to change daycare. Julian had had enough problems adapting to Little Bo Peep; besides, it was convenient for me, being so close to home. I was now teaching full time, managing the house, looking after two children, taking Polly to weekly piano and swimming lessons, and I was exhausted. ABC Nursery School, which I'd never heard of, would mean at least another half-hour of travelling in the morning. More stress on me meant more stress on Julian.

I could hear my voice getting higher, shrill. I twinged with guilt at seeming selfish. I should be thinking of the benefits of a small setting to Julian. I just did not want to admit that Jules was not fitting into Little Bo Peep, even after two years. He was an outsider, ignored by the children and May Carruthers did not know what to do about it. But I wanted him in with all the "normal" kids. *Still give him a chance, May! Act as if all is well.*

I was hanging out six pairs of Fruit of the Loom underpants daily to get air through them before I decided to consult Dr. Geene. Julian had mauve rings under his eyes, was thin and listless and had a thin sort of diarrhea that seemed to have gone on and off for months, yet it was difficult to pin down exactly what was wrong. I felt resentful. Why couldn't he be like his cousin Brett, with a stomach of cast-iron?

Dr. Geene diagnosed fecal impactment. Julian had a hardened stool the size of a grapefruit at the top of his rectum. The runny poop had presented as "diarrhea" from liquid loosening constantly around and from this stool. I had brought him in just in time. Any later and it could have become extremely serious, diverticulosis. As it was, the muscles of the rectum had collapsed.

"I thought he had diarrhea," I said weakly.

"It's a common mistake," said Dr. Geene quietly.

I could not necessarily blame Dr. Geene, except that advice had been given initially over the phone, a common enough occurrence for minor ailments not involving a high temperature. I had misled Dr. Geene by stating that Julian had diarrhea, and Dr. Geene had assumed, wrongly perhaps, I knew all the facets of severe constipation as opposed to diarrhea. There was no time to waste on recriminations. I was to begin treatment promptly. Julian was to be given Senokot before and after every meal to help loosen the stool from one end and a pediatric Fleet enema twice a day to work on the other end.

While I worried about Julian's health, a part of me felt relief: now we knew something definite, physical, and treatable. Being severely constipated for so long must surely have affected Julian's alertness, might even be the cause of emotional problems. Dr. Geene agreed it certainly wouldn't have helped, and he estimated Julian must have been like this for over a year, the gradual nature of a fecal impactment making it hard to recognize.

Weeks later, after two daily enemas and endless bottles of syrup of figs, the huge stool finally broke and dissolved. Jules leapt up and ran half-naked into his bedroom where he whooped in circles, a new child.

This could be a turning point. What I had learned was that I had a sensitive child with several difficulties, not just in the language area: he had an over-sensitive digestive system and bowel. I determined from now on to apply myself with diligence to Julian's diet.

Julian was never so happy. He began to talk more, still single words or two-word combinations, but an increase in vocabulary nonetheless. I began to keep a more precise list of his new words in my diary, and one wonderful day, he said "Daddy."

"I knew he would get it! Clever Jules! Clever clever boy! Daddy!" I longed for the first time he'd say *"Mommy!"* but he didn't.

There was one afternoon when Alec came home and asked, "Where's Mommy?"

Without glancing up, Julian replied, "Thelma in kishen."

I enthused to Miss Nugent over a coffee that he was copying so much now I couldn't keep up. Miss Nugent was doing a follow-up from our visit to The Creche the previous fall. She said cautiously that she did not think speech delay was influenced by constipation.

"But it wasn't ordinary constipation, Miss Nugent."

I quoted my standby, *Up the Years from One to Six:* "Illness or serious undernourishment can interfere with a child's readiness in wanting to talk." And that was the Department of Health and Welfare, Ottawa, speaking.

"I'm certain there'll be a big change in Julian once this is over, Miss Nugent," I told her. "No wonder he wasn't talking — he wasn't getting the proper nutrition for his brain."

Miss Nugent tactfully did not mention the millions of starving children in Africa and India who nevertheless learned to talk on time. But I was certain there was a link between severe prolonged constipation and speech delay. It was the only thing that made sense so far.

Miss Nugent said that she had been in touch with Dr. Geene and was still interested in offering Julian a placement in The Creche the coming year, and providing emotional support for me.

"But he'll be starting *school,* Miss Nugent."

My words seemed to transfix mid-air, as if I was being propelled towards some climax, some confrontation not long in coming. Miss Nugent looked concerned. It was May 1981, and Jules was four and a half. Kindergarten registration was taking place in the local schools for fall enrollment. Time was running out.

Perhaps this was the final propulsion towards confronting Dr. Geene once and for all. Whatever was wrong with Julian, we believed it was temporary, some sort of emotional immaturity that was affecting his language development. We needed the professional expertise and guidance of a specialist. To our surprise, Dr. Geene agreed, as if he were expecting us to ask. He quickly arranged an appointment with Dr. Adelina Rakka, "the best in the field," he assured us.

Seven

As I look back, I understand, at last, how inevitable was
the ultimate conclusion; inevitable to everyone, that is,
except Alec and me.

I n the follow-up interview after Dr. Rakka diagnosed Julian, Dr. Geene shifted evasively, obviously feeling as awkward and uncomfortable as we did.

We had just read *Son-Rise* by Barry Neil Kaufman that a sympathetic friend had given Alec, saying, "These parents brought their kid out of autism, and he sounds just like your son!" *Son-Rise* was published in 1976, the year of Julian's birth, which meant it had already been out on the market five years. Barry Neil Kaufman and his wife Suzi had brought their baby son, Raun, out of autism. A key factor was that they had ignored all the doctors' and experts' negative predictions. Instead they had devised their own program of treatment called "Options." Kaufman had a doctorate in psychology, which had to have helped. He certainly spent enough pages on his excursions into Jung, Adler, Perls, Horney, Gestalt, and Skinner, and especially a new psychologist called Dr. Ivaar Lovaas, whose early intervention techniques in autism the Kaufmans instantly recognized as valuable.

The Lovaas technique was not well known among professionals, even though it was purported to be the most successful method in the treatment of autism to date. Dr. Lovaas, a psychologist in California, had developed certain behavior modification techniques to bring children out of autism. His technique worked mainly with children age three and under. Lovaas' manual, *The Me Book*, had been published in 1981, the year Julian was diagnosed. Yet the Kaufmans were among the few who had already been aware of the techniques and had integrated many of them into their own approach.

Suzi Kaufman had logged eight hours a day, seven days a week, locked willingly inside a bathroom with baby Raun because he needed to be in that kind of confined space to concentrate. There was a photo in the book of Suzi sitting resolutely on the floor between a toilet bowl and a bathtub, four feet by six feet, relentlessly going through the program that was to bring Raun out of his autism.

I agonized over what I realized was wasted time by putting Julian in Little Bo Peep, and now it was too late. One didn't cure a five year old of autism. It seemed treatment had to be given early, while the behavior patterns were still new and unentrenched. The difference between Raun Kaufman and Julian was that Raun's autistic symptoms had been recognized and treated at seventeen months, giving rise inevitably to the question as to why Julian had not been diagnosed earlier.

It was the issue that consumed us as we faced Dr. Geene. I felt confused, pained. Surely pediatricians were trained in medical school to identify the signs and symptoms of developmental delays in a baby as well as of chicken pox and meningitis? And out of all the professionals involved with Julian, surely a speech and language pathologist should have recognized symptoms of autism in the language delays of a three year old. Yet Mr. Corsen had hedged, got away with that "year behind" cliché.

As I thought it over, I realized that Dr. Geene had never once actually sat down with me during a well-baby visit and given me an explicit warning. He had never once said the words, "I suspect this child has symptoms of retardation and autism; let's get him checked by a specialist right away." Dr. Geene had professionally done the right things, as he would carefully remind us: He had referred us to appropriate professionals, audiologist, speech and language pathologist, and a child and family clinic, The Creche. Yet the crucial element of time, according to Kaufman, had not been recognized. My fault was that I had feared to confront Dr. Geene.

My Sad Is All Gone

Jules might not have necessarily shown the remarkable results like Raun Kaufman; there were so many variables, and it was hard to say whether Julian was retarded or appeared retarded due to autism. (Raun had been designated *severely* retarded as well as autistic.) But the opportunity to at least try some approach had been denied us, though admitedly not with any malicious intent on Dr. Geene's part. That was what was so hard to understand. But as Kaufman had pointed out in his book, why would doctors rush with a diagnosis when they believed that autism was incurable? It made no difference in Dr. Geene's opinion whether we were told when Julian was one-and-a-half or four-and-a-half: *the outcome was the same,* even though the Kaufman's had proved otherwise. So we could only sit in Dr. Geene's office in the follow-up consultation, tense, accusatory, sad, waiting for answers that could not be given. We sensed an impasse, that the outcome had been decided for us long ago, choices made.

Dr. Geene was visibly irritated. He had not heard of *Son-Rise,* nor intended to read it. It was likely the Kaufmans' son had been misdiagnosed, easy enough to do in a baby, Dr. Greene pointed out. Autism was incurable.

"You have to realize, Mr. and Mrs. Orchard, parents like the Kaufmans will believe in any so-called miracle, understandably of course.

"My advice to you is to accept the placement in Thistletown, if that is what Dr. Rakka recommends."

Eight

Thistletown Regional Centre, once called "The Children's Psychiatric Hospital," was a dark brick institutional building with dreary rows of windows. There was a whiff of antiseptic inside. Before the 1950s it had been a convalescent and rehabilitation hospital for children with chronic illnesses such as polio and TB. My guide assured me that Julian would not have much cause to be in this administrative section but this was where I imagined him, plaintive and lost during admission.

I was viewing the program at Dr. Rakka's suggestion. I knew I had to see it for myself. The program was regarded as a model for the rest of Canada, assured my guide with visible pride. The autistic unit was part of a program called TRE-ADD: "Training, Rehabilitation, Education of children with Autism and other Developmental Delays." It concentrated on two areas: language development and behavior modification.

The guide showed me the school wing first. I was allowed to look through the observation window in the door at a sunny open room with windows overlooking gardens. There were large round tables, casually placed, at which sat groups of two or three children reading or doing puzzles with teaching assistants. "We only treat a small number at a time," my guide explained.

A boy of about six was being pulled to his feet, then pushed back into a chair, over and over, presumably to teach him to sit on request. His head wobbled. A worker stood behind the chair grasping the boy's shoulders from behind, so there was no eye contact. "Sit!"

"Oh, I know it seems terrible, but you have to break their will," said my guide, sensing my anxiety. I was watching aversion therapy in action, she explained. It lasted for about five minutes, then the worker tested the boy to see if he would sit when asked. If he resisted, the treatment would resume.

"I know it's hard for a parent to accept it at first. But you'll understand when you see the good results eventually. He'll be able to sit and learn."

I thought of Miss Nugent's words at The Creche, "He'll have to *sit!*" Surely I could get Jules to obey me without resorting to this. I reminded myself I was seeing a superficial slice of programming without understanding the full background of the boy and his parents. But the incident troubled me, reminding me this was a treatment center, pleasant though the grounds were. Though Julian needed treatment, I didn't want aversion therapy used on him. The Kaufmans based their program on love not on breaking a child's will. My guide answered my scepticism dubiously – would the Kauffmans be happy if their son was mutilating himself? Many of the autistic children in the center were self-abusive; some tore their faces. Some had to have their hands bound, and even then they'd break free and inflict bloody wounds. Others banged their heads against walls and floors and had to wear protective helmets. The parents of such autistic children were desperate. Not only could they not cope, they needed respite from the stress. Parental training and counselling had to be undertaken if the child were ever to return to the home. Regardless, many stayed in the residential setting.

We went outside and crossed the grass to visit the group home where Julian would be placed until he went on to senior group home out in the community, she explained. A worker passed us across the grass, accompanying a young boy of about twelve. The boy's wrist was shackled to the worker's. He'd committed a serious crime and was housed in a different section, for young offenders.

It turned out that Thistletown was a center for several government social agencies, not just for autistic children. The boy pulled at his chain, making a grunting sound, low-throated. It was terrible and sad, and frightening.

"Yes, I know it looks that way, but he has to have a certain amount of exercise in the fresh air, so it's for his own good. He goes swimming and plays basketball too," assured my guide.

The group home was a relatively spacious modern bungalow — white walls, nice wood floors, pastel decor, abstract pictures on the walls — but it wasn't our cozy home. My guide eulogized on the kitchen's modernity, its cupboards and latest oven, and on the lovely bedrooms — each child had his own room.

"The kids love it here," she cried. "It's better than their own homes for some of them. He'll soon settle in."

Something about the way she said that alerted me. It sounded so cheerful, optimistic, convincing. Yes, a mother could leave her little boy here without too many qualms, if she didn't look too closely. It depended how desperate a parent's needs were.

I tried to be objective: Thistletown was genuinely struggling to develop programs for difficult children no one else seemed able to cope with. This is what I told myself.

I considered the future. Julian would eventually adapt, adjust, settle in, forget us over the years. Some counselor, kind enough, would be his housemother, group house "C" would be his home; Thistletown, his world; and TRE-ADD, his treatment. Eventually he would move on to a group home for adults. He would become who and what others shaped him to be, not necessarily better or worse than what we could provide as parents, but he wouldn't be *our* son, growing up in *our* family, loved by *us*.

My visit left me searching for more options — there had to be some alternative. I rang the Board of Education, first to inform them Julian would not be attending kindergarten at his local school after all. I was to meet with Miss Ellis, Coordinator for Special Services, responsible for the education of special needs children in the region: retarded, physically disabled, learning disabled, emotionally disturbed, and behaviorally maladjusted.

I confided my fears about the autistic unit at Thistletown to Miss Ellis, my dread at the thought of having to give up Jules.

"Well, we do have a small segregated kindergarten operating out of Dewie Public School, Mrs. Orchard. Julian could go there," she offered. She said that first she wanted to spend some time with Julian observing him, perhaps in our home or a playground, with my permission. Miss Ellis struck me as kind, informative, and clear.

"It's your choice, Mrs. Orchard," she said.

"You mean I don't have to place Julian in Thistletown or The Creche?"

"No, you don't. You are the one who decides. You know your son best."

"I'm sorry, I guess I'm confused, I've had the wrong impression; there's been so much to deal with."

"On the contrary, you strike me as coping very well in the circumstances. We have mothers coming in here wringing their hands absolutely frantic, in denial. I think you're doing remarkably well."

Mrs. Ellis went on, addressing my hesitation about sending Julian to Thistletown. "Those particular programs are excellent in their way. The Creche, for instance, was started up for autistic and other developmentally delayed children in the inner city of Toronto at a time when the public school system did not provide services for special needs children. But now we do."

Dewie Public School was but a ten-minute drive from our house, and Julian could be bussed in a special education bus provided by the Board. I had no objection to that. Lots of kids were bused all over the place. Yellow Catholic Separate School buses trailed the neighborhood picking up Catholic schoolchildren at pick-up points; blue Transhelp vans picked up the physically disabled. I had no objection to his class being segregated, with some integration in the regular kindergarten class. At least he'd be in a normal school mixing with normal kids . . . *and he'd live at home*. It was the best option yet.

But Dr. Rakka did not seem to think so. In the final consultation, she urged me to accept placement at Thistletown. I had little idea of the difficulties involved in raising an autistic child, she warned. Julian would not be capable of giving the love I'd expect as a mother; he could not cope with shifts in emotion. She insisted that he needed someone strict, objective, completely stable, and highly self-disciplined – as I so evidently was not. Dr. Rakka glanced at me as I sat tense and anxious in the chair. She said she was sure of Alec, but not so sure of me; she doubted I would last the course.

In making a choice for Julian counter to what Dr. Rakka had recommended, I sensed I had somehow, in one deft stroke, shifted authority from her domain to mine. Julian would attend public school the coming fall and thereafter be serviced by the Board of Education. I would be answerable to its mandate, but it would also be answerable to me, as parent, an implication I could not yet fully grasp but that perhaps Dr. Rakka did.

I clung steadfastly to one gleam of hope, the half-forgotten words of the audiologist, Dr. Saul, ringing in my head: *"This is not a slow child. This is a bright child. An intelligent child!"*

Part Two

Nine

On September 3, 1981, little Jules set off in the small yellow bus at the bottom of our drive. He was clutching his new Snoopy lunchbox to his chest, his long lashes sweeping his cheeks as he pressed his face to the glass.

I rang Elsie at work as soon as I got home from visiting Julian's class his first big day at school, that vital new beginning I so wanted to be successful. I asked the receptionist to put her through at once; it was urgent.

"The kids can't do anything, Else, they're non-verbal," I told my sister.

"Non-verbal?"

"They use a sort of sign language, but they're not deaf. Banging their fists together seems to mean 'toilet.' " I was disappointed and angry.

"Thel, it's imperative you get him out of there!"

Other than that brief visit to Surrey Place and Thistletown I had never had an opportunity to be in contact with "retarded" children. There weren't any special ed classes in any school where I'd taught in. When I was growing up in Wales, any child with a disability was kept away from public gaze in special homes behind tall hedges. Occasionally, I saw a child in town suffering from infantile paralysis wearing frightening leg irons, but never at school. Once I'd seen a teenager in a wheelchair who had been born a "blue baby" which had terrified me. I never thought of them as real children like myself, with mothers and fathers – not out of superiority but ignorance.

Now I found myself forced to come to grips with issues I struggled to grasp.

During my visit to Julian's class I tried not to look too closely at the other children. They were seated on the rug for "circle time," some clapped hands to a song. Others turned to look at me across the slanting sunlight; they had abnormal-looking features, some with drooling lips. The drooling upset me — why couldn't they close their mouths? One little boy, Lonnie, could not sit up, he seemed to have no spine. He lay in a sort of lolling helplessness, his face turned up to me in a vacant smile. He kept smiling at me while these cruel uncharitable thoughts surged through me. I was a mother in their midst. The littlest one, "SARAH" printed on her dress, ran to me, thin arms flailing. She also could not speak. She clung to my legs with all her strength as if she understood I was a mother. Perhaps they wanted their mothers, and some like Jules started to rock. "There now, Sarah," said the aide gently, releasing her fingers.

"They look so strange . . . misshapen," I confided to my friend Judith afterward. An Irishwoman with the gift of second sight, a widow who lived alone with a cat and bird, Judith had once been a social worker and a counselor for disturbed children and youth in the '50s.

"Don't let it bother you," she said comfortingly. Her grey hair fell softly round a kind face. "Yes they look different and it frightens you at first, but Julian won't notice that. He doesn't see that in people, only you and I do. Julian will be able to relax with them and that's what is important. They might do him good. Give it a chance."

I did not want to see or know more. I didn't want to get to know other parents.

Yet I had to admit that compared with Little Bo Peep Daycare with its cramped quarters the TMR (Trainable Mentally Retarded) kindergarten room was heaven. Dewie Public School was like any small suburban school, and the TMR classroom was like any other "normal" kindergarten room, open and sunny, well-stocked with games, books, puzzles, sand and water tables, dollhouses, rocking-horse, a rug. It had its own cloakroom with bright cubbyholes named for each child, and a washroom. Julian had already gone "pee-pee" in the toilet, an encouraging sign.

There was something called "the gross motor room" adjoining the kindergarten. It contained apparatus familiar yet strange: a specially large tricycle screwed to the floor, a huge double mattress occupying central place with a mound of cushions, towels and sponges, a wooden platform of steps Julian would be able to run up and down in seconds. There was also a huge softball (a pediatric ball) that had been provided by the occupational health department at the local hospital. The department sent resource workers regularly to advise the teacher on strategies.

But at four-and-a-half years, Julian was lithe and agile. He didn't need a gross motor room. Warning signals flashed through me. How low was "low functioning"?

There were only five children in the class. A ratio of five to two meant lots of individualized attention and guidance from Mrs. Wilkins and Mrs. Lilly. Mrs. Wilkins, who liked to be called "Wilkins," was an experienced TMR teacher in her fifties. Mrs. Lilly, "Lil," was heavy, maternal looking, solid, knowledgeable. Together, they were a team that inspired confidence. Julian would spend most of his time with these teachers, though he was also to be integrated into regular kindergarten down the hall for library and music. I tried not to think of him as segregated in a negative sense. If he'd been in a class of twenty-five kids he might have been overwhelmed and likely to withdraw into himself. It would be Little Bo Peep all over again. I decided to think of it as a special small class that would help him through this difficult period, help him to talk and socialize so he could move on. It wasn't going to be this way forever.

Julian bounded off the bus that afternoon clutching his lunchbox:

"Sawah . . . Trisha . . . . .Wicky . . . Lonny! Seatbelts! Seatbelts pliss!" He already knew the name of every child.

Marvelling, I checked the little blue communication book that from now on would be my link with his kindergarten world via notes from his teacher. Mrs. Wilkins had written:

> *Julian had a successful first day. Talked about school bus. Played with Fisher-Price school bus. Sang bus song. Painted school bus. In the gross motor room Julian pulled Lonny in the wagon, just for a minute. Enjoyed your visit, glad you came.*

I read the words over and over. Julian talking, singing, painting, having fun with a little playmate? He had done more in one morning in the TMR kindergarten than he had in two years at Little Bo Peep. I kissed the book, read it again, and wrote back *"Wonderful!"*

I now looked forward, eagerly, to the daily communications from Mrs. Wilkins. Greedily I pored over each comment, each precious word of progress, each item of development that told me Julian was improving, that his speech was developing, and that some form of social relationship, however infantile, was beginning to bud. *"This morning Julian painted and was singing while he painted."*

I couldn't get enough. I especially noted details such as: Julian's skills: *"Julian cut using scissors along a thick 2" line today."*

Julian cutting, learning cube shapes, stamping leaves, making french toast. Julian fighting! This most of all.

"We are getting some appropriate spontaneous speech from Julian especially at playtime. He said "NO Ricky!" and pushed his hand away when Ricky tried to take the stroller off him."

Thursday's entry: *"We began reverse integration today. Kerry came in to play from grade one, and Julian and Kerry had a great time together. Julian did what Kerry did and consequently did many things he had not done before."*

I was home on a year's unpaid leave of absence so that I could be on hand for Julian after he finished school at eleven-thirty. I decided to visit the class again one morning.

"He's talking a lot now," enthused Mrs. Wilkins.

"He is at home, too."

"Well, when they're with other children . . . "

This seemed contradictory considering the children were non-verbal, yet there was no doubt Julian's speech was being stimulated from spending time with these classmates and being in a small class setting.

It was circle time again. This time I found I could look more calmly at the children — Jules' little friends. Something drew me to them, a sort of flower-like tenderness welling up, the way their broken faces turned to me implicit in trust. They smiled and waved from the rug. Kerry, a firstgrader, was obviously the "normal" one joining in "reverse integration" for an hour. He was an alert child looking curiously at me, and smiling at Julian. I felt relieved he was next to Jules and at the same time shame at what seemed a subtle rejection of these others, tender wilting ones wanting my attention. Yet I looked eagerly at Kerry, his good looks, his healthy body, glad that Jules had chosen him to share a game with, the closest he had come to friendship. Could it be that he sensed Kerry was someone he could get a verbal response from, without understanding why? He talked to Kerry, built an elaborate house of LEGO bricks with him, but it was clear as I watched that Lonny was the one he loved.

"Lonny no walk!" he chuckled over and over, watching Lonny flounder in his wheelchair, trying to do a puzzle. Lil was guiding Lonny hand-over-hand to place one piece in the tray. It seemed to take hours. Each time Julian went by, Lonny's face lit up.

Ten

I was to meet the mothers of the children sooner than I expected. At Thanksgiving, Mrs. Wilkins organized a "Get to Know Each Other" lunch for parents and students at McDonald's. She thought it high time. All the children loved McDonald's and the restaurant was on the school boundary, next to the yard. I was nervous. What conversation did one make over fries and a burger with a mother who had been through the pain of diagnosis? "How's your child doing?" the usual cliché that got conversation rolling, seemed incongruous as I watched Sarah slam her head on the tray, and Lonny struggle to hold his fork with the "hammer grip." (This grip mastered meant your child was progressing in fine motor skills and could graduate to the proper pencil grip.)

Each mother sat with her child at the long table. "We thought it would be more comfortable for everyone as you know your child best," Mrs. Wilkins had smiled brightly

I did not note any warmth or appreciation in the guests, and two of them scowled at Mrs. Wilkins. The parents did not talk. Lonny's mother, who looked like a teenager, sat between Julian and Lonny. She lifted Lonny's glass for him to sip, lifted his fries, one by one, for him to nibble off the end of her fingers, the ketchup dribbling down. She cupped his lolling head in her hands and slowly squeezed juice between his thick blue lips. It trickled down his chin onto his neck. Mrs. Wilkins and Lil both rushed with napkins.

Suddenly a little girl, Patricia, shrieked and shuddered. She started banging her head on the table.

"Now Patricia!" her mother tightened, we all tightened. She glanced at the test of us looking away, her body stiffening as she pushed Patricia's head down.

"Watch! She's choking, Marg," said Sarah's mother. Sarah was making humming noises. We all tried to carry on as if none of this was happening.

The girls' mothers were flushed and agitated, they frowned at Mrs. Wilkins who was proffering comfort like, "Yes, she does that sometimes, doesn't she?"

No child was eating except for Julian. Julian was silent, working his way through his fries. He loved McDonald's food. He ate carefully using the wooden fork to spear each fry , and used two hands independently to hold his burger. I was suddenly conscious of these ordinary skills so taken for granted.

Suddenly he looked up: "More fries pliss. More fries, more burger. Dwink for Juyan."

"Oh, he can talk!" exclaimed one of the mothers.

At once, every mother's eyes seemed to swivel on Julian in the caboose.

"But this is very good, very good talking!" interposed a mother, Mrs. Malotitch, "He good boy, very advanced. My girl Nadia not talk. Not yet. She autistic, you know that?"

"Julian is autistic, too." Nadia, had not stopped rocking and moaning the entire time. Her body shuddered in little spasms every so often. There was something familiar about the way she did not look at her mother, or me.

"Julian is autistic?" Mrs. Malotitch got very excited.

There could be differences between autistic children. Nadia, very pretty with glossy black curls and bright dark eyes, was non-verbal and violent, even at six. I was yet to understand the constant sudden tightening that seized her body might be minor convulsions. She screwed up a french fry.

"No Nadia!" Mrs. Malotitch slapped Nadia's hand.

"Yes, Julian is beginning to talk a lot more, now, thanks to this class." I mumbled in a low voice. I was hating this, hating the uncomfortable stares of envy and regret from these mothers whose children had no speech, none emerging.

Nadia dropped the fry and let out a blood-curdling screech that seemed to slice through the caboose.

"Now stop that right now, Nadia!" shouted Mrs. Malotitch.

A server, a youngster from the main complex, stood in the doorway with more Coke. He stared fascinated at us all: mothers bent nurturing over their too-big children attempting to feed them, fry by fry, the youngsters rocking and moaning, spitting out pieces of fries, jerking their mouths obstinately. Fries scattered around, ketchup oozed everywhere. You felt anger, shame. Surely, Mrs. Wilkins must have known it would be like this, nothing but an embarrassment for the parents. How could anyone imagine that were we enjoying this? My head throbbed, my eyes ached from trying to smile so much, from trying so hard to make kind remarks, to keep up a semblance of happiness as if it were not so bad.

I said desperate things like: "She likes that fry, doesn't she?"

Only Lonny's mother, Betsy, was honest. She turned to me, and I saw a worn young face. She was a single parent and worked only part-time as a waitress in The Blue Duck, so that she could be home when Lonny got off the bus. She never had any time for herself, she said softly. Sometimes her mother took Lonny to give her a break. She lived in a two-room apartment. She was gentle, kind, and loved Lonny.

What could I say? I still saw Lonny by his disabilities, by his weak scrunched-up human body I could not bear to look at. I could not see, not yet, the beauty of his life, only the fleeting reluctant tenderness that took me by surprise at times, the way he curled his finger round his mother's waiting to be fed, like a nestling. Julian loved Lonny, you could see. He kept touching him, giggling.

But wouldn't I have preferred that Julian show preference for Ricky — smarter, brighter, handsome Ricky, with the "borderline" I.Q.? I was hoping Ricky's mother would invite Julian over to play sometime: Julian and Ricky, the ones with the most promise.

In the parking lot at McDonald's, I had my first taste of teacher bashing.

"They're useless teachers!" The mother of Patricia glowered. "This has to be the lousiest program in the whole district!" she said grimly.

Sarah's mother joined in. "Sarah has learned absolutely nothing in this class! She can't say a word."

We stood by the fence overlooking the schoolyard. Both mothers were ugly with anger as their little girls rocked and thrashed about in their strollers. Time to go home, but to what?

"Don't you just *hate* TMR?" Sarah's mother spit out the word. " 'Retarded! *Trainable Mentally Retarded! Brain-damaged!*' That's what the kids call our kids out in the yard. 'There go the brain-damaged kids.' Wilkins needs to get rid of that compound, too!"

Patricia's mother glowered again: "Patricia still can't speak either!"

Patricia's mother gritted her teeth. There was a stiff wind. Early snow began to fall, a thin veil over us all; I wished I were oceans away, far, far.

Their names were Helen and Olga, they said. Helen and Olga wanted their children integrated into regular kindergarten, with normal children. Then their daughters' terrible behaviors, the head-banging, screamings, scratching, throwing things would lessen, maybe stop.

A bell rang. Children began to run up the slope to form lines at the doors: normal children, wondrously verbal, normal children, normal I.Q., shouting and jostling, joking and singing, laughing and talking wonderful language, each word, each phrase, catching the air. How had they learned it? Their zillions of brain cells computing, absorbing the scintillating words they so took for granted. We watched in silence against the fence, keeping a firm grip on our children.

It was what Helen and Olga wanted for Sarah and Patricia. To run up that same slope with those others, laughing and singing into the light, even if scrabbling on their hands and knees, broken and weak.

Mrs. Malotitch invited me for tea for Tuesday. She wanted Julian to play with Nadia. Mrs. Malotitch was another angry mother, her anger coming from great pain that Nadia was not at Julian's level, that she could not speak like Julian. If Julian played with Nadia, maybe Nadia too would speak.

But I did not want to be drawn into more pain, bear her pain, which was like a burden over my chest and face. I preferred to get to know Ricky's mother, so Julian would get to improve himself. Ricky was not autistic, so had better social behaviors for Julian to model. I was caught by Mrs. Malotitch's plea, "Julian will be good for Nadia." But how good would Nadia be for Julian? Wouldn't he pick up her bad behaviors?

But I need not have worried. Julian seemed not to be even aware of Nadia, nor she of him. As Mrs. Malotitch and I sat at coffee they circled the dining-room table, wary and distant. They seemed not to recognize each other even though they spent every morning together in class. They passed each other by within inches silently, without pause or glance. Yet surely each must know the other was there!

A huge Doberman pinscher came bounding into room. "Down, Casper, down!"

Nadia quivered and tightened, clenching her body. It was obvious the dog terrified her. Her eyes squeezed shut, not unlike the way Julian tensed up, tightening himself when Alec and I argued, our voices zinging uncomprehendingly over his head. Oh, this was awful, why had I agreed to come?

It would be so much more peaceful and quiet without that dog, any dog. Why couldn't Mrs. Malotitch, Vera, see that? Why did she deliberately hang on to the dog? But then why did Alec and I argue with Julian around? As if he could cope? As if he were not there?

"Do you think the dog frightens her, Mrs. Malotitch?"

"Vera. Call me Vera, Thelma. No, Nadia she loves the dog, the dog loves her."

Vera herself was a powerful strong heavy woman from Eastern Europe. She had been through much, had been an engineer in her own country. She had immigrated to Canada for Nadia's sake.

"Now stop that, Nadia!" She slapped Nadia's arm, and shook her. "Stop! Stop!"

"Stop stop," laughed Julian. He was fascinated with Mrs. Malotitch. "Stop, Nadia, stop."

Nadia's distress was probably due to our intruding on her routine, her space. I hinted as much, but at once Vera swept this aside: Nadia had to get used to people. It was no good giving in to them. You had to make them come out of their autism. It sounded like the Kaufman's, except that Raun had been a baby at the time; I did not want to get into that again.

Vera wanted Nadia and Julian to play outside in the yard. There was a swing-set and climbing frame set up for Nadia and friends. Toys, balls, a wading pool, a sandbox, the sand in it smooth, untouched. Lonely little Nadia. I wondered if they would "play." I worried that Nadia might attack Julian, scratch his eyes during one of her seizure-like contortions. I could not feel altruistic about Nadia all the time. I was more concerned with protecting Julian than about her suffering and needs when it came right down to it. I was concerned about the dog attacking them too. Didn't nervous excitable children set these dogs off?

Vera insisted Caspar was trained, he loved children. She was determined to put the children out because she desperately wanted to talk about Mrs. Wilkins and Lil, what bad bad teachers they were, and what a useless program they ran. "Nadia, she learn nothing with them!"

But could any program teach Nadia? I had no knowledge as yet of teaching autistic children, but it seemed obvious Nadia's violence would have to be treated somehow before she could learn and develop. I had only a vague concept of the term "treatment." Hadn't this been the one of the objectives of the program at The Creche and Thistletown? "He'll have to learn to *sit* first." I could see now the kindergarten class was not suited to Nadia; she might benefit from the more intense treatment-oriented programming at The Creche or Thistledown; but Julian was coming along well. A lot of credit for his progress was due to Mrs. Wilkins and Lil and the children. Somehow those little ones, speechless themselves, stimulated Jules. I shared my thoughts with Vera, but instantly regretted it.

Nadia's mother looked so envious, so sad. What was the right thing to say, the way to be, with a mother like this? It was so obvious her little girl was not at the level of Julian yet, may never be; that Nadia had no special friend.

"Julian good, very very good boy."

Once again my eyes ached from trying to smile kindly so much. I tried to think of some incident, some illustration, to show how difficult Julian could be too, that there was hope for Nadia. That was what Vera wanted to hear, wasn't it?

"Well, Julian once ate a dead seagull."

"Never never never eat dead seagulls, or anything else off the ground!" I had cried passionately, wiping feathers from his mouth that Sunday. We'd been by the river in Port Credit.

"My God, he's eating a *seagull!*" Elsie had screamed — "Brett stay back, don't *touch* him!"

"Never! Never!" Julian had echoed, mimicking the expression on my face. Was that what I looked like — that ugly contorted mean face tensed with anxiety? Much like Vera's face right then.

Vera put down her cup.

"Yes, Nadia also! She eat her own shit!"

"Yeah, well, it's called *pica,* Vera."

So you began to see it, how close Nadia and Julian nevertheless were, that two children from completely different backgrounds and countries yet displayed outstanding characteristics unlearned from each other. Nadia seemed just a more extreme form of Julian. What part of the brain dictated eating dead seagulls and one's own feces? Why couldn't they understand not to eat carcasses and poop? Every other kid could.

Anger surged through Vera.

"Hah! Theory, theory! But what they doing about it, Thelma?"

I sipped desperately at my coffee. My eyes and face ached all the more from all the smiling. I wished I had never agreed to this visit. This was painful, having to face this unpleasant ugly woman's anger and pain. I also recognized that her suffering was what made her ugly, and that the ugliness would turn people against her.

She hated Dr. Rakka who had also diagnosed Nadia. But unlike Alec and me, Vera rejected the diagnosis. She felt Dr. Rakka was fifty years behind the times. New ideas and theories were out about autism in America, in California. Vera had read not only *Son-Rise* but Dr. Lovaas's experimental work with autistic children, *The Me Book*. Nadia could be worked with, but not in the kind of stupid class she was in. Autistic children did not have to be autistic for life.

The Kaufmans had done it, but could Vera be a Suzi Kaufman?

Vera was daring to challenge not only Dr. Rakka and the entire medical profession, but also the Board of Education and the whole concept of special ed.

"You just think! They say polio incurable once. All those cripple children now have cure. What about before they find out about bacteria and virus? They torture people, believe in bad spirit. Now they discover bacteria and have penicillin. How we not know there is cure for autism?"

When I asked Mrs. Wilkins at my next visit if Julian ever played with Nadia, she wrinkled up her nose and said Mrs. Malotitch had gone off to the States looking for some cure in California.

Nadia was worse than Julian, said Mrs. Wilkins. She was very autistic, and her chances were seriously limited. Was Nadia's brain more damaged than Julian's, then? That whatever was not connecting connected less in Nadia's brain, but was the same in essence as in Julian's? It was disturbing. I would liked to have studied them in school side by side, observing closely. What was going on with Nadia, and was it the same in Julian?

"Poor Nadia," murmured Mrs. Wilkins. Her mother just could not face the prognosis, could not accept. I sensed tacit approval of myself: I was a realistic "good" mother who understood the diagnosis and Julian's future, and was bravely facing up to things.

But I'd admired Vera's guts and anger. I was sorry she had gone as if some opportunity, some chink of light, had in a small way presented itself.

Vera was a fighter. She was determined to have something better than was being offered and she was remarkably daring. Why wasn't I? Partly because I was satisfied for now with the class. I saw improvement in Julian in every way and Mrs. Wilkins must too. It was a good time to bring up the possibility of a higher functioning autistic-type language program for Julian next year.

Mrs. Wilkins hesitated. There was the opening at Thistletown. It was still being held open for Julian, she hinted.

So Mrs. Wilkins knew about the Thistletown placement for Julian. Well, of course, she would. She had access to his OSR, (Ontario School Record) in the office; she would have read Dr. Rakka's report. Information was passed along like a secret code over your head, and there was nothing you could do about it.

Carefully we skirt around the issue. I need to assure Mrs. Wilkins how much I recognize Julian's wonderful advancement without seeming to be dissatisfied. And I want him to keep on advancing, who knew to what exciting level? Juli printing and singing the letters of the alphabet, Juli learning numbers and colors and the days of the week, cooking, and hammering nails on a cobbler's bench, his latest achievement. Mrs. Wilkins smiled. "Yes, Julian was doing wonderfully," she said.

But was it enough? Enough to get him out of TMR? Out of the label "brain-damaged" for life. Re-diagnosed. It all had to do with language. Somehow I had to raise the level of his language skills from that "low-to-moderate retarded" to "borderline." He could then be placed in SLD: Special Learning Disability. Wasn't that what he had, intrinsically, "a special language learning disability"?

Eleven

W ell, you certainly handle him beautifully, Mrs. Orchard. You echo and guide his language well, but watch the complex sentences though."

Nancy, the speech therapist at Erindale Oaks Treatment Centre, was observing Julian. He was there for a speech and language assessment ordered by the special education department of the Board of Education, to ascertain whether TMR-kindergarten was the appropriate placement for him. The results would be important, influencing the choice of placement next year.

The therapists were young, enthusiastic, knowledgeable, fresh out of university, and the Erindale Oaks was modern, full of new toys and equipment, bright and innovative, with a large carpeted play area. The decor was pleasing, peaceful. I had been invited to bring one of Julian's toys, so I chose the Fisher-Price bus as the most likely traditional toy he might play with now that he went on a school bus himself. It had little wooden figures he called his "dollies" that he loved to put on and off the bus.

We were invited to sit on the floor and play together, while Brenda, another therapist, watched quietly from the side. Julian was at ease right away. I was careful not to get too close to him, allowing him plenty of physical space. He was busy at once with the bus, putting the dollies on one by one, naming them and solemnly re-enacting his experiences. "Bye bye," he echoed. This was real imaginative play, and he was tolerating me next to him. There was tremendous improvement, not just in his language but social skills, already in the months since Dr. Rakka's diagnosis in July. Brenda was pleased.

Next we had a snack together at a small table, to demonstrate interactive skills and social relationship, while Brenda watched through a window. Everything continued smoothly, beautifully. Julian even helped put the tea things away and fold the cloth.

Afterwards, Julian went to a smaller testing room with Brenda to do language testing; they were using the Peabody and the WISC-R, standard psychological and I.Q. tests that Dr. Rakka and Dr. Bland the school psychologist had used. "It might not be any different to Dr. Rakka's assessment," hinted Brenda. The remark niggled at me, that Brenda had been privy to Dr. Rakka's report. It seemed I could never get away from Dr. Rakka. But again it all went so well, and Jules had loved being in the beautiful facility with its large airy rooms overlooking the valley. If only it could always be like this. If there could be one small area set aside for the treatment of children with autism. I did not want to give up Brenda now I had found her. I needed her input, her guidance, her continued example relating to Julian.

The testing now moved into the physiological workout to check why Julian kept walking on his toes (even though I insisted toe walking was part of autism). We were in a large exercise room, like a huge gross motor room. The focal point was apparatus specially designed to develop strength and mobility of limbs. There were ramps at each entrance, extra wide doors. Julian bounded through the session. He ran over benches, hopped through hoops, climbed sets of steps with ease and agility, swung like a monkey over bars, balanced gracefully along the beam, followed the chalk line.

"There's certainly nothing wrong with his hamstrings!" proclaimed the therapist.

As Julian continued to be tested, executing dance-like steps over the wooden balance beams, I was becoming aware of an eerie silence in the room, the stillness of children who could barely move, their silent mothers who avoided each other's eyes. These mothers bent assiduously over their babies, their faces furrowed in concentration, working their babies' limbs, massaging joints, moving tendons, extending a muscle here, turning their babies' heads with infinite care and weariness on frail necks, slowly, with attention, bodies caught in the flow of light and shadow across the floors.

These parents carrying their whimpering, weak little ones in their arms, looked wonderingly at Julian executing pirouettes over the trampoline, being evaluated for muscle tone. I turned away feeling guilty about his prowess, his physical normality among these parents whose suffering was etched on their faces. Wanting to yet turn to them, connect, but how? One had a baby on her shoulder shuddering at intervals like a limp doll.

"What's wrong with your son?" she snapped. "He don't look like he belongs here!"

I now realized the Centre serviced the physically disabled, and Julian was hardly that. "They are worried he walks on his toes," sounded feeble. How to explain Julian's tirade of red versus yellow boots, the shirt that had to be buttoned up to the top, knives and forks laid in a certain order, one brand of Colgate over another and placed in the exact groove above the basin otherwise intense tears, screams — how to explain this in the face of her great burden?

But he needed the Centre, too. I was horrified to feel a momentary flash of resentment against these mothers and their children for having these facilities all to themselves, when Julian had to be turned away. There was no specific treatment center for children with autism in the region, despite the high taxes we paid. There was also a shortage of speech and language therapists, the very thing Julian needed.

Brenda and Nancy hesitated, ready for the summation. Brenda chose her words carefully. Julian could continue to make great strides, but the focus had to be on ensuring a response to exactly what I said. Echolalia — echoing and repeating words — was not necessarily wrong; it was his means right now of acquiring language and was not to be discouraged, but I had to keep his mind focussed on comprehending the meaning of what was said to him. His receptive and expressive language and general cognitive abilities were still in the retarded range at the twenty-month level, said Brenda gently.

I felt tears coming, weariness and unexpected disappointment. Still only at twenty-months! It seemed that no matter how hard I tried, I could never get him out of that twenty-month range so predicted by Dr. Rakka. Despite all the acquisition of vocabulary he had made the past five months, it seemed he still could not use language at a normal meaningful level of interchange. Would he ever? At least Brenda was going to make recommendations to the board for Julian to be placed in a special language class for autistic children, should such a class exist.

Later I watched as a child outside in the parking lot was being slowly lowered out of a van. His mother waited patiently, even cheerfully, by the ramp for this tiresome long maneuver to be done with. It would take Jules and me moments to hop in the car and be gone. I was ashamed – of course the Centre was deservedly for these ones.

"Nice place for them here," I attempted a smile.

"Ah, yes we are grateful they built this place, they do so much for Enrico."

The mother looked curiously at Julian, who had begun to tug at my arm. "Dummy, dummy," he insisted, asking for his favorite toy.

"He's autistic," I offered.

"Ah, he so beautiful."

I felt I should say the same about her son. And he was beautiful. Despite his soft thick legs hanging inert as the attendant lifted him out, the shapeless mass inside his pants, his luminous eyes fixed on us welcoming, filled with such light. You forgot about the deformed body that no longer mattered. Somehow we were all radiating around this Enrico. "Enwico!" laughed Julian, touching him.

The Speech and Language Communication Report, when it arrived, was five pages long, clear, succinct, helpful, divided into sections listing the instruments and protocols used. It said wonderful encouraging things about my speech work with Julian. But what I still needed was a real live speech therapist in my living room, to show me, help me. I was told to try the Geneva Centre for Autism, which served the greater Toronto area.

The Centre provided excellent informative workshops on autism for parents, but no actual hands-on help in our home. It turned out we were not under their mandate either.

I visited the lending library in the old Geneva Centre on St. George Street. There were tomes on autism to read: books, pamphlets, journals, text-books on the etiology, symptoms, pharmacology, theories of mind, methods of teaching, means of controlling through behavior modification and aversives; summations by experts in the field of autism, often contradictory.

It did not help to read at one point: *"Baby's brainpower set by the age of one."*

Nevertheless I went out and bought a bright red play table, two painted chairs, and a soft beige scatter rug similar to the ones in the play area at Erindale Oaks Treatment Centre. Alec cleaned out the basement, set up the new play area in a cozy corner for Julian and Polly. I laid out plasticine, puzzles, a music box, the cash register, and the Fisher-Price toy bus with its little wooden dollies.

"Oh, Mommy, it's so nice!" cries Polly excitedly. "I can bring Stephanie and Krystal in to play!"

At once I had a vision of Julian and Polly and little friends busily interacting and playing for long happy hours together, with me facilitating on the side.

But Julian had other ideas. Without a word he seized the yellow bus and dollies and stomped back upstairs, setting them up once again in a row on the coffee table.

"Mommy dolly, Daddy dolly, girl dolly, boy dolly."

Twelve

nd so it began, on and on with the little dollies, his new passion, day after day, the minute he ran in off the bus. The dollies were waiting where he'd placed them that morning in a line facing the window.

Was this what I should be encouraging? Was this the way out of "severe" delay?

"Sarah fall down! Poor poor Sarah!"

He knocks down the girl dolly — *thud.*

So now I know, without looking at the communication book, what happened in school that morning.

"Julian fall down. Bad Juyan!"

I am shaken. Is this how he sees himself? And is this still language operating at a twenty-months level? The same quality of play as the rigid little boy's only months ago at Dr. Rakka's? And a year ago with Mr. Corsen?

He has placed the dollies in another order, so I have to pay attention if I want to know what's going on. He takes the mommy and daddy, and what does he do with them? Puts daddy dolly against mommy dolly: "Tiss."

Finally he becomes fascinated with the boy dolly as time goes by, but does not make the connection with himself, but he is careful to give boy dolly an extra piece of cookie and an extra sip of juice from the tea set.

Suddenly I was weary of the dollies. My voice ached, and something else more nebulous. Early snow streamed down the trees sprinkling the lawn, misting the river, everything out there bound in fine ice. How long I have been going on with this, the months passing in a smothering silence? The house suddenly hot and heavy, brooding and still. I feel its somberness, which is my own – the subtle misgivings, the insidious dismay closing in, a restless yearning. For myself, I needed time for myself. *Why isn't this enough?* I tighten anxiously. Yet it was so important, these hours with Julian now, this chance so precious, the drama of little dollies, the spurts of passion, the fire of his needs! Words spilling forth. It was wonderful..

Is it February, now? March, with the glowering sky? At once Julian herds little dollies under the shelter of the ashtray.

"Big storm!" he pants, not without pleasure in his anguish. "Little dollies f'ighten."

"Julian frightened of big storm?" I echo.

"Don't be f'ighten, Julian!" His voice takes on a new falsetto that indicates Mrs. Wilkins. "Don't be f'ighten, Lonny. Lonny f'ighten! Sawah f'ighten, don't cwy, Sawah."

And the little dollies cower under the ashtray. I note this, thrilled – this is real play, passionate creation, Lord Julian in his realm!

He takes out "Daddy" dolly and stomps him back to the fore: "Doc'r Bland not f'ighten!"

And what must Dr. Bland, the school psychologist, have been doing in the TMR kindergarten? Examining, observing, probing, deciding – the final judgment. Surely, he must be observing the wonderful improvement in Julian, the advancing facility of speech and thought, the grasp of relationship, the involvement here.

Excited, I watch little dollies creep out of their hiding place. Storm gone. *Yes, surely this is enough, this satisfaction sufficient,* I urge myself. *My precious one, little Juli, Oh Jules, so busily probing, adjusting, the deepest recesses; surely my own heart can be quieted, misgivings assuaged, selfishness burned in these holy fires:*

"Oh dolly, dolly, cwying tears!"

Dear Mrs. Orchard, This morning Perky the canary got out of his cage — we suspect the new boy — Julian was most concerned and actually told Mrs. Dunn, "You put that bird back in cage right now!" Can you believe it?

I didn't want to get my hopes too high, but it seemed obvious Mrs. Wilkins must be noting the great strides Julian had made this year. I felt such hope.

"Funny to hear his voice at last," observed Elsie. "I always wondered what it would sound like. Now we can't shut him up."

She was exaggerating, but I loved to hear it. "Oh, you think Jules is talking more, Else?"

"Oh for sure. What a difference from just six months ago, there's no comparison," said Elsie generously. Meanwhile Brett was to play the part of the giant in the kindergarten play at his school, Holy Rosary Separate. Could Alec lend him his black belt?

Carefully I check the guide to children's speech and language development given me by Brenda and Nancy. I didn't want to deceive myself again about Julian's advancement. I wanted this to be real. "Causes for Concern" in language development at age two cited: *"Does not use common objects for intended purpose in pretend play."* It meant Julian was now at least at age-two level. He was nearly six and a half.

Gusts of snow beat against the blurry window, the world whitened and faded . . . It was a shock. Still only "two."

Yet I saw hope. I saw pronouns being used now, an emerging sense of identity, commands that were at a four-year level. He was using correct order of syntax like any other child. I seized at every-thing, every small gain, each minute success, every pronoun, conjunction, hopeful he was overcoming, bit by bit, at least one of Wing's terrible Triad. This famous Triad of impairments found in autistic children was designated by Lorna Wing, a British specialist in the field of autism. Her Camberwell study done in London in the '70s with Judith Gould, had concluded that autistic children, retarded or not, had three outstanding undeniable indisputable features: severe social impairment, specifically the inability to engage in two-way reciprocal interaction with children their own age; severe communication deficits, and an "absence of imagination, including pretend play."

Wing noted that instead of "pretend play" the autistic child substituted repetitive ritualistic stereotypical behaviors and stim-ming, such as Julian waving his fingers back and forth in front of his nose hypnotically. This was something still to work on.

There was also his ongoing obsession with order, another aspect of Wing's terrible Triad. Everything in the house had to be ordered just so according to patterns the rest of us barely noticed: the mail had to be in its exact place on the coffee table one inch behind the ashtray; our seating arrangement at the breakfast table followed exact configuration, Alec to the east, Jules to the north . . . etc. He demanded the buttons of his shirt be done up in exact order from the bottom up to his throat. If this didn't happen, Julian would unleash screams of torment, clench his fists and beat at us. But this was not the anger of a spoiled child; it was one of distress, anxiety. It was so weird, and so stressful, I often wanted to scream.

"Oh-h, yes, he has to have everything buttoned and zipped up to death," Mrs. Wilkins agreed.

I was disturbed that Mrs. Wilkins had been aware of Julian's obsession but had never mentioned it as if it was somehow a part of his autism that could not be changed. The only reference to autistic behavior in the interim report card half way through the school year was in a general though ominous way : *"Julian must learn to deal with frustration and to adapt to changes."*

"Reciprocal" was another very important word, perhaps the most important, the key, according to Wing. One had to encourage two-way reciprocity when working with an autistic child.

He still would turn his back to me as he set up his little dollies. At once I was obliterated, as if I just was not there for him. *But I am, Juli, I am. Let me have a turn with you.*

Anxiously I consulted the language guide again. Taking turns is not just a social nicety, it's the vital ingredient in a social relationship comprised of listening, talking, sharing minds and hearts. So far, Julian only talked and listened to himself. Yet he'd made progress, and I concentrated on that.

It was May, the time when the In-School Placement and Review Committee (IPRC) was to make a decision on Julian's placement for September. Mrs. Wilkins looked at me, perplexed. I had asked whether Julian was going into regular kindergarten next year or, even more wonderful, grade one.

"Oh! But my dear — "

My dear, what? Mrs. Wilkins looked agitated, concerned again. "He'll be going on with the others. To primary TMR."

"You mean, he really is retarded then?"

I meant "retarded" like Patricia, like Lonny.

"But my dear! Well, yes!" fluttered Mrs. Wilkins as if there could never have been any doubt. Julian was designated to go on to the Primary TMR program at Sunny Acres Public School, as close a placement the Board of Education could find to our house.

Pain glowed through me for Julian. How could he be so retarded? He was going to be with Patricia and Sarah, and Lonny and Alphonse and others for life. He would attend this Primary TMR class, then at nine years of age switch to Junior TMR; at eleven to Intermediate TMR, forever and ever. There was even a senior segregated school for the retarded somewhere out on Fifth Line.

I protested: but what about the outstanding gains he had made? The improvement in behavior, the endless hours I had worked with him on his vocabulary, his pronouns. The dramas of his little dollies? He could talk, communicate meaningfully, play imaginatively. I was aware of my voice thickening in an ugly tense, urgent way.

"There are other children in the 'new' class who can talk, who will even be ahead of Julian, who can say things like the time and the weather when asked, Mrs. Orchard."

I sensed she felt I was becoming difficult. God forbid, a "Difficult Parent."

Julian had certainly improved, went Mrs. Wilkins smoothly. He was coming along. But that was all. The diagnosis remained: "low-to-moderate retarded and autistic."

"What are you hiding, Jules?"

Julian hesitated, giggled, and thrust out his arm.

"Oh, it's a caterpillar!"

"Juyan's cattypillar." Jules stroked it softly. It was soft green with wavy bristles crawling up his elbow.

"Your own caterpillar. Well, I guess he can come along for the ride, Jules."

We were on our way to Fritz's Deli for a drink of pop, coffee for me. The sun blazed in the hot clear sky, the trees heavy with end-of-summer foliage. Jules hummed happily to himself as we walked down into the village of Port Credit. He was slim and lithe, his thick dark curls clustered round his neck; a gentle soul. He held his arm out rigidly all the way to Mr. Sun's, moving the caterpillar back to his elbow whenever it reached the sleeve of his T-shirt.

"One day the caterpillar will turn into a butterfly, Jules, and fly away." I introduced the idea tentatively. I could see problems when it came time to remove this caterpillar and leave it on some leaf. "He needs to eat and rest on a plant, Jules, when we get to Fritz's Deli. Caterpillars don't like ham and cheese bagels, Jules, they need leaves."

Surprisingly Julian conceded to leave the caterpillar outside in a tub of petunias.

"Turn into buttfly," said Jules happily to Fritz.

Thirteen

It was Julian's first year in the Primary TMR class. We received the results of the psychological test that every student was given by the end of their first year in a TMR program. Julian's scores put everyone in a tizzy: what was little Julian Orchard doing being placed in a TMR Primary Class with scores like that?

At six and a half years old, he had presented at the level of a seven and half year old on the McCarthy Scales of Children's Abilities, Puzzle-Solving Subtest. He also scored a high-average in the WISC-R Problem Solving Block Design Subtest. Dr. Bland had been impressed. The McCarthy Scales were considered the best estimate of non-verbal intellectual potential. No one questioned McCarthy.

This part of the test was "non-verbal," cautioned Dr. Bland, who had conducted the testing. Dr. Bland had a corpulent body and a glistening bald head, with steel glasses over protuberant big blue eyes; a few sprouts of reddish hair sprung round a jocular pinkish face, and he had a bushy moustache. Beads of sweat trickled down his brow.

Julian's *verbal* I.Q., stressed Dr. Bland, was still "low-to-moderate retarded," as expected. "Expected" because splinter skills were typical of autistic intelligence: high-functioning in this, retarded in that, up and down. For instance, when Dr. Bland had asked Julian "What is Mummy's name?" Julian had replied: *"Mommy is Daddy."*

Well, there you had it. Everyone in the meeting round the kindergarten table relaxed, except me. *"Bizarre,"* Dr. Bland had written on Julian's report. Bizarre and retarded remained the general consensus. In fact, Dr. Bland opted that Julian seemed to have problems with emotional identity, period. He was going around kissing lampposts on community walks. Kissing and hugging, and having conversations with every lamppost on the street while never thinking to hug Miss Hodge, his new teacher. Perhaps I should have stopped it right then but hadn't I hoped that if he at least loved a lamppost then one day he might love Mommy. Wasn't it better to love a lamppost, Dr. Bland, than nothing at all?

Of course, wheezed Dr. Bland, bemused, there was always the possibility Julian couldn't tell the difference, heh heh! Everyone laughed. Dr. Bland had a repertoire of autistic anecdotes he loved to regale.

The real point was that Julian could not survive life with autistic splinter skills, emphasized Dr. Bland. Geometric block designs were not going to see him through, and, therefore, he did belong in TMR.

But Dr. Bland was too clever and astute a psychologist not to recognize the implications of Julian's testing. Above average in the normal range was above average. What was needed, he realized, was for the Board to start up a higher-functioning autistic class specifically for children like Julian. There were four or five other PDD-autistic children across the region. Julian's intelligence was becoming more apparent and disturbing as he progressed through the primary years in TMR.

By age seven Julian was no longer the frightened anxious little boy with the thick curly fringe who had stepped off the bus two years earlier from kindergarten. He was now tense, hyperactive, even mischievous, and highly verbal in an echolalic way. Having Julian in the classroom was something like having the radio stuck on the same station, sighed Miss Hodge. Jules had become fascinated by *Sesame Street,* and it was like listening to an unending, idiosyncratic version of the TV show. For Jules had discovered Bert and Ernie and Oscar the Grouch!

While Patricia painstakingly pegged her way through a hundred pegs slowly, laboriously, on the pegboard and Lonny was learning to raise a cup to his lips by himself — activities that Julian could do swiftly, unerringly — Julian was prancing round the classroom chortling "Throw Miss Hodge in the garbage!" He would sing "I love TRASH!" By a certain logic I deduced he loved Miss Hodge and wanted to throw her in the garbage can as a sort of compliment. Miss Hodge did not look flattered.

A normal child knew instinctively not to go around shouting "Throw Miss Hodge in the garbage" in front of her, but social niceties are precisely what autistic children have most difficulty with. The most one could hope for was to train him each time, incident by incident, what not to say or do. It was tiring and time-consuming because he had no idea of status, or hierarchy; "Jules, do not say that. Miss Hodge is your teacher, we don't talk about teachers like that, it's not funny," sounded obvious, but Julian laughed all the more. It was Wing's Triad again: language confused by social deficits.

But Miss Hodge had never heard of Lorna Wing or her Triad. She just wanted to stop the incessant acting out. But Jules *was* acting out imaginatively, enjoying the same TV programs as thousands of other kids in the world and that was surely exciting. He was actually *imagining himself to be Oscar.* Just as he had done with little dollies, he came running in from school to grab his dolls, Bert and Ernie, and begin his "play," listening to the Bert 'n Ernie record I'd bought him. Julian chuckled to himself as he put on his favorite record, naughty Ernie teasing solid implacable stoic Bert. "Ernie's BAD, Mommy!" Julian's eyes glittered with delight, "Now don't be bad, Juyan!"

"Jules, you're a good boy," I smiled, not wanting to spoil his fun but concerned at the connection he was making, which wasn't exactly what we wanted. "A very good boy. You can enjoy Ernie but don't act like him, Jules." But Julian only laughed all the more.

So I could see how much Julian's difficulties stemmed from his "autism" rather than from his retardation. He exhibited weird behaviors that were often hard to explain, behaviors that a teacher just did not expect or was not trained to cope with, especially if she'd never actually come in contact with an autistic child. And Julian was the only autistic child in Sunny Acres.

"What's he up to *now?*" fumed the aide.

We were at special needs swimming, the weekly leisure swim for the TMR class at Grayson Secondary School pool. I was teaching three-quarter time then and I'd offered to come as a parent volunteer to help out. The children always were required to line up against the wall until Miss Hodge gave the signal to jump into the pool, a safety measure. But though Julian was naturally athletic and a good swimmer, he had difficulty lining up, following directions. He jumped about, fussed and protested, unhappy, distressed, ignoring the whistle. He would not get into line because the line was *not in the same order* as the previous week, I tried to explain to Miss Hodge as I held on to Julian. It sounded insane. If Lonnie was not next to Gerda, for instance, Julian would shriek and beat his head in frustration.

"That's nuts!" said the aide. "He's insane."

Would he always be like this?

Fourteen

D on't be concerned about why he has these behaviors, why
he's breaking every pane of glass in the music room door,"
said Jill Blais calmly. Behavior modification regarded that kind of
agonizing as a waste of time, she explained, even though the panes
were antique and irreplacable! Jill was the behavior training therapist assigned to us by the behavior management services
department of the hospital, personally recommended by Dr. Bland.

Jill was the mature mother of two teenage sons. It was
wonderful finally to have someone, a real live person sitting in our
living-room, solidly and matter-of-factly to advise us while Julian
zinged around the room, definitely upset at the sudden change in
routine. He kept pointing to the mail on the coffee table, which had
inadvertently got pushed to a different "place" behind the Kleenex
when Jill put her purse down. He kept up a high painful whine.

We were not prepared for this "Don't question, don't analyze the
cause" approach. Our instincts, like most people's, were to try to find
the "cause" of a behavior. If you found the cause, you could then
surely set about changing the behavior, a traditional view of child
rearing that had worked for centuries. Jill shook her head. We were
to look at behavior in a different way from now on. Forget the cause.
Just deal with the behavior directly, one step at a time. We were to
model the desired behavior we wanted and as soon as Julian cooperated we were to reward him with a favorite treat such as Smarties
candy. This was followed up immediately with hugs and praise.

"Catch a kid looking good," was the motto.

To our surprise, it worked even with Julian hurtling food and
shoes. "Ignore the offending behavior, give a clear alternative" went
the additional advice.

"Always put the boots on the tray in the hall, Jules, the *running* shoes go in the *closet*." Saying "always" was the key. It was like using his autism, his love of order, to work for us, a small thing, but powerful and effective. Candy was the decoy. It gave him some power to start off with, because he was getting something he liked, but it was his autistic love of order that was the draw.

"Watch Mommy, Julian."

"Mommy, Juyan." Julian's eyes were slanting away, yet keeping me in his peripheral vision. For one thing I had his red running shoes in my hand.

"Put the RED shoes in the closet, Mommy."

Promptly I obeyed myself; I put the shoes inside the hall closet. I showed myself the box of Smarties. "Smarty! Smarty!" went Jules, predictably.

"Mommy good girl. Mommy put shoes in closet. Mommy gets a Smarty," I told myself.

"Good girl, Thelma," said Juli, catching on. "Julian have Smarty."

"Julian put *red* shoes in closet first."

At once Jules put the shoes away after months of hurtling them across the living room. I gave him two Smarties. He did not need more, which was interesting. Even one Smarty would have worked because the principle worked.

"Now put BOOTS on the boot tray."

Julian loved it. Boots on boot tray. Slippers beside bed. Red shoes in closet. Always the same closet, always the same order. So he did not mind being directed to do things if the direction was limited, concise. It was making life predictable for him, safe. Could this be why he was always so good going to bed, putting up no resistance? Bedtime involved the same routine night after night: bath-time, bedtime songs for Jules, stories for Polly, following the same pattern.

"Sing *Ma Bonnie Lie Over th' Ocean* again, Thelma," Jules would go drowsily, his lashes fluttering closed.

Then, just as we thought we were getting things under control with behavior modification: "Mommy, Julian's chewing the back-seat again!"

What was it about our new purple Pontiac Le Mans, the biggest, smartest-looking, second-hand car we'd ever owned? Julian gouged his teeth into the upholstery whenever he sat back there with Polly. Was it switching lanes on the highway that upset him? Julian with his strange autistic memory seemed to have every lane, turn, ramp and verge to Willowdale photographed in a vast mental grid in his head. One deviation on the 401 caused paroxysms of rage in the back, more tearing and ripping. The covering was savaged with tooth-marks, as if an animal had been trapped back there. He beat the windows and bounced angrily around, screeching until we reached Willowdale. As soon as he got out of the car he was quiet.

Was it the radio he disliked, or a particular station? Or our conversation along with the hum of traffic? Was it traffic itself? Or, worse — us?

"What he needs is a good spanking," said my father-in-law, pouring himself a Scotch. We were not strict enough parents. After all, he was nearly eight.

"You should have patience, speak to him softly," advised Ma. He never chewed their car, an eight-cylinder Chevy.

"You could try Ritalin," advised Dr. Bland. "It'll settle him right down, take the edge off his hyperactivity. Lots of kids are on it successfully."

But we were horrified to even think of drugging an eight year old. Then the Le Mans broke down and had to be given to the scrap yard. The dealer "whewed" when Alec took it in: "Looks like some animal's been at this."

The new car, a second-hand Lada, was spacious and airy, with big windows all round, giving excellent visibility. Julian sat quietly, smiling throughout our first run, looking out. He was the same on the second trip, and the third. It had been the windows! The old Le Mans, a sports-style car, had had thin, slitty windows in the back. It must have given him claustrophobia. And he had not been able to say.

Julian now had a vocabulary of thousands of words, but he had not been able to use them to protect himself. He still had difficulty communicating his needs directly, even if he was under discomfort or pain. Autistic children were cited as having little sensation of pain, "a high pain threshold," but I wondered if the problem was an inability to express it verbally, to focus on the words needed to actualize what was going on in their bodies? It was as if Julian had no sense of himself at crucial times of need. How to give it to him?

But even here there was hope, glimpses of redemption. He ran into the kitchen from the garden one day, holding up his finger. "Finger fall off!"

There was a deep cut with blood, and the fingernail was hanging off. I washed it and bound it up with Elastoplast, noting the absence of tears or wincing. I hinted at appropriate emotion: "There! Don't be sad, Jules, Mommy fix it, Mommy kiss it better."

Gaily Jules pranced out the door holding up his finger, newly bound. "My sad is all gone, Mommy!"

Dr. Rakka had been right about the evenness of tone needed to maintain Julian's equilibrium. But it was wearying. We had our irritations, too, our passing animosities and sudden explosions – our aggravations.

"You're always writing away at that stupid journal!" growled Alec.

"Well you're always holed up in the TV room watching the *Johnny Carson Show* with a six-pack every night!"

I could hear a dangerous edge to my voice, feel inexplicable tension rising. Julian picked up right away.

"Six-pack, six-pack," he chanted, hitting his face. I actually felt like screaming myself, I couldn't take this! Perhaps Dr. Rakka had been right about me, that I would never last the course.

Fifteen

Dr. Bland had finally succeeded in getting the Board to start up a primary-junior autistic class. Dr. Bland knew most of the autistic/PDD children in the region through the IPRCs. A teacher had been hired, the school chosen: Riverlea Public School. It over-looked the river and willows. The class was to start with four or five students, three boys and one girl who were all autistic/PDD, between seven and eleven years old.

"Nice new class, Jules! New school, new teacher, new little friends to play with."

"New seagulls," said Julian, looking up at the sky, a different part of the sky from what was over Sunny Acres P.S.

We were excited. There was a speech and language pathologist attached to the class. At last, Jules would be getting the intensive language programming he'd always needed. By age nine he could write words and short sentences in his daily journal with help, recite the days of the week, months of the year, tell time to the half-hour, read the pre-primer reader, *Pig in a Jig,* count to one hundred, do one-step operations up to ten with concrete aids, cook a cheese soufflé, use a cobbler's bench, and read the menu at McDonald's from the pictures. But there was so much more to his ability, we knew.

The autistic class turned out to be similar to TMR. Miss Laverne even used the same canary-yellow TMR curriculum as her guide. Cooking, shopping at No Frills, small motor activities — peg-board, hoops, sorting cups, counting blocks, weaving cards — personal hygiene, some printing exercises that Julian had already mastered with Miss Hodge. Miss Hoeffel, the speech therapist, turned out to be the regular Board speech therapist who serviced half the special-ed classes in the region. The autistic class was one of many in her

Julian at age 9 or 10

workload that she visited for a half-hour once a week for "consulta-tion" with the teacher. Where was the one-to-one intensive Lovaas-type intervention, the minute-by-minute non-stop style of programming the Kauffmans had done with Raun that I'd hoped would be going on?

For a long time, Miss Hoeffel worked on teaching the children to distinguish "social absurdities," an important skill in meaningful comprehension. Perhaps it was important that Julian see that it was "inappropriate" for a bicycle to have square wheels. Did Jules get that? Did Dylan?

Dylan was Julian's personal friend. He was a high-functioning lively boy with Asperger's Syndrome who could read at a grade-four level, although it was not clear if his comprehension was at the same level. He also worked on a computer at home, he told me.

I came to pick up Julian from school one afternoon to get a sense of the other students. It was a brief glimpse, but fascinating and informative. After all, these were the first autistic children I had seen apart from Nadia. These were Jules' daily playmates, the most influential in helping him learn and relate. The third boy was quite different in temperament and ability from Julian and Dylan. Aaron sat hunched, withdrawn, at his solitary desk enclosed by screens. "He likes it that way," explained Miss Laverne. The one little girl was mute and severely developmentally delayed.

It was obvious from the bond between Jules and Dylan that Julian had met an intellectually challenging but also lovable child who enjoyed his personality. This was the closest to personal friendship based on a certain equality that Julian had ever had. He talked about Dylan at home in brief recollections – "Dylan naughty in school!"– chuckling to himself. Dylan and Jules, Jules and Dylan. I could hear them coming as the bus veered the corner of the drive, larking about together in the back seat of the bus. The autistic class was worth it just to hear Dolly the driver's exasperated, "Those two drive me nuts!" *Those two.*

Unfortunately, Dylan was leaving in June, his father informed me at Meet the Teacher Night. Mr. Purdis was putting Dylan into private school that specialized in one-on-one tutoring for children with learning disabilities, costing thousands of dollars in fees. He wanted Dylan learning the prime ministers of Canada, he said, not how to lay toothpaste on a toothbrush.

It was not necessarily Miss Laverne's fault. There was no information available from programs like TEACCH (Treatment & Education of Autistic and Communication Handicapped Children) at the University of North Carolina at Chapel Hill, Chapel Hill, North Carolina; no Ivar Lovass Behaviour Modification Programming, and no one had yet heard of the Higashi School model in Massachusetts, least of all Miss Laverne. Dr. Bland did offer to go down to Boston to do some research, but the Board would not finance the trip as there were too few autistic children to warrant the expense.

How was a teacher to get four nine-year-old autistic children to interact when two of them were shut off, deeply absorbed in private rituals and stimming? We had been so eager for an "autistic" class to be the answer that we'd ignored the fact that Julian had no other playmates other than Dylan. Children were friendly to him out on the playground at recess and in grade three integration for music, but Julian was unable to sustain friendship on his own. He could not relate to these normal children the way they were used to, and they were too young to have the patience or insight needed to bridge his deficits. When Dylan left in June — what then?

"Aw heck," said Alec, "he might as well go back to Miss Hodge and the TMR program next year. At least he'll have more kids to mix with."

The Junior TMR program had had eleven students of varying ability, some "borderline," high functioning. They had challenged Julian. In retrospect we could see that the different personalities rubbing off on each other had provided lots of social interaction. As well, there were the security afforded Julian from the core children who had been with him since kindergarten. It was a difficult decision; all the more sensitive because we were making it on Julian's behalf. When we said to him: "Jules do you want to stay in Miss Laverne's class or go back to Miss Hodge?" he had answered. "Lonnie in Miss Hodge," which seemed to indicate Miss Hodge. But then he cried, "And Dylan!" We explained that Dylan was leaving in June, but Julian could not seem to comprehend the idea of "gone."

We had expected that Miss Laverne would have had specific knowledge of programming. This was a high-profile job, the very first classroom for autistic students in the entire school system. But Miss Laverne had been chosen for her knowledge of autism rather than for teaching techniques and expertise; this was actually her first year of teaching. She had formerly been a case worker facilitating meaningful dialogue with parents in the home setting. It had taken a while for us to realize that Miss Laverne actually had few basic prerequisite teaching skills. Music, especially, an essential tool for getting through to autistic children, was relegated to an itinerary teacher who came one period a week. It was not central to the programming. Shopping for groceries at No Frills was. Somewhere Miss Laverne had learned that autistic children needed their own space. The classroom was divided with partitions, effectively blocking one child off from the other "to prevent distraction" she explained.

Yet on "Meet the Teacher Night" the parents of Aaron and Matilda, the two non-verbal children, enthused over Miss Laverne's programming; they felt their children were really benefiting from the fine motor skills program and the focus on behavior modification. They liked the screens, feeling they helped Matilda and Aaron to focus. You realized, a bit non-plussed, that there was no one approach to accommodate the differences among autistic children.

I hoped to figure out how to have a more rigorous approach for Jules in academics. A look in his printing book showed me Jules still working on trite "name and address" exercises he'd mastered years ago with Miss Hodge. I was anxious for Miss Laverne to know of these abilities. Jules could write sentences with accompanying little illustrations, funny gnome-like creatures with big pointed ears. It was some time before I'd realized they were self-portraits. But what Miss Laverne wanted was for the parents to view a video she'd brought along, "It's Not the End of the World," on repressed parental rage and hostility.

What was it about people in this field? I struggled to get it, because basically Miss Laverne was a decent young woman, like-able, eager to do her best as she saw it, which seemed to be to counsel *us*. How else to explain autistic children but through their weird dysfunctional parents?

Miss Laverne turned on the video. We parents sat back, resigned and confused, as the film began focusing on parental anguish over their child's diagnosis and the need for "closure," hinted Miss Laverne. But shouldn't we be discussing whether she was teaching the new "spiral" math (she wasn't), and when she planned on starting "Baker's Dozen" on the switched-off Commodore 64? The video whirred on . . .

Alec and I were undergoing stresses of our own in teaching at this time. I had missed several vital years of teaching after the births of Polly and Julian, causing me to lose touch with what was happening in the teaching profession. The Hall-Dennis Report, "Living and Learning," that had come out in 1968 had been the beginning of a revolution in teaching methodology that culminated in the '70s and '80s in a radical change from the old teacher-centered approach of the '50s to a new child-centered approach to learning in which the teacher was a "facilitator." In the old method, the teacher tended to stand at the front of the class talking and using the blackboard as a main teaching tool, students seated in silence in rows facing the board. Discipline was of the essence.

In the new child-centered learning, the teacher worked at the pace and style of the children. It involved hands-on experiential learning and a whole language approach to teaching reading and writing. The children now sat in groups and did "group work" and projects, the focus of learning primarily centered on themselves and their emotions and experiences. Spellers, drills, phonic charts, multiplication tables and rules of all kind were tossed out the window. I found it difficult at first to abandon techniques like memorization and drills that I'd always thought gave the children strong foundations and intellectual security. (No one seemed able to explain how we had yet produced Canada's brilliant writers and thinkers, theologians and scientists, with these dull old '50s methods.)

Gradually I found myself enthusing over the whole language approach – the burning golden hours spent painting, modelling, writing rough draft, revised draft, so intense, the room rocking like a ship, while at the same time keeping a synthesis of older rote methods. Yet just when the new approach was well under way, the computer era took over: instant communication, instant excitement, instant gratification somehow at odds with the homemade little story books the children painstakingly produced in the whole language approach. But computers were here to stay, and it meant new skills to master, more teaching courses to take at night.

Meanwhile Alec had stresses of his own as a technical teacher at Brockley High School, one of the few Basic Level, technical schools left in the Greater Toronto Area. He was trying to do his best to adapt to the new "credit system." Students now chose whatever subjects they wanted, at whatever level they were at. It meant a grade-12 student could graduate with grade-9 level equivalent math.

A result of this choice was that students could effectively shut down programs. If too few students chose a particular program, it would be cut. Students often chose their programs based on which teacher they liked best, or who gave them easy, high marks, and dropped subjects that were "boring."

Many technical shops closed down as a result of low interest from students.

At the same time, special education programs were on the rise as children were increasingly being labeled with various newly-named learning disorders teachers had never heard of such as "specific reading disability," "discalculia," "specifc arithmetic disorder," and "attention deficit disorder" (ADD).

The ADD students were being prescribed a staggering three billion dollars' worth of medications like Ritalin each year. Alec and I tried to adapt to these changes and keep ourselves open to new opportunities in education for Julian. We could only hope all was for the best.

Sixteen

U nder Bill 82 in Ontario there were new changes and opportunities for Julian. The Pilot Project was the latest initiative of the Board of Education. The plan called for integrating, or "mainstreaming," a chosen few "special needs" children into regular classrooms fulltime.

The Association for Community Living (formerly The Association for the Mentally Retarded) advocated for full integration for all children, regardless of disability. Many members favored phasing out all segregated classes like the Primary and Junior TMR classes seeing them as outmoded and prejudicial. Furthermore, Community Living's new slogan "People First" had brought everyone up short, startling parents, psychiatrists, psychologists, social workers, and educators. Suddenly everyone in the field was scrambling to read Wolf Wolfensberger's *Principles of Normalization*, which had fueled the process of deinstitutionalization, desegregation and the "normalization" of the mentally handicapped into the community begun in the '70s. We parents were part of something much bigger than ourselves.

"Words have power," urged Community Living. Nomenclature now changed: old pejorative epithets like "retarded" were replaced by "developmentally challenged" (D.C.) Jules was "D.C.," Lonnie was developmentally delayed, "D.D." instead of physically handicapped, and Sara was visually impaired, V.I. "TMR" classes were now labeled "D.C."

Part of the hope of the Pilot Project was that full integration would eventually counteract old attitudes and concepts about developmentally challenged individuals and be an example to other Boards. But the children in the schoolyard soon caught on. *"There go the D.Cs . . . "* went the new refrain.

Patricia's mum was hoping Patricia would be chosen for main-streaming, and Sarah's mum wanted Sarah. But naturally the best behaved would be selected as they were deemed most likely to benefit. The Board wanted this to be a success.

So Patricia and Sarah were not asked, and certainly not Lonny ...

But Julian was offered a placement in a grade four classroom with thirty other students; a personal "aide" would be provided. It was an honor to Julian and it sounded impressive. It was certainly the politically correct thing to do, but we found ourselves questioning what the actual benefit of being in a grade four class with thirty strange children would be to Julian other than us being able to say "Julian's in regular grade four now." Only a few chosen schools were to participate in the project, and Sunny Acres was not one of them. This would mean a change of school, teachers and students for Julian. But the friends he already had was what was important to him; he'd learned so much from them.

The Catholic Separate School Board had begun to accept special needs students in the '80s. From the outset they were dedicated to mainstreaming. A few parents I knew in special needs swimming had children in the Separate School system; they enthused over full integration and insisted there was no other way. These parents were young and their children had only been mainstreamed in kindergarten or grade one where intellectual differences were not as noticeable and the program was less focused on academics. I asked other parents and teachers about older students mainstreamed and heard stories of D.C. pupils consigned to the back of the classroom with the aide so as not to disturb the class, or, conversely, the teaching assistant taking the student outside into the hallway to work where it was quiet since the noise level and group-work activities of the students was upsetting the child. What was the advantage of such scenarios? The younger parents at once insisted that socialization, not academics, was what mattered and such incidents were in the minority. We agonized over the decision again, instinctively wanting to protect Julian, though the provision of an assistant was important for an insecure child like Julian, a bridge with reality he needed.

However, at the same time we already had years of experience with Julian being fully integrated with "normal" kids in the summer day-camp programs run by Parks & Recreation. Community Living had provided a "worker" for him much as the Board would now provide an assistant, named Nick. Julian had been always in a smaller group of children within the larger framework. By now, he'd spent six summers and spring breaks singing in pow-wows, swimming, hiking, making bead necklaces in crafts, joining in Wednesday night sleep-overs, going to movies at Cinesphere along with sixty other boys and girls of all ages, having a grand old time.

There had been one unfortunate incident this summer when his worker had let him go into the washroom alone, thinking it inappropriate to watch over a big boy going on eleven. Jules was beginning to develop. He certainly was "well-endowed," chuckled Alec.

Nick had been leaning against the wall outside in the sun when I'd arrived to pick up Jules. Out had come a group of giggling little boys, about six and seven years old, from the boys' washroom.

"Hey," one said, "Did ya see his cock?"

"Yeah, did you see the size of it?"

Just then, Jules came ambling out flushed and smiling, zip undone.

"Julian did you show your pee-pee inside the washroom?" Nick asked.

"Everybody laughing," said Jules.

That was an exception, of course, one hoped. The kids in general were undeniably nice to Julian, the worker made sure of that. But inevitably it was Nick that he had related to, Nick that he spoke about fondly at home. At summer's end, when Nick returned to university and the sixty kids went back to their schools with their friends, Jules did not have one personal friend, not one "normal" one, that is.

These memories naturally made us hesitant about the benefits of socialization that the Pilot Project stressed as its strong point. So we didn't in the end choose the Pilot Project. Julian was transferred back to Junior D.C. from the autistic/PDD class. In a way it seemed Julian was going backwards. Yet, our decision was not carved in stone. Julian could always be mainstreamed later on, perhaps in middle school or high school. The future was promising, we told ourselves.

Julian seemed happy to be back in his old class after being away for a year. I went along the first morning for a half-hour for his settling in, but I needn't have worried. Julian excitedly called his friends by full name. He readily joined in circle time, now called "opening exercises and personal sharing." He was able to give the date and the weather, and understand the class was going on a trip to the apple orchard that week. He settled down at the writing table to start a new journal, with the help of the teaching assistant. He wrote: "I am gld be bk."

The core of children that had been with Julian from the beginning was still there: Lonnie, Sara, Patricia, Khadish. Sara could now talk despite her visual impairment and she would run up to you and shout : "Hi you Julian's mum, you got lip'sick on!" She had a high singsong voice much like Julian's in the early years.

"Sara, you can talk!"

"And sing," said Miss Hodge proudly. How marvelous to hear Sara singing *Can't Buy Me Love!* from her Beatles album.

Patricia was still non-verbal. She sat concentrating on her signing cards, picture communication photos she used to express her wants. Lonnie could now feed himself with a spoon, and work his stiff finger on a Bliss Symbolics board.

Had Julian missed these children? Did autistic children emotionally "miss" people?

Leo Kanner, the famous psychologist who had first defined autism in the 1940s, had noted an "alone" quality to autistic children's relationships. When had Kanner's aloneness changed to "loneliness" in Jules? That he wanted and needed friendship and human relationships? There was a whole slew of neighbors, I now discovered, that he had understandings with. Julian seemed to know that the Craddocks who lived opposite us kept their cookies in the Ovaltine tin by the gas stove. Julian would sneak over after school. "Ah, he knows!" smiled Mrs. Craddock . She had papery-thin skin with fine mauve veins threaded through, and crinkly eyes.

It seemed Julian also knew where Moira McTavish's shortbreads were tucked away, and where Sam the fireman down the road kept his strings of black licorice. Julian regularly appeared at Francine's back door for a bowl of pasta. Maybe they thought I didn't feed him properly. I pondered on this private life of Julian's in the neighborhood, where he was privy to all the treats going.

It was the same in the village. Many a business proprietor had come to know Julian over the years. Ben at Rabba's let him smell the magazines; Zim of Polsky Deli kept him a pepperoni tucked away. Giovanni the barber called out through the glass door *"Ciao! Jiuliano, my friend!"*

If only Mother could have understood this.

"Thelma, I wouldn't go *talking* about Julian if I were you. After all, he doesn't *look* retarded so why spoil his chances, and your own?" she had advised on her last visit, full of concern.

I understood the love behind Mother's feelings, and the decades of thinking behind it that demanded anything imperfect, not up to par, be put away, denied, but there was so much to hide in that kind of thinking. It was such a strain. There was, in fact, a whole part of me that did not actually live up to Mother's wonderfully high standards, if she but knew.

On the last day of a visit Mother had her suitcase packed, and was holding back tears.

"Oh Nana, you're such fun!" cried Polly, hugging Mother. Mother had french-braided Polly's hair, taught her the art of make-up, tweezed her eyebrows – "You can't go round with those bushes, Pollywogs!" – given her perfume, "Surrender," and a bright red skirt. At fifteen Polly and her friends were into "black."

"They look like a bunch of Satanists coming up the street," said Mother, worried.

"Nana leaving! Nana leaving!" Julian's eyes had filled with tears and he tried to hold back the suitcase.

"Hey, I do believe he likes me!" Mother looked quite cheered. "Well, imagine. Old Jules."

"She'll come back next year," I coaxed.

"Nex' year," echoed Julian, tears wetting his cheeks.

He kept a firm grip on the suitcase; this was going to be difficult. At the same time I was surprised, excited. He began to sob.

"You're going to have to let go of the suitcase, Jules."

"Well, it just goes to show!" fluttered Mother, quite chuffed. She suddenly bent and gave Julian a kiss on the nose.

He gave a long wail as the taxi turned into the drive, to Mother's delight.

Something about Mother had touched Julian, despite her carelessly hurtful words: "I really think it's time you should look into putting him away somewhere, Thelma. That Dr. Rakka was right, get on with your life!" It was happening again just as it had in Wales when he was a child. Perhaps it was her gaiety he loved, her suit-case, or the pillow she tucked under her feet on the sofa as she smoked and ate chocolate truffles. "Want one, kiddo?"

She began sending me snippets from articles on autism in the British newspapers: the effects of vitamin therapy on autistic children, the use of "the electric prod" to stem self-abuse in these children and information on "farming communities" in Britain and Europe where special needs children like Julian were placed to live and work.

"See what they do with them over here, Thelma, and the parents are free."

Seventeen

H e thinks we intend to put him here," said Alec, as we toured the grounds of Oakleigh House. Oakleigh House was a small institutional setting outside Toronto, not too far from Port Credit and one of the few places that offered residential services to autistic/PDD clients. Community Living was supposed to be pressing for Oakleigh to be closed, in keeping with its philosophy of normalization. An institution, no matter how small or attractive, was still an institution.

But we did not want to "put" Jules anywhere. Alec and I hoped to be house-parents one day using our house as an "associative" home with live-in help, under the aegis of Community Living.

"If you're alive, Mr. and Mrs. Orchard," Sophie had droned. Sophie was our caseworker with Community Living.

We had attended the Community Living workshop : *"Where Will Your Child Go If You Drop Dead Tomorrow?"* Members had been urged to attend the seminar on wills, estates and trusts to learn how to set up a will with special provisions for their child, in the event of sudden death. Putting Julian's name on waiting lists for a group home now could ensure him a "place" some time in the future when we would no longer be around to look after him ourselves. It was a necessity, we were urged.

Oakleigh House consisted of a white main building, and small cottages spaced around the grounds, each with its own garden — so far so good.

The staff had been expecting us. They were mostly young people in their twenties and thirties, casually dressed in jeans and sweat shirts. We were pleased to see young men — male role models. Jim showed us the dining hall, the recreation room, where one old man sat slumped alone in a wheelchair watching TV. Most of the residents were out at "Work Experience," if they were older, or at school, explained Jim.

We went on to view a large indoor swimming pool. "Well, Julian would love that. He's a great swimmer." If it ever had to come to it, I thought cautiously.

Jim showed us the bungalows where some lower-functioning autistic residents were housed.

"So you understand autism, then?" asked Alec.

"Sure do!"

Jim glanced at Julian who held my hand, in silence. We were back in the entrance hall of the main building, a low echoing room. Jim assured us it was alive, no shortage of action when everyone was back, when we commented on the eerie quiet.

"Well, it certainly seems a nice place," Alec said reluctantly. I felt Julian's grip tighten on my hand. "I'm sure Jules would be well looked after here, and could get to like it if the worst ever came to the worst, but hopefully that will never happen."

Jim glanced again at Julian. "Ya know, he doesn't seem like he needs institutional care. But of course we'd be glad to have him if that's what you ever needed . . . you can't sacrifice your entire life."

"No-o-o-o Mommy!" Tears filled Julian's eyes. He gripped my hand harder, trying to wheel round and guage the expression in my eyes. He did not want to let go of my hand.

"No! No! Mommy!" he said, again, in anguish. Looking up at me earnestly, doing his best to lock eyes with mine. He faced me determinedly:

"Juyan go home! Juyan go home wiv Mommy!"

Tears of immense sadness trickled down his cheeks – the tears of a child who is going to be left behind in an echoing hall and does not know why.

Suddenly the place was vast, empty, unloving, seen through his fearing eyes. But he had called me "Mommy," had looked into my face urgently, locked eyes, out of great need. He needed me, loved me, was choosing me. I cherished this moment. For the first time since he had been born he was showing that he recognized I was his mother. The wondrous realization swept over me in waves.

"It's OK, Jules. You won't live here. Julian will stay with Mommy and Daddy always. Always, Jules."

The next two years went by swiftly as things came together for Julian. He moved on to the next stage of his schooling, the intermediate developmentally challenged class in Lymewood Public School, age range ten to fourteen years. The intermediate class approximated to middle school, the transition between junior level and secondary school. The final step would be a satellite class in our local high school. Jules was growing up. But the precious moment in Oakleigh House shimmered inside me; it was what I held on to that summer when something in me broke.

I could not go on, and just when Julian was coming into this wonderful phase at eleven – he'd never been so good.

Sunlight slanted through the classroom window touching my desk, The Teacher's Desk. Perhaps that was the defining moment. Something about that desk, that solid oblong, its values, its security, its assurance – its tedium – suddenly filled me with alarm, and my life crystallized in a flash. I longed for release, as if a part of me had been buried for decades.

"It's an illusion, Thel, escapism, not wanting to face things anymore," Alec pleaded hopefully. "It's stress . . . "

Lots of parents with autistic children went through this, he pursued, but we had always relied on friendship in our marriage, working together, a delicate balance, and now I was wanting out. Alec was confused.

I took a small flat near Toronto, but not too far from the house. Waves of heat beat the streets a somnolent pink as I urged myself through that long strange summer. I felt I had failed Alec, yet I needed this time alone to come to terms with something deep within myself that I could not explain to him or Elsie or anyone right then. It was something that had to be resolved by going back over my childhood, and it had to be done by myself alone as I sought out a new life. Alec decided to wait it out.

"I still love you, Thel . . . " Alec mumbled. "It's not the same without you. You're the only reason I keep going, you, and the kids. The house is empty without you."

At the same time I came over to see Jules and Polly each day, tried to keep up the usual routines, especially Julian's. I brought him back and forth to day camp and sang to him at bedtime.

"Mommy's gone," I heard him say clearly one day, as he stood in the doorway. "The books are gone."

Something about the factual way he said that smote me. *He had noticed I was gone.* How could I have thought otherwise?

Alec and I had agreed to tell Polly I had moved out for the summer for a "break," but Polly had too many teenage friends with parents in the process of divorce not to understand the significance of what was going on. One afternoon I glimpsed Polly on the river in Port Credit as she rowed bravely up-stream doing her best — she always did her best — unaware I was watching from the bank, her strained eyes blinking in the bright sunshine. Something about her strained wan face caught at me sharply. She worried about me, I knew, alone, unprotected by Daddy, out there somewhere in some room that was not home, cut off in a large city in a large world, which meant her own unprotectedness.

I felt a flash of pain. I knew then I had to return. I determined that I would try to heal all that was fragile and broken that summer away from home. And I was ready. I could now put the past aside and dedicate myself anew with Alec, and put heart and soul into helping the children, especially Jules.

"She's back," said Julian. "The books are back." Smiling to himself he tapped the volumes along the shelves and smelled them. Books with their bindings well worn, frayed, rows of them where they should be, familiar, loved.

It was strange but it was a relief for all of us to be together as a family again. We had somehow come through, little suspecting what yet lay ahead, that an agony was soon to be upon us, the ultimate test of faith and love.

Part Three

Julian, age 14. This school photo was taken
just before the violent stage of his life began.

Eighteen

Y*ou fucking bloody no-good liar, you!"* Julian glared across the living room, his cheeks unnaturally flushed and blotched in that ugly way. Blood oozed from his gums.

"Am I a bad boy?" he yelled, his newly breaking voice crackling, tense. Tears filled his eyes. He raised his fists again – thud – thud. Instinctively I raised my arms, too late, he noted the movement.

"Am I a bad boy to Mommy?"

Pounding his face, there was no stopping now – bam – thud. Blood gushed suddenly from his nose.

"Don't Jules, don't! Don't hurt yourself," I pleaded, struggling to keep my voice smooth and even, calmness was essential. But too late again, he had caught the edge of concern in the tone.

Nearly fourteen, tall and strong, the new Julian towered over us. Alec crouched down behind him, not sure what to do, what was going on, he had just come out of the shower. We had learned by now that too much intervention, too many voices, inflamed him further. He was like an animal, trapped. *"Aaaaaah!"*

I flinched to ward off the blow I knew was coming. Oh Jules! Don't hit me, I am your mother! Mommy. He bit himself instead, slapping his cheek all the while.

"Those people!" he yelled, getting into it. *"Those kids over there! Are they laughing at you, Julian? Yes they are! What will happen if they hit me, Mommy?"* Thud – thud.

"What will happen?"

He was pounding his knuckles at the "kids" on the wall. What kids, Jules?

"Those kids! There!" pointing harshly at the wall. *"Those bad kids there!"* he wept.

And this was the worst – the most frightening, the most eerie – the people he claimed to see.

"You're nothing but a fucking no-good retard, Julian Orchard!"
The words bounce off the walls, his flushed face dark with emotion, tears on his cheeks.

"What does *fuck* mean, Mommy? What does it mean? What does it ME-E-EAN?"

"It's OK, Jules, it's OK, OK . . . "

I manage to get away. "Gotta go to the toilet a minute, Jules." *"She's gotta go to the toilet, if you gotta go you gotta go!"* I'm careful to lock myself in the washroom. I can still hear his panting, furniture being banged, Alec's low tone, "There, there, son."

I turn on the taps full-blast, it would be too terrible if he heard sobs, and sink onto the seat holding my head, shaking with the strain, the terrible sadness. My arms ache, blue with bruises turning dull. My back hurt. I wept. What was happening? What had happened to our son, and where had we gone so wrong? It had to be something we were doing.

"What the hell happened?" said Alec.

We stood at the storm door watching Julian pacing outside now – he'd gone hurtling out and was stomping round and round the apple tree in full view of the neighbors. A deep diagonal path was worn across the grass similar to the one in the living room carpet.

"Fucking assho-o-le!" he was yelling. Old Mr. and Mrs. Craddock were peering out of their front window opposite. We were anxious about Jules, anxious about the Craddocks, about everyone on the street, how long they could be expected to put up with this up and down their properties before calling the police. And the scene there'd now be trying to get him back inside.

"I don't know," I turned to Alec.

"You must have said something to set him off like this." It was a hell of a way to spend Saturday morning, he grumbled.

"Why do you always blame me, why is it always something I've done?" I flared.

"Because it always *is* to do with you," said Alec complacently. "Just think about it. It's always around you he gets like this."

"Like this" . . . It was true. I seemed to have an effect on him, just being near him.

I tried to think back, relive every moment of the incident, what my voice might have sounded like – querulous, critical? – trying to come to grips. We usually made pancakes together Saturday morning, his Aunt Jemima Pancake Mix and one egg still out on the counter ready for him. Mixing bowl, wooden spoon, spatula, frying pan, the usual accoutrements of his pancake routine in a neat row.

I'd just finished shaving him . . . "You're handsome, Jules," I'd said.

"Handsome," he'd agreed in that robotic mechanical way, staring at his face in the bathroom mirror. I'd been showing him how to use his first razor, a Philip's Philishave 805 electric with the circular motion guaranteeing a close shave.

"Oh Mom, look at Jules' fuzzy little moustache, it's so sweet!" Polly had peered in. "Hey, Mom, he's good-looking." Polly had sized up her brother with the knowing eyes of a peer. At fourteen Julian was "cool" with his slim figure and dark good looks, like one of those East Indian film stars in Hindi movies that seemed to go on forever.

I wasn't sure what exactly happened after that. As I cleaned the hairs out of the sink, Polly had come agitatedly back upstairs, "MOM! *Do something* about Julian!"

He had gone down to the living room HALF-NAKED, she'd hissed, his pajama bottoms all open, "*you* know," her girlfriends were there. All I'd done was try to explain to Julian not to do that, but he'd at once clenched his fists — my voice had had an urgency to it I supposed and he hadn't liked Polly's flushed face and excited tone of voice either, unhappy-excited, and the way she and her friends had gone scuttling down to the basement with their cassettes.

"He's nuts, Alec . . . " My voice trailed away miserably, because what had my expression been, my tone of voice that had set him off?

It was so unfair! But what was fair?

"Mommy's mad again!" yelled Julian. He was back. His fists hammered at the storm door, which rattled tinnily.

"See! You've set him off again!"

"But — "

"Mom, we're going over to Charlotte's," said Polly sheepishly, emerging from the basement. She and her friends were carrying cassette boxes and a black boombox. They slunk out the back way, heads down. "See you later. . . "

"Bad ! Bad! Bad!" Julian was weeping, beating his head against the metal door.

"Hey, he's gonna break the hinge," said Alec, ever practical.
"F-U-C-K. You witch's tit, you mother-fucking . . . "

Picking up a wet sponge, I ran and wiped down his face; he was calming down. I put a cold compress to his throbbing wrists, told him Mommy loved him — over and over, my voice low, urgent.

Gradually it subsided, whatever "it" had been, whatever took over him, possessing him at such times. A chill fear passed over me, not for the first time . . .

Nineteen

Things were no better at school. Mrs. McDougall, Julian's teacher in the Intermediate Developmentally Challenged (D.C.) wing at Lymewood had reported a dramatic change in Julian's behavior this term. "They didn't know what to do with him."

"Just can't go on like this, Mrs. Orchard."

Dr. Bland paused in the interview. As the Board of Education psychologist, he was the most important person at the table, more important than Mr. Dickson the principal was, definitely more than poor Mrs. McDougall. He felt that what was called for was a new psychological assessment on Julian. He hadn't had one since kindergarten.

It wasn't just that Julian was going round the school calling Mr. Dickson "Dickhead," accompanied by loud manic laughter, explained Dr. Bland.

"Don't say he doesn't *know* what he's doing, Mrs. Orchard!"

Mr. Dickson frowned. "Dick-head-Dickson" was bad enough. But of late Julian had extended his range of metaphors to include — and here Mr. Dickson stiffened ramrod straight — he was tall and thin with a clipped moustache, hair sleeked sideways — "Suck-my-dick-Dickson!"

Dr. Bland hid a quick smile. "Ugh-h, yes, well, Ernie . . ."

Admittedly one could see how awkward and embarrassing that must all be for Mr. Dickson to be continually called "Dickhead" etc. up and down the halls — persistently — for Julian was persistent. I tried to be conciliatory, sympathetic towards Mr. Dickson. That was the nature of echolalia and after all Julian was autistic, echoing over and over a loved phrase "Suck-My-Dick-Dickson" to the horrified delight, no doubt, of the grade eights who likely had set him up to it in the first place — couldn't Dr. Bland and Mr. Dickson see that? Julian was integrated into woodworking class.

Mrs. McDougall fluttered large worried eyes. She was weary from teaching Intermediate D.C. She had eleven developmentally challenged adolescents this year, including a student in a wheelchair and Julian Orchard, she said.

"But he also goes around the house saying he's 'nothing but a fucking Paki,' " I pointed out, though wasn't the implication of Julian's new self-awareness, for an autistic, mind-boggling and important? The word, the latest in his school vocabulary, explodes from him at home. "Paki! Paki!" Jules had no idea what an East Indian was, or a "Paki," or a Sri Lankan for that matter; he didn't realize that, in fact, he was neither but "mixed." How to explain that! But he had grasped the implication. So now he partly knew this new thing about himself he'd not been aware of before. That he was that word, somehow, "Paki." And that it was bad, unlovely. Not loveable. And you are, Jules, you are!

"Well, if parents will demand integration . . . " drawled Dr. Bland.

Should we cancel integration? Alec was all for it. "What the shit, if this is what he's learning."

It was essential to appear calm, objective, keep all this in proportion. This dickhead business was just a phase of adolescence, not so unusual or different from normal teenage behavior except Julian did not know how to hide and dissemble his. I held to this point. The "phase" we could get through if we only worked together, Mrs. McDougall. It was essential to have her on our side here, being Julian's teacher. He'd been doing so well under her the past two years in the junior and intermediate program, I reminded everyone. Until his moustache had grown in at thirteen. Big Jules with his fuzzy new moustache, smacking his head against the board, the chalk flying. " . . . *a danger to himself and others, Mrs. Orchard.*" The only thing that seemed to work was giving Julian Play-Doh at his desk in the corner; kneading the plasticine somehow helped "ground" him, work out his aggression, she hesitated, but for how long could that continue?

"Look, Mrs. McDougall," I appealed to her directly. "Just try to keep the lid on this year — that's all we ask."

I went on earnestly: "We don't expect you to teach him academics." (Though did what took place in Room 9 pass even remotely for academics?) "He just can't cope with it right now. It's a stage he's going through — adolescence — I appreciate how difficult it is and it's the same for us at home . . . "

I pulled out the article I'd seen in *Life* about a special school for children like Jules down in Boston. I'd have to proceed carefully, of course, not to seem to be imputing criticism at the DC (developmentally challenged) program.

"There's this special school in the States, in Boston, Dr. Bland, called The Higashi School, with the latest approach to teaching autistic children. I don't expect Mrs. McDougall to be running a Higashi School program, but some of the ideas sound like they could work for Julian."

The school, which cost $36,000 a year, conceived of and run by Dr. Kitahara of Japan, focused on outdoor activity and exercise that Dr. Kitahara had discovered raised the endorphins, something autistic children needed. The bottom line was that the children were taken outside — I stressed "outside" — to run for miles each day along the beaches of Boston to raise those endorphins. Running, riding, gardening, exercises, outdoors in the sunlight for hours, apparently prevented autistic children from lapsing into typical autistic behaviors. The intensive physical program was balanced by an equally invigorating arts program — painting, music, dance — a wonderful synthesis of activity and creativity so needed by tense high-strung over-emotional autistic teenagers like Julian. Again, I did not expect Mrs. McDougall to take Julian running down to the beach off Lakeshore, but if Jules could only be taken *outside* to run freely, say across the playing fields, for a good half-hour twice daily . . .

Mrs. McDougall looked dubiously at the glossy picture of autistic children streaming across the sands down in Boston . . . autistic angels dissolving into light . . . the wind blowing back their hair, their eyes startling, their faces shining like stars. Dr. Kitahara, the directress, had managed to do it, had succeeded with Daily Life Therapy, so why not Mrs. McDougall? Maybe all Julian needed was to raise his endorphins. That seemed to be Dr. Kitahara's secret.

It needed more than raising his endorphins to get Julian Orchard under control, drawled Dr. Bland.

Nevertheless, as much out of respect for my new position as teacher of an autistic class myself (in a new school) rather than any faith in Dr. Kitahara, Mrs. McDougall agreed to take Julian out, on trial, for two twenty-minute runs a day.

Julian the gazelle, that first morning, bounding across Lymewood playing fields only to disappear in a trice through distant woods, and, further, over some stream, followed gamely by stout Miss Stead, the aide, in brogues. "Stop! Stop!" Mr. Dickson had hovered anxiously on the sideline of the soccer pitch, cupping his eyes. "Out of sight . . . . gone. . " He scanned the horizon. Julian Orchard had not stopped running, and would not. After all, no one had told him to.

Yes, I was now teacher of the primary autistic class myself, a challenge I'd never expected. *"Thelma, do you think that a wise move for your career teaching children like that, with all your education?"* wrote Mother. Five autistic partially non-verbal little boys fresh from kindergarten . . . Five little Julians.

"Go for it! You're the ideal person for the job," my former principal enthused. "You've taught everything from high school English to kindergarten! And you can sing!"

It was true. Over the years I seemed to have moved ever "downward" in the teaching hierarchy, to Mother's increasing consternation. "Thelma, I don't know why you're wasting your talents on . . . " But the kindergarten and other primary teaching hours had suited Julian's bussing as special needs children were home at three o'clock. But it was teaching elementary that taught me to teach, that gave me an infinitude of skills and approaches, practical knowledge – songs, finger plays, mimes, stories, plays, dances, so that when the right moment came, I got the job.

"But how would they feel about a parent, a mother of an autistic child, teaching the class?" I'd still been hesitant.

"All the more reason to hire you; you'll understand the parents, where they're coming from," insisted this principal. "You can do it. Believe in yourself."

The five little Julians gazed away from me that first morning in circle time. You knew right away that had to be the focus of your work: language development.

I threw out Miss Laverne's old screens and partitions, grouped the desks together in a square block, "group work" style, each child always facing another. So when Bobby looked up he saw Giorgio doing puzzles, writing, counting. I had the big sand table – our old wading pool from home – given center-place in the room. This was where it was all going to happen . . . It was up to me to give lots of time for it to happen!

When Betsy, the teaching assistant, went to intervene in a fight that first week, I held her back. "No, Bet' – watch – and wait. Let them fight and squabble!"

"But Thelma, it's unfair what Georgio's doing. He's so spoiled!"

"Well, let *them* deal with Giorgio! That's how they'll learn that words mean something." The precious words that give them what they want and need, Giorgio's Nintendo action figure, Mattie's racing car. Words that were not echolalic.

"*My!*" Rory clenching the little action figure in its plastic cape.

"Mama . . . Mama!" screamed Giorgio, grabbing it back. He hides it down his chest, heaving. Mattie, the elective mute, wails, but no words. But wailing won't get his action figure back, nor his favorite dinky Porsche. Words will. By the way, make sure there's only ONE action figure available, one red Porsche, one bucket and spade! And we'll sing about wanting and sharing in circle tomorrow.

"Wow!" said Betsy. "This is so different."

Forget the old discipline for now. We were not here to make them sit quietly in their seats – quiet little autistic boys were definitely not what was needed. That could come later. We were there to get them talking, laughing, looking *at* each other, – sharing, developing their talents, growing in language, relating.

"Look how these kids are coming along!" marvelled Betsy months later, as we actually had them putting on "Three Billy Goats Gruff" with Giorgio playing baby billy goat with paper horns taped to his brow!

Yet I couldn't seem to help my own son . . .

Once again, Julian was pacing the living room after school, seemingly reliving the events of the day, imaginary, or real, and the metaphor that came to mind was that of a caged animal, a tiger or panther, lashing its tail. His face had that remote intense look, yet at the same time wary, absorbing each nuance of our expressions, tone of voice, mien, as if ready to pounce, on us, his parents. His eyes gleamed. His face was flushed, hands sweating, jaw clenched; again we thrilled in horror with the sensation that we were witnessing a sort of madness. I sat tense on the sofa, watching, waiting, Alec kept a grip on the newspaper keeping up a semblance of normality. Jules was panting as he tread back and forth from doorway to dining alcove.

"She's *watching* you, Julian. You behave yourself!"

Julian snarled, spinning round. He beat his head, then slowly, excruciatingly, tore his nails down his cheeks. Livid little marks filled with blood, flesh torn apart. "Don't! Oh, God, don't, Jules!"

I sprang up. I couldn't stand this, not one moment more.

"What the hell − ?" Alec dropped the paper.

"What the hell? What the hell?" screamed Julian, panicking.

"It's OK, Jules, OK." I realized my mistake, tried to soothe the situation, prevent it escalating. Julian pushed me against the wall; his eyes glazed, this was moving quickly into another dimension, one we could not enter.

"Bad, bad, bad!" He howled, ripping his face again.

"Jules!"

Alec fell, hurtled against the fireplace. Julian slapped his hands spread-eagled against the wall and began banging his forehead against it. *Bam − bam.* Luckily Alec long ago had the foresight to check every inch of wall in the house for odd nails sticking out, and removed them. What would Julian do next? What was going to happen? We tried hemming him in, keeping close. Sometimes if I put my arms round him, or stroked his arm it had a calming grounding effect; it would "break" the sort of violent trance. I put out a hand.

"Fuck! Fuck!" Jules was incensed. "You KNOW that's an F-word, Orchard." Suddenly without warning he ran full-tilt at the big picture window. There was a creak, then a crash of glass. Julian's head and upper torso went right through, hanging out over the cobbled walk. Shards of glass flew into the living room. There was a sickening moment of silence, of shock.

"Oh, my God."

"Call Pino."

I ran into the kitchen. Trembling, I rang our neighbors Pino and Francesca. They lived around the corner and had always maintained an interest in Julian. Within moments, they arrived with their oldest son, Raphael, a tall young man now in university. Pino and Raphael had helped out before to calm Julian down. They seemed to fill the living room with their presence, hesitating round our sofa, eyeing the shattered glass, not sure what to do this time. Yet something about the way big gentle Pino said softly in Italian, "Ah, Jiuliano, *bene, bene,*" seemed to halt Julian, jerk his brain momentarily out of its spasm.

Then: "Kill Thelma!"

"Hey hey hey, that your mama. You don't say that about your mama."

"Yeah, that's your mama, Julian," snarled Jules, his face smeared with blood and tears. Oh Jules.

Pino smiled. He patted Julian.

"What'll happen if I say 'balls' to the bus driver, Pino?"

But Julian's voice was already weakening. Whatever spasm had taken him over was waning. The presence of father and son together, both big calm men, was having an effect. "Does Raphael say 'balls' to his bus driver? No he doesn't, Julian."

Raphael shifted awkwardly, glancing wryly at his dad. Pino maintained an easy mild expression. Meanwhile, Francesca appeared with a wet paper towel doused with antiseptic. "Here, let's wipe your face. Remember Francesca from when you were a little boy, Jules? You used to play with Raphael and Pier."

We were lucky that Pino and Francesca had known Julian from babyhood, had seen the phases he'd gone through, believed that this, too, was a phase that would pass. How much this meant to us at the time, the faith and hope of these good neighbors.

Eventually we coaxed Jules into his pajamas, got him to clean his teeth, the routines an essential part, we'd learned by now, of the calming-down process. Suddenly Julian fell asleep instantly, against his pillow, a miraculous deep baby sleep. In the morning he would remember nothing of the episode, would ignore the gaping hole in the window – Pino had fit a piece of plywood into the pane.

Equally miraculously, his wounds and bruises would heal quickly in a phenomenal way. There would be little trace of the horror. A new pane of glass would replace the old. But our own bruises remained.

"Uh, we're battered parents, that's what we are," grunted Alec. The irony of our situation couldn't be denied, but the humor hid a desperate anxiety. Nothing had prepared us, or our doctors, for this violence and self-mutilation in a child. At the walk-in clinic one physician had actually asked fearfully, when we'd brought Jules in for a tetanus shot, "Will he bite?" as Julian lunged in the small cubicle. He balked at having Julian as a patient any longer; the rest of the family, yes. Julian needed a "specialist" to handle him, he hinted, maybe a psychiatrist. "We're just not trained for this, Mr. and Mrs. Orchard."

A petite Filippino nurse finally stepped in to give the shot.

"The fact is, Mrs. Orchard . . . "

Dr. Bland rustled the psych report. His eyes narrowed. We were in a circle once again round the table in Mr. Dickson's office; this time it was serious, they hinted. "Julian, I'm sorry to say, seems to have deteriorated . . . "

Dr. Bland was knowledgeable about autism. In fact, he found the autistic/PDD population fascinating, he said. He'd been dealing with autistic students for decades, so he'd had to develop a wry sort of humor. "Let's face it, how else do you survive in this business?"

The report was covered with miniscule hieroglyphs only trained psychologists could interpret, know the full significance of.

I tensed in readiness, for something, because this was what decided everything: the school Jules went to, which special class — special needs in one such school, special needs in another. Or an "extra special" placement you would never want your son in, ever, that Dr. Bland knows about but will say only in his own good time.

Julian's level of functioning this time round at age 13.6 years, according to the Stanford-Binet Intelligence Scale (Fourth Edition) showed: *moderate range of retardation*, said Dr. Bland.

The Raven's Coloured Progressive Matrices assessing non-verbal reasoning: "below five and one-half years of age equivalency, I'm afraid, Mrs. Orchard."

But that had been his strength. He had achieved above-normal scores the last time in the non-verbal reasoning; I was confused.

"Ah, but that was when he was six, Mrs. Orchard. A lot can happen . . . "

"Does one get less intelligent, then, as one gets older, Dr. Bland? I was under the impression one's basic I.Q. never changed."

Mrs. clever-puss-Orchard, thinks too much for her own good.

Dr. Bland frowned.

"But we must remember, Mrs. Orchard, that had been only in a very limited area: the Puzzle Solving Subtest of the McCarthy Scales and, well, yes, the Block Design subtest. Yes, that had been in the high average range, as I recollect."

He flicked back a moment through the old Psych Test, 1981.

Everything was there in the dossier, everything he needed to know about Julian.

"The truth is, Mrs. Orchard, we maybe should be looking at a more suitable placement for Julian in the near future."

At the bottom, under RECOMMENDATIONS, Dr. Bland had noted: *"A psychiatric referral is strongly recommended to the parents . . . but they are not willing to pursue it at this time."*

And there you had it.

I wanted him to stay at Lymewood in the Intermediate D.C. program! It was vital to keep Julian's self image intact by keeping his world intact. Moving him would imply something was wrong with him. "But there *is* something very wrong, Mrs. Orchard . . . "

But Jules liked Lymewood, and despite everything he liked Mr. Dickson, I pleaded. Julian had been in the program for two years, he had been doing so well up to now, I stressed. His math graphs alone — surely they counted — "Measuring Marvelous ME," for instance. Jules had measured himself on full-length brown kraft paper and written: "I am 170cm tall." He had traced his hand with a pencil and measured it using unifex cubes: "8 unifex cubes long" he had noted. His foot was 12 unifex cubes. And what about his Thanksgiving diagram in language arts, "Time To Be Grateful"? I was sweating. He'd drawn pictures and underwritten he was grateful for "trke" (turkey), "Bre" (bread) and "SDFN" (stuffing). Besides, it was important that he finish his year with the others and go on to the Satellite Class with them — Jules a high schooler!

"But Mrs. Orchard, Satellite Classes demand a certain level of academics and behavior. They have to *sit!*"

But I can't stop. There are his "friends," Sarah and Khadish, Patricia and Lonnie, he's been with forever. That cannot be discounted. He loves Lonnie! He's always loved Lonnie ! You can't take him away from him! He's entitled to finish his year!

I heard my voice trembling. I sounded so frighteningly like Toby Farlane's mother. Toby had turned out to be the "terror" of my autistic class. He was an "experimental placement" from a treatment center where he'd eaten his feces — after smearing it over the aides. I had already regretted my rash decision to remove the partitions. Toby was "on trial" from the center, but Mrs. Farlane hoped nevertheless it would work, that we would survive, that it was a phase Toby was going through and he'd end up like Giorgio and Mattie . . .

What is it about mothers? My voice tense with hope, like hers.

"And Lymewood has the lovely row of poplars," I heard myself going on desperately about the trees, as if they mattered.

Dr. Bland tapped a pencil thoughtfully . . .

I began to sob. At last, I was alone. Alec had taken Julian out to his special needs swimming lesson. It was important to keep up normal routines, to keep Julian in the community around people, normal people, in the hope his behaviors might become transformed into more normal ones too, even though it was so evident this was not happening.

I took out Julian's old school journals I'd kept, the test of time surely these past few years, to compare with his current writing that Mrs. McDougall had sent home at my request. My body hunched over the table in a sorrowful way. I read one recent entry first: *"I Am a doy."*

Which month, which day, did his writing change from the innocent delightful reports of his daily life to these intense blotched scrawls across the page, these jabs of pain that verified only too clearly Dr. Bland's surmise that Julian had "deteriorated"?

"My NAmE I S JulIAn I AM A dOY."

The letters clumsily enlarged on the large manilla drawing book Mrs. McDougall had wisely given him.

Where the luminosity, the promised resplendence, that was to have changed him forever back in the primary class?

I turn to the report cards of the last year or so even more anxiously to compare with his latest, puzzling as over some mystery. It had been a certainty he'd go on to a satellite class.

> *Julian now has 30 high-frequency words from the Dolch word list in his Dolch word box.*

Mrs. McDougall had written this the previous year when he twelve, obviously pleased with Julian's progress.

> *Julian will write independently using invented spelling technique . . . He will build a sight word vocabulary of at least 50 words . . . "*

Again the words of a proud approving teacher.

Mathematics: Julian will complete the requirements for the Grade 2 Math curriculum.. . Julian completed a sewing project in Family Studies . . .

(He'd made a cloth pencil case that year.)

I turn to his most recent reports. Gradually things begin shift, other forces coming into play . . . He's older, not so loveable, not so excusable. He's thirteen, he's five foot seven, he has a moustache, he sweats . . .

Julian will learn to control loud unacceptable laughter . . .
He will not put foreign objects in his mouth.
Julian has been highly vocal in the classroom this term. His behavior is inappropriate, and he has been asked to leave the class on such occasions . . .

How much unspoken anxiety, and teacher duress are in the next amazing but surely sad words:

Our goal has been successful somewhat in curbing Julian's continual inappropriate requests for hugs and kisses . . .

I felt dismay. I should have followed up more closely on this, seen the warning signals. At the time I'd laughed it off, not unpleased. *Jules wanting to kiss Mrs. McDougall!* It was something he'd suddenly started last year at home, innocently enough. "Tissies, Mommy!" he'd say, bending down to my level. I'd kissed his cheek awkwardly at first. Was this the delayed affection of a little boy who'd not known to ask at the proper age: one, two, three years? It was the first time he'd ever sought physical affection, that he was not stimming on my perfume! You just hadn't expected him to transfer it to stolid, dull Mrs. McDougall! She hadn't known what to do with all this unwanted "inappropriate attention" as she called it. And, as usual, Julian did not ask for just one kiss. He went on and on about it round the classroom, over and over, "Tissies, Mrs. McDougall, tissies! Tissies"

You felt such confusion, a mixture of amusement and despair and, once again, a certain sadness.

If only the laughing would stop, the insane-sounding bursts accompanied by rapid excitable pacing as he talks over conversations with imaginary boys: they are always male, always violent, or deformed. Strange, frightening, still more frightening than the rages.

"There'll be nothing left of the carpet soon," noted Alec, computing the cost of new broadloom. This was no joke, he objected, we couldn't afford this behavior much longer. But Julian was lost, gesticulating at someone, some non-existent boy he laughs at, loudly, as if we are not there but nearby on the sofa.

"Who is this Ricky Morris he's on about all the time?" whispers Alec.

"I don't know. He's not at Lymewood."

"Don't go laughing at Ricky Morris," says Julian as if Alec never spoke. That chill wave grips me again. *Psychosis:* first symptoms. "I really do think we should be looking at a psychiatrist for Julian, Mrs. Orchard," Dr. Bland had intimated at the last meeting.

Julian was gripping a popsicle stick, part of an ever increasing collection of items that now formed a mound of collectibles in the corner of the dining-room – garbage ties, bus tickets, candy wrappers but not "appropriate" collections of hockey cards, for instance. He just was not interested in organized sports, had no boyish heroes, the rock stars or hockey idols of most boys his age. He just wanted these everyday items that most people threw out as junk.

Of course, he'd had funny little collections as a child I reminded myself; the little "family" of sticks carefully laid out on the front lawn when he was five, his little dollies. That now seemed so far away. There was a new disturbing obsessiveness to this collecting. He had to keep every popsicle stick in a certain order known to him – how did he know? But he did. "Where's my popsicle stick?" he insisted, clenching. He'd forgotten about "Ricky Morris."

"But you've got fifty or more sticks there, Jules."

"But I want my popsicle stick!" It was getting unbelievably tense, at once.

"House looks like a bloody garbage dump," muttered Alec.

"Sh-sh, Al."

We lived in a new subliminal fear after the smashed window episode. (We had since placed the sofa strategically in front of the window as a buffer.) I tried to sound and look casual about the popsicle sticks, hoping it would pass off. "You can't keep all of them, Jules, there's no room. Mommy has to tidy them up sometimes."

"But my popsicle stick's GONE!"

It was vital to keep the tone relaxed, unshaken, but it was as if we were creeping around verbally and paradoxically this sometimes only created further tension. The slightest anxious inflexion in my voice, in particular, could always rouse Julian, fuse his own anxiety quickly into the rage we dreaded.

"*He*'s controlling *us!*" muttered Alec again; he was tired of this, he wanted to watch *Sixty Minutes,* he wanted a normal life.

"Did Alec use the word 'bloody'? Yes he did!" It was starting up again. It would be laughable if it were not so tragic. Cautiously we edged round the sofa. Jules tore at his fingers. The ends were now permanently calloused and blackened, the nails tender. He had a long bluish hang-nail he compulsively bit, chewed at over and over. This was the worst anguish, Julian's ongoing self-mutilation that he did not seem to feel. I felt my body tensing.

"What happened to the bumblebee, Mom?" yelled Julian, tearing his nails. "Just keep still, Julian. Don't make an issue it. The bumbly will go away," he admonished himself, switching his tone to mine of long ago, so long!

Suddenly he shifted to the kitchen and out the back door to the garden, bolting for the willow. We watched, relieved, as he paced the tree round and round, flicking the popsicle stick as he went. You could hear him droning to himself in a monotone.

"Mom, Dad, I know his behavior looks insane, but I honestly don't think he's psychotic, it's just his age and that he's autistic. He can't process what's happening to him," insisted Polly, coming up from the basement, her arms full of clothes. "I mean he's going through the stuff any teenager goes through, feeling insecure about himself and everything, only he can't express it so it all comes out like this. He's acting out his thoughts and feelings about kids and people . . . "

These were the very words I too longed to believe. But Polly was away in residence most of the time at University of Toronto, her "reward" for helping us out with Julian over the years, especially putting him on the bus in the mornings so I could keep working. I'd been determined she was to have a few years' respite, at least, away from her brother, and have fun like any other student as she deserved it. So I'd put money aside for years for residence fees. "Oh Mom, that's the best gift you could ever have given me!" She had so many new friends! On the other hand, she didn't get to see Julian on an ongoing basis; just odd weekends when she came home extra hungry from residence or had a load of laundry to do. She did not get to see the full extent of Julian's rages and strangeness. Hearing about the smashed front window from us second-hand was not the same as living through the event. How could Polly or anyone know?

But he'd been violent as a little boy at times, Polly reminded us gently.

"Mom, Dad, remember all the window panes he smashed in the door of the music room that time?"

He'd once put his head through every antique pane of glass with their exquisitely carved flower whorls — irreplaceable — when he was six or so. But it had not seemed to have the relevance of now. Now that he was nearly fourteen. I recalled Dr. Bland saying once: "Behaviors you can put up with when they're three years old are quite different when they're thirteen and six-feet tall!"

Still, Polly had given us an important "outsider's" view. We clung to it, that this was only a phase, Jules was not going over the borderline, that delicate space between understandable frustrated behavior and psychosis . . . I tightened again, watching him under the willow. I loved Jules so much, wanted him to feel that security of feeling worthy: that was it. He saw himself so much as "bad," something his very own behaviors ironically created, it was so frustrating. Yet he was "the best boy on the bus," Deanie the bus driver always insisted loyally. It was true, an aspect of Jules few knew. The whirring motion of the bus lolled him always into peaceful somnolence, as in a car. Deannie never saw "the other Julian" of home and school. I'd remind Jules of this, that he was the best, on the bus at least. It counted for something, a start.

"He's the best boy on the bus," I mumbled to Polly. "Deannie said so." It sounded arcane, though, desperate in the circumstances, a desperate parent seizing the slightest desperate pretext.

"But that's just it, Mom! Look, don't cry Mom, Dad, I'll take Jules out to the mall for the afternoon and then to McDonald's, he'll love that. You guys have a break."

Polly was just so great, so solid, confident, and kind. She was right; a break was what we needed. But then, what after that; after she'd gone and "it" started up again?

"Julian frightens the younger children . . . "

Mrs. McDougall appeals to me as I hasten down the hall in response to her call — another suspension for Julian Orchard, this time for two days. (I suspected she needed the break, as probably did Julian.) I would have to take time off, using up my allotted "sick days." As usual, I received a formal letter on grey paper confirming the suspension, the opening words now familiar: "This will serve to notify you that Julian is hereby suspended." It was approved by the Superintendent of Schools who had had to be notified and it would be recorded in Julian's OSR (Ontario School Record). And what did that mean? Right then, I didn't care.

A class of grade ones press their backs against the wall outside the library fearfully, excited as Julian charges by — "Just keep still, everyone!" A monster in their midst, a real live one with black wavy hair and a funny moustache, foaming at the mouth, whose mother has come to take him away. I tense angrily. Mr. Dickson hovers nervously at my side. "Try to steer him into the gross motor room, Ethel. Mrs. Orchard's here."

"They're gonna beat you up!" screams Julian even when safely maneuvered into the gross motor room to cool down, the O.T. room where he has a trampoline, exercise bikes, massage mats on which to supposedly work out his excess energy for how else would we even get him to the nearest exit? Mr. Dickson peers through the window in the door. He's worried. Julian is slashing at the "faces" he says are laughing at him, the evil "boys," the violence, the anguish on his face catching at us, his tear-stained cheeks. *But there is no one there, Jules. No one is out to get you. Everyone loves you. Mr. Dickson loves you — Mrs. McDougall — Dr. Bland too, honest.*

How many times have we re-enacted this terror: Jules cowering behind the big orthopedic ball, refusing to come out. *It's OK, Jules, it's OK, let's get your coat and hat and Snoopy lunchbox.*

"He doesn't *belong* here any more, Mrs. Orchard ... "

Why can't I get it?

Twenty

M aybe it's time to look at an alternate placement for Julian, a more TRE-ADD-type setting under Section 27, given the psychotic-like symptoms developing . . . " murmured Dr. Bland. So Dr. Bland recognized it too. Of course he did, he was trained. But Jules would never get into a satellite class once he was designated "Section 27." Students "ended up," were "sent to," the specially segregated class like a prison sentence. Because no one knew what to do with them. They were beyond normal classroom management, the "end of the line." They disappeared from the regular D.C. class in a flurry of permission forms and IPRCs, rarely to return.

"Section 27" was classed as a "Care and Treatment" program. It was under the Ministry for Social Services in partnership with the Ministry of Education for "high-needs" individuals still in school. There was a Section 27 class for young offenders as well as the Section 27 class for Autistic/PDD students. The assistants in the classroom were childcare workers rather than teaching assistants, specially trained. It sounded serious. It was serious.

There was a Junior/Senior TRE-ADD class, age range eleven to fourteen, Jules could fit into nicely before Christmas, hinted Dr. Bland.

TRE-ADD (Training, Rehabilitation, Education of Children with Autism and other Developmental Delays) operated out of Thistletown Regional Centre, so we were back full circle to where we had started with Dr. Rakka in 1981, so long ago. The program admirably suited a certain autistic clientele: lower-functioning, often non-verbal, severely behavioral, very "needy," which was why they were not in the usual D.C. or Autistic/PDD classes. Many had severe attention deficit disorders. But Jules was highly verbal, he was bright! "Ah, but violent, face it, Mrs. Orchard. Bordering psychotic."

Dr. Bland subsequently set up an appointment for me to visit the Primary/Junior class. Julian could benefit from the rigid regimen, the one-on-one monitoring.

I observed the class, finding the strictly regulated programming claustrophobic. How would Jules feel in this room? There was no *time* for a child to "act up"! Tasks, such as folding laundry, or doing a puzzle, or working on a peg-board, were rotated in short, strictly segmented work units of five minutes' duration. The children were kept strictly "to task" with rewards or aversives, following the principles of behavior modification, explained the director of the program.

Most of the children in the class were so quiet, so compliant, one wondered why they weren't in a D.C. class. Ah, but they were "good," meaning "under control," *because* of the strict monitoring, smiled the director. All aversives were used in accordance with the Child and Family Services Act, she assured me. Workers were bound by the Act to place a gym mat on the floor before applying restraints, holds, or bite-guards. The "box," a tall box-like wooden structure in the corner of the room with a door in it was reserved for special "out-of-control" cases.

The box sounded and looked more terrible than it actually was, she pointed out, not unreasonably. What else could be done with a violent exploding pre-adolescent tearing his teeth through his arm – or savaging yours – but isolate him as quickly as possible into some empty contained space for his own protection, and that of others? It was the lesser of two evils. No one *wanted* to use it. The coordinator had steady cool steely eyes, unflinching. Oh, Jules!

How far did a child – did Jules – have to go before being finally designated? How many self-beatings, slashings, punches, merited "severe"? That's what I wanted to know. More than anything. *And at the same time, I did not want to know*. Don't tell me! Not yet. How much "worse" he had to get. For there was no doubt in Dr. Bland's mind, Julian Orchard was getting "worse."

"You could castrate him," said Judith.
She was my kindly elderly friend in her seventies, who was

sorry for Julian ranting up and down the street. She sat on the sofa observing him, fearful at times especially when he pushed his face up to hers in an ugly way, hitting his own. "Judith!" he yelled at the wall. Suddenly Julian dug his teeth into his wrist. Dark purple teeth-marks edged his artery, which bulged, bloody. One day he was going to go right through, blood spurt, what would I do then? How would I even get him to hospital?

"It's the death wish," said Judith quietly. She believed she had the Irish gift of the "second sight" which afforded her intuitive power. Judith had worked as a counselor in homes for delinquent youth and young women in the '50s and '60s. The hostels had also housed mentally handicapped girls and schizophrenics, that was how she knew, she said.

"They all do it, they all come to it in the end," she sighed. "It's the death wish of the human race."

She meant the death wish of the mentally-insane, of the disturbed, of paranoid schizophrenics . . . It started young, she said: she had seen it so many times. On the wards, seen them brought in . . .

There were places in the States I could take him to get it done, she went on in a low voice. "You and Alec should not have to go through this, Thelma. And think of Polly, the effect of all this on her, think of your health.

"Castration will make life better for him, settle him down. Do you think he's happy like this?"

But I couldn't do that to him, no matter what.

Twenty-one

Y ou felt so helpless, so lacking in real knowledge about what was happening, what these sudden surges in Julian meant — their strangeness — whether he really was psychotic, whatever that exactly was, as Dr. Bland said. It was the sort of word one associated with mad obsessive types who committed violent rape and murder, so terrible.

I have to know, seek out the truth, verify the research for myself. I go to the Gerstein Library Saturday morning while Alec takes Jules to the barber: The Gerstein Centre for Science Information at the University of Toronto. Top university in Canada, top of Maclean's list of Top Ten Universities. The library is housed in a grey stone building on King's College Circle; there are carved portals with great black wrought-iron brackets across the heavy doors.

Inside a tapestry hangs in the dimly lit entrance hall, a gift from the Princess of Wales, 20th November, 1908. A kingly figure of a man on a flashing white horse with flossy mane, holds a flag with some German words emblazoned on it. The banner says: "King Edward III is represented on the battlefield of Crecy pointing to his son, the Black Prince, the flag of the dead King of Bohemia . . . exhorts him to pledge his life to the service of mankind . . . "

"Her Royal Highness, the Princess of Wales," the inscription goes, hopes "that her Banner may inspire Undergraduates . . . to adopt for the guidance of their lives the motto 'I Serve' . . . *Ich Dien*"! It's so sincere for a moment you actually believe it, the Black Prince on bended knee bowing his head before his father.

The banner so thick and soft as velvet in the glass case, and sad. I want to believe the Princess of Wales meant it, that Edward III was anxious to give his son, the Black Prince, the highest moral impulse to serve and uplift mankind!

Inside I descend to the stacks with my call numbers, I have a whole handful of them. I find my books and lift down the tomes grey with must from the shelves: *History of Psychiatry, History of Psychoses, Neuroses, American Journals of Psychiatry, Journals of Medicine . . .*

Schizophrenia: Psychogenesis, Diagnosis and Prognosis . . . symptoms first recognized by Benedict Morel in 1852 in France . . . followed by Emil Kraepelin, in the nineteenth century,(1856–1926). Kraepelin noted adolescents with hallucinations, delusions, bizarre behavior, deterioration and psychosis.

Then Bleuler defines it for good in 1908, the same year the Princess donated her Banner, as "schizophrenia," the "splitting of integrated functions." Basically schizophrenia is "disruption," that is its terrible distinguishing feature. In general*, the earlier the age of onset, the worse the outcome is likely to be.*

Is that what is happening to Jules? Can't hold it together, just can't. I would rather know all this, be prepared for any outcome. It's late October, The IPRC will be in motion by the end of November to place Julian somewhere, "somewhere more suitable."

But Bleuler claims that sometimes there can be social recovery from a psychotic episode. He'd seen it.

"So is he any better now?"

Elsie eyed Julian cautiously. The coffee shop was full, mainly of after-churchgoers. Jules sat down with us for a moment then jumped up again restlessly and went to stand in the corner by the men's washroom, talking to himself in an urgent way.

"*. . . and you know what will happen to you . . .*" Mrs. McDougall's tone, it was eerie. People were looking, though was his self-talk any different in essence to Brett's yelling to himself at the video station? He was playing Pac-Man.

"How come Julian does that, Aunt Thel?"

Brett knocked off some asteroids whizzing through space. The game was Asteroids.

"Jules has problems, Brett, right now," I said, as if they were temporary, and all we needed was patience and he'd be out of it by eighteen.

"He's not the only one!" said Elsie gruffly.

She was not pleased with how Brett was doing at school since he'd gone into grade eight. He was bored with the work, hated the kids in his class, calling them nerds and White Supremacists, hated the teachers, even Mr. Lystrom who took a personal interest in him and gave him a role in the school play. "It's his age, I guess," she sighed. She had got him a part-time job Friday nights as busboy at St. Hubert's Chicken Villa picking up trays. "Keep him occupied, out of trouble. Plus he'll learn the value of a dollar."

But Brett just laughed, used to this heckling and teasing, the sort of mother-son camaraderie I envied.

At fourteen Brett was still small for his age, blond, freckled, tense and shy. He was bored now at our Sunday coffee mornings without Polly. Polly had rebelled long ago — "Mom, I'm too old for that stuff any more!" She had had exams to study for, as well as her grade ten piano exam at The Royal Conservatory of Music in Toronto. She'd been learning Beethoven's sonata, *Opus 27, No 2,* Elsie's favorite. Brett had to understand that. Now that Polly was away in first-year university, he missed her. Polly was in the vital "in" crowd at Victoria College, she wore cool black clothes, lace-up granny boots, and two sets of earrings. Brett wanted to be like her boyfriend, Todd, and have a stud in his ear. Julian was a complex oddity who now towered unexpectedly over him. "Ma, how come Julian's taller 'n' me?"

"Well blame your father not me!"

"HIT!" yelled Brett.

"Hit!" yelled Julian hitting himself.

"It's only a game, Jules."

"Why does he keep doing that, Thel?"

"Dr. Bland says he's . . . psychotic."

Elsie took a long drag at her cigarette, glancing out at the early snow-bound river, the boats caught tight in place in the icy harbor. Seagulls flapped over the masts. Thin sleet sheeted the sky. It was disconcerting the way things were shifting between us. I had always been the one helping Elsie out.

"What's that mean, then . . . exactly?" A psychotic was a terrible thing to have in the family.

"Well, as far as I can figure it out, it's sort of thinking that's 'divorced from reality' according to Bleuler." I tightened, anxiously.

"Who the hell is Bleuler? And who the hell lives in reality?" snorted Elsie.

"He's . . . some famous psychiatrist in the nineteenth century, he sort of defined schizophrenia." (The most terrifying word in the English language.)

"Oh my God, what next?"

She lit up another cig and got out her latest Rosamunde Hartley romance. The cover showed dedicated but rebellious young Nurse Dinsmore, her long tangled curls breaking recklessly out of her nurse's cap, stethoscope askew, as she tried to resist the embrace of young Dr. Paul: *"Conquered With A Kiss."*

Oh, if only it were that simple, Else.

Julian had come running into the house off the bus, tossed down his bag yelling "ASSHOLE," and gone straight outside. He was stomping up and down the street in his big boots still shouting expletives and hitting himself as we watched, tensing, at the front window. Now he was outside Sam, the fireman's, house. It was a new unexpected problem that demanded immediate attention, but complex, for the demography of the street had changed over the years. Young families had moved in as elderly neighbors had moved out to condos and nursing homes, or passed away. The new younger parents tended to keep an eye on each other's children as part of "Neighborhood Watch"; they did not expect to be including a big, pacing, restless thirteen year old with a moustache. There were still a few older neighbors who looked out for Julian in a good-natured way — "We're keeping an eye on him" — but how long could that last? In particular, we were coming to rely more and more on Pino and Francesca at the end of the road adjoining ours to come over in times of crisis.

We were anxious not to take advantage of the leeway given, this neighborly concern, not take it for granted. We were sure the Craddocks in particular must be tiring of Julian's tirades. They were the oldest residents in the neighborhood. "What's happened to poor old Jules?" Mr. Craddock had trembled one day. "He's a big boy now." Had that been a hint? He watched with interest all that happened on the street as he slowly speared the last of the leaves on the opposite lawn.

We tried to keep Jules involved in outside activities as much as possible. One evening of the week was taken up with Special

Olympics for developmentally challenged individuals, age range thirteen plus. The program was run by two volunteer Catholic high school teachers, Rozie and Dan, soon known as Rozie'n'Dan to Julian. They had the use of the gym facilities at Mary Immaculate Separate School. The program was excellent and well thought-out for the developmentally challenged: activities were varied weekly, from soccer and baseball to volleyball, swimming, indoor golf, and bowling, with track and field in the spring. Also included were parties at Christmas and year-end.

But would Julian participate, or be an on-the-fringe spectator circling the gym and "spoiling it" for everyone else?

Rozie, a matronly, kindly figure, looked dubiously at Julian.

"We don't want to be teachers, having to discipline difficult participants, Mrs. Orchard. We're just volunteers, this is meant to be fun."

"Julian has an excellent eye," she reported puzzled when I came to pick him up later.

It seemed Julian had scored the highest number of strikes for his team in bowling – without even looking at the pins as he took aim. Another example of his strange "autistic" skill.

"We'll give him a try this season . . . "

It was the beginning of a relationship that Julian was to cherish for twelve years. He never failed to remind us every Monday evening: "Julian go to Special 'lympics at Mary Maclit." We were thrilled. But right now that only took care of one evening. Six evenings loomed ahead, with Julian pacing at the door in the hallway to be let out on the street.

A long evening walk to McDonald's was the answer. It would use up Jules' excess nervous energy, which seemed inexhaustible, and at the same time put him in a happier mood. Having a burger at McDonald's invariably had a calming effect I'd noted, with some dismay. But I had to push aside my own instinctive misgivings about too much fast food for now. It was more important to keep Jules part of the community and fast-food restaurants unfortunately were the only place that Julian's excitable behaviors seemed to be less notice-able or of less concern to others. We devised a safe route along the Lakeshore away from neighbors, yet out and about Port Credit. Jules would experience people going about ordinary tasks, we fantasized, shopping at Safeway, picking up six packs of beer at the liquor store, or just ambling by with their children and dogs.

Somehow most evenings we managed the three-mile walk to McDonald's and back, assessing Julian's state of mind the whole way, ready to divert him down a side street. It was essential to keep on top of any quickly flaring situation.

But it was often hard to pass teenagers knotting the sidewalk, bringing home painfully that if he had been normal, Julian would likely have been out with them instead of with his mother and father. Perhaps he sensed this too, he kept walking half a block ahead of us, understandable but worrisome. Yet he also seemed frightened.

Suddenly the evening inexplicably exploded. Had we missed some clue? Julian was striding his usual half-block ahead, waving his fists as if he were defending himself against someone, yelling at them. We called out anxiously, but too late. A police cruiser had slowed down. We could hear the officer as we ran up, "Hey kid, what's your name?"

Julian walked on all the faster, muttering "What's your name, what's your name?"

"It's OK officer, he's with us."

"He's with you?"

"We're just having an evening walk, officer."

A second officer, an older man who looked in his late fifties, got anxiously out of the cruiser, walkie-talkie in hand. I was aware of a gun in his holster, surreal, the incident was surreal, unbelievable, but it was happening. This could be a showdown with a possible paranoid schizophrenic, I heard his low voice contacting someone.

"It's the POLICE!" yelled Julian suddenly, unnerved.

"Jules!" I tried to lower my tone, sound conciliatory,

"You don't walk away when a police car comes by and the police officer talks to you. The police officer is a nice man, a good man. He is Julian's friend. He wants to help you. So when the nice kind officer says 'What's your name?' You STOP and say 'Julian Orchard, sir.' "

I paused, gasping, knowing his love of order. "And you say your address and telephone number." This was uttered in what I hoped was a low soothing tone at break-neck speed as Jules' pacing renewed down the sidewalk. Alec meanwhile was trying to explain that Julian was autistic but the officers were suspicious, hesitating. I could hear urgent words from the cruiser, *"Yes sir. . autistic. .no, not a schizophrenic. . registered at the hospital . . . ?"*

Things were escalating at a rapid pace. If only they'd let us handle this by ourselves.

Julian wheeled round, startled, quivering with unmistakable accusation, fear: *You're supposed to STOP, Julian!*

He punched wildly missing me as the officers closed in. "OK kid, OK."

"Watch it, Jake." The young one had handcuffs which he quickly snapped on to Julian's wrists.

"Oh, don't hurt him! This was all a misunderstanding; he's harmless, he doesn't mean it."

"We just want the best for him, ma'am."

The old officer nodded sympathetically that he had not heard of autism, he knew about schizophrenia. He was a kindly man. The police had all the those suffering from schizophrenia in the area on record on a computer, he explained softly, so they would under-stand how to respond if called in a crisis. "We get lots of calls from schizos gone nuts."

He sighed. "Sorry, we'd better take him in, ma'am. It's a shame, nice kid like that."

Julian was sitting quietly now in the back of the cruiser. "Am I going to jail, Mommy?"

Finally the officers agreed to escort us home, instead. The old officer put Julian's name and particulars on the computer, adding it to the quick tally of troubled "mental patients," so they would know him next time and respond appropriately, he added.

But Jules wasn't mental, we wanted to cry out.

Twenty-two

A ctually, we don't talk about childhood schizophrenia any more," drawled Dr. Bland.

It was recess time. Dr. Bland was in my classroom for student observation. I'd shown him the book I was reading right then, *The Schizophrenic Child,* by a Dr. Sheila Cantor, one of the mountain of books on autism and schizophrenia from my ongoing research at the Gerstein library. This Dr. Sheila Cantor had been a Child Psychiatry fellow of Belleview Psychiatric Hospital, New York, in the '70s. She was assistant professor at the University of Manitoba Medical School, and had personal experience of schizophrenic children at her hands-on clinic, so how could she be wrong?

Her description of the symptoms of schizophrenia in children was so uncanny: identical to those of autism. *The Schizophrenic Child* read like a blueprint of Julian. It was all there — impoverishment of language, the rituals, the stereotyped behaviors, *echolalia,* lack of eye-contact, the lack of self . . . "disintegration," that word again, especially the danger of total disintegration in adolescence/early adulthood.

"But that's old hat now, Mrs. Orchard, pre-1980 thinking," said Dr. Bland. "We're in DSM-111 now. DSM-111-*Revised!*" he added, not uncomically. Couldn't I understand that the DSM, the *Diagnostic Statistical Manual* put out by the American Psychiatric Association, was the psychiatric equivalent to the King James Version of the Bible?

"It's 'Pervasive Developmental Disorder' now, Mrs. Orchard. "PDD." The PDD umbrella. He had to keep up with all the new terminology as a psychologist. "You'd be better off reading Frith."

Una Frith had written the highly regarded book, *Autism: Explaining the Enigma,* published in 1989. Every parent with an autistic child was supposed to be reading Frith and her "theory of mind," but I was more interested in her claims about childhood schizophrenia. Frith actually stated it was non-existent in children before the age of five, yet here was Dr. Cantor only a decade before describing schizophrenic *infants* in her ward. "The symptomatic infant," and yes, Julian seemed to have had all those symptoms too, Dr. Bland.

"Don't you think you should stick to teaching alphabet soup, Mrs. Orchard?"

But I needed closure, something definite to hold on to for Jules, to be prepared. According to Frith, it seemed Julian was *on* an autistic continuum, and *under* The PDD Umbrella, whereas schizophrenia was something else. It had everything to do with "age of onset." And suddenly I was afraid.

Which is it better to be: continuously disintegrating from birth, or suddenly psychotic, at fourteen?

For Frith had touched on a truth I dreaded: schizophrenia *could be superimposed on autism*. A psychotic autistic, an autistic psychotic, not forgetting that current research pointed to schizophrenia being likely genetic, passed on through the generations, noted Frith. That's what Dr. Bland liked about Frith. She was so succinct.

"Of course, Dr. Bland no longer quite believes in Kanner's 'psychogenic' theory though one felt it was always there lurking around . . . the 'refrigerator mother' as the cause of her child's psychosis . . . No doubt about marital stress found in couples with autistic children . . . marriage breakdown, total emotional mental breakdown . . . some mothers even ending up killing themselves and their autistic children . . . " Dr. Bland droned on. His personal view was that parents of autistic children probably start out as normal as anyone else, and the stress of dealing with autism makes them end up as abnormal themselves. Heh, heh, heh!

"The fact is, Mrs. Orchard, sometimes in life we have to face very unpleasant, painful truths about our children and even ourselves."

Which was why it was important to attend the Symposium on Schizophrenia before things got more serious for Jules at Lymewood. The workshop, "Focus on Schizophrenia in the '90s," was being offered by the Psychiatric Department of the local hospital, supported by Friends of Schizophrenia and sponsored by Meyers-Squibb Pharmaceutical. It was cited for the benefit of professionals and lay people like myself with an interest in schizophrenia in "family members." This would be a chance learn from psychiatrists themselves who would know every avenue of treatment available to Julian, the latest advance in medicine and psychiatry, even what exactly "psychosis" and "anti-psychotic" medication meant. I still wasn't sure. If Julian was not psychotic as Polly maintained, why was Dr. Bland wanting to put him on "anti-psychotic" medication?

Nervously I sat down in the hospital auditorium. On the way in, a group of individuals calling themselves "Psychiatric Survivors" had been gathered in the lobby and the foyer waving disturbing placards: "Psychiatry Psucks!" protesting against this very workshop, to which they claimed not to have been invited to present their views.

The evening's topic was: "The Pharmacology of Schizophrenia," to be followed by "Personal Perspectives." There was a ripple of interest in the audience. Real live schizophrenics were to go up on the stage, and we could judge for ourselves, smiled Dr. Cruikshank. He was the head of schizophrenia at the hospital, and he was very excited about the whole thing, having an open forum for the public like this, "new beginning for the '90s," he chuckled.

Dr. Cruikshank looked in his sixties, as did Dr. Abernathy: both tops in the field of schizophrenia. "This is a venture," said Dr. Cruikshank appreciatively, "not like the old days." He hesitated. It had to be brought up, he coughed, "the old days" . . . Deep insulin coma . . . repatterning . . . inklodon gas treatment (you wouldn't want to know about that particular experiment) . . . metrazol convulsive "therapy," tried out on deserters in the World Wars. Banned now, of course. But how many of us in the audience knew that?

Dr. Abernathy was here for the pharmacokinetics of drugging. Because the symptoms of schizophrenia are dangerous in outcome, and are never to be overlooked or underestimated.

Positive Symptoms and Negative Symptoms of Schizophrenia, often referred to as "PANSS" in the field. This classification, we learned, had been proposed by T.J. Crow in 1980, defining patients in terms of the presence or absence of "positive" and "negative" symptoms. Although this was not formally adopted as part of DSM classification of schizophrenia, the clinical distinction of the two types had had a strong influence on psychiatric thinking and research.

Of course, it was the "Positive" ones you wanted to know about. Does he or doesn't he have them? *Oh Jules!* The "Negative" were the more serious to treat, said Dr. Abernathy. Much more serious, but not the more dangerous.

Positive did not mean positive in the sense of good, explained Dr. Abernathy. It meant *something that was there that should not be there*. Positive/dangerous meant violent, excitable, filled with inexplicable rage and outbursts, talking-out, hallucinatory, deluded, raving mad starkers from hell, paranoiac — *"They're gonna kill you, Julian!"* — The negative state was the more difficult to treat; to medicate, that is, observed Dr. Abernathy. Because whereas you can blank out something bad or violent that is there, you can't drug "happiness," "involvement," "enthusiasm," *into* someone. No, you can't, Dr. Abernathy. Was Dr. Abernathy brilliant, or not?

Negative symptoms were: apathy, withdrawal, poverty of thought, blunting of emotions, the state of unhappiness.

It still might be only a passing phase with Julian, I thought. He was still only fourteen, his primary diagnosis still Autistic/PDD. I tried not to dwell on Frith, that schizophrenia could be superimposed. But the evidence was compelling.

It seemed DSM defined schizophrenia as a "disturbance" of at least six months' duration, with two or more symptoms active for at least a month. Disturbance manifested as disordered thought processes ("Mommy is Daddy") including echolalia, perseveration, "clanging" (repeating words similar in sound but not in meaning); there were also the repetitive stereotyped behaviors, aggressive and agitated behavior. The list of criteria for schizophrenia went on, only too familiar, strikingly similar to autism.

"Psychosis" itself was defined as the inability to distinguish reality from fantasy. The indicators of a poor prognosis were: young onset, withdrawn autistic behavior and assaultiveness, said Dr. Abernathy calmly.

Dr. Abernathy was obviously the one to trust here, who knew what he was doing, guiding us so we'd know and recognize the symptoms and what to do about them. What drugs to give was stressed at the outset.

First guest speaker: Harry Odelle, to be followed by Ms. Heather Spence. One was an unsuccessful patient who did not manage his meds; the other, an office worker, successfully maintained on medication. Young, bright, and on chlorpromazine, she was pert, pretty, with a dazzling assuring smile and natty earrings. So right away she's what you want your child to be, and naturally they put her on last because last impressions are what an audience always takes away with them. It's obvious Harry had likely never cooperated with his psychiatrists from the loud belligerent way he grips the mike, in a panic.

"Drugs done me wrong, all my life," he wheezes.

He's as old as Dr. Cruikshank. It's hard to say of someone who has spent most of his life institutionalized, who has been through "everything," been tried on "everything," *psychiatry phsucks!* he trembles. His voice is thin and cracked, grating; he twitches continually due, he rasps, to "them drugs" they shot into his ass, what they done to him, what the drugs done, what Haldol done. See his tongue? Haldol done him no good, the drugs was bad. He drones on and on, gripping the mike, his tongue flicking horribly, like a snake's. Now he has T.D. Know what that is? Tardive dyskinesia. No one told him "about T.D." and now he had it. Now he can't remember nothing, all those things they done to him locked up. And his mouth opens to tell us, and we strain, waiting, waiting to know before it is too late. But something dissolves in his brain, it strains and the words do not come, the very words he needs to say and we to hear. We strain with him, *tell us, Harry, tell us.*

The psychiatrists pick their way through the almond tidbits in the interval. Everyone needs replenishment. There is punch and coffee put on by the Friends of Schizophrenia and Merrill Dow Pharmaceuticals in the foyer. The pharmaceutical companies have their booths set up in aisles with their wares and brochures. Eli Lilly, SmithKline Beecham ... *our products guaranteed ... extra-pyramidal effects minimized ... smooths the way for enhanced compliance* ... Dr. Abernathy probes a bracelet of shrimp, pinkish, peeled.

The middle-aged woman sharing the windowseat with me suddenly slumps, her eyes brimming with tears, which means I must say something to her, one can't just ignore something like this. Because she is a mother, the mother of a twenty-four-year-old schizophrenic, she sobs. Bill had delusions, persecution mania, hallucinations, everything "positive." He'd once chopped down her kitchen door with a hatchet. I stiffen.

Madge has never heard of DSM. She only knows she is fifty-nine, a widow, overweight and puffy-faced with dark circles under her eyes. That she never sleeps for fear that Bill will come back and kill her. He is out on the streets starving because he won't take his medication any more. He can't look after himself, doesn't wash or dress himself properly, doesn't cook, or clean the room he has in some ratty rooming house in Parkdale. He breaks into her home at night, steals money, food; she has only a small pension but if she objects, he beats her up, his own mother. "He can't help it," she sobs harder.

The police at Station 52 have urged her to change her locks for her own good. She hates locking out her own son, knowing it is his life or hers.

"Is he any better on the — the medications?" I ask. Shouldn't Dr. Abernathy know about this? Dr. Cruikshank? They are still spearing shrimp from the pink crevette frilled with lettuce, only yards away. There is the hum of conversation, low, modulated — psychiatrists rarely get excited.

Madge, her name was Madge Hodgeson, she says, shakes her head wearily. "They all know us." Her son had tried every medication. Largactil, Mellaril, Haldol, every one in the book, "They don't make no difference."

Just then a protest group in the lobby began advancing, waving signs and chanting in unison, *"Hey hey, CPA, how many kids did you drug today?"*

Some members were from The Ontario Coalition Against Electroshock, others from Voice of Women demanding: "Food not bombs," "Hugs not Haldol." Everyone seemed to fear Haldol.

"SHOCKED TO DEATH! — PSYCHIATRY KILLS! — TORTURE NOT TREATMENT!! — L'HOSPITAL DES PRAIRIES MERDE! — JUSTICE IN MONTREAL FOR DUPLESSIS ORPHANS!" — screamed the billboards.

One woman they called Hettie was shouting in a trembling voice: "SMASHED THE STATE IN '88!" But Hetty looked as if she couldn't smash a potato let alone the psychiatric state.

They were weak and they knew it; the marginalised, the poor, pathetic survivors at best, mocking in some frail attempt to show what? Their leader was a fierce yet gentle man with fine grey hair waving out like a prophet of the Old Testament: eloquent, fiery, dressed in frayed old pants and a worn jacket covered with buttons, *Chemical Rape, Psychobabble.*

Yet something in the strained eyes of these ones I recognized, yes; a frailty, a brokenness that was mine.

It was all so different from what had been presented on the stage, what you wanted to believe in. Madge began to sob all the harder, perhaps because it was obvious where her son belonged here.

Her hand gripped mine, plump and wet, the cuticles ground down. I let her keep hold of me. What else was there to do, what say, my own heart so tight as we sat in the windowseat. Because what I wanted to know so desperately now was *when* had been the onset of Bill's psychosis, and how had she known — known for sure?

"Oh you'll *know* . . . "

Twenty-three

J ulian should go on some kind of medication, like other
students." Dr. Bland said the words for the first time. "Many of
our students have had success with Haldol, try a low dose to start,
of course . . ."

Mr. Dickson and Mrs. McDougall nodded in agreement.

On Haldol Julian could possibly be transferred — mid-year
transfer — to The Meadows, said Dr. Bland *sotto voce*. It was
November; the all-important IPRC was to take place shortly. The
final stamp.

The Meadows was the segregated senior school for the developmentally challenged (mentally retarded) out on Fifth Line. So
Jules was not to make the satellite class, then.

But The Meadows was still better than a Section 27 classroom, I
thought, quickly seizing the offer. The Section 27 senior autistic unit
was completely segregated with its own time-out room and padded
mat for the aides to use for the ones acting out. The aides took crisis
intervention techniques; it had its own separate washroom, kitch-
enette. The Meadows was middle-of-the-road, not a satellite
program in a regular high school, but not a Section 27-mandated
program either. It was segregated, yet open to the community with
a big work experience program. The students in the satellite classes
came over every Friday from the feeder schools for school assembly
and for dances. It was a compromise. A compromise for Julian that
we grasped at gratefully, the best the Board could offer in the
circumstances thanks to Dr. Bland's intervention, as long as Julian
started on some sort of medication . . . the unspoken assumption,
the other half of the equation.

"It is the preferred medication of choice, Mr. and Mrs. Orchard."

"You wanna get him under control . . . "

Dr. Sol smiled. He was the psychiatrist recommended by Dr. Bland, crisis situation. We sat in his office in The Child and Family Clinic, Psychiatric Services. Dr. Sol was casually dressed in an open-neck purple shirt, soft corduroys, brogues, as if he were in his den at home. He seemed in his late forties, attractive and intelligent.

"I suggest 0.5mg twice daily to start."

Dr. Sol reached for his RX pad.

"Isn't there some sort of medical examination first, Doctor?" asked Alec.

We were vague about this, whatever it was a psychiatrist needed to know about a patient's health before putting him on drugs. What about Julian's kidneys? His liver? Dr. Sol seemed so relaxed about the prescription.

"Thousands are on Haldol. This is an extremely low dose with little or no side effects, Mrs. Orchard."

"But don't you want to observe him more, Dr. Sol?"

Dr. Sol shrugged, lounging back in his easy chair. What more was there to see? He already could see "what Julian was all about." Dr. Sol couldn't exactly have a conversation with Julian, could he? He couldn't ask him how he felt, why he did what he did, or get any insights from Julian himself. It always had to come back to parental input and observation. I supposed psychiatrists did not actually do physical examinations; he didn't seem to have a stethoscope on hand. Still, should he not be concerned about Julian's heartbeat, the way he was pacing agitatedly outside the door so red in the face?

Julian had grasped Dr. Sol's hand in the first moment of intro-duction and at that instant you were aware of Dr. Sol's reservation, even fear; this was a psychiatrist who also walked the wards of Queen Street Mental Health Centre downtown Toronto as part of his job. Quickly he'd loosened his hand and backed away, suggesting Julian feel free to walk around outside, we did not need him listening in to our discussion about him, reasonable enough. But that wariness, swiftly hid, resumed whenever Julian came to the doorway.

Dr. Sol shrugged. Julian did not need a physical examination to go on Haldol. "However," he concurred in a soothing way – this was definitely a psychiatrist who did not want adversarial confrontation – "If you insist, and it's going to make you more comfortable, you can certainly have your family doctor check him out."

But then who would be responsible for the actual drug monitoring other than ourselves if Dr. Sol prescribed the drug and Dr. Geene examined his reactions? The two men didn't even know each other.

Dr. Sol looked startled. "Well I guess he could send the results on to me."

But surely Jules should have a physical check-up before going on Haldol to compare his progress or physical reactions, otherwise what proof would we have how Haldol was affecting him, we persisted.

"Mrs. Orchard, as I've said, there's little chance of side effects given the minimal dose Julian will be on. Side effects happen after being on high doses for a number of years. But it's up to you. I'm not forcing Haldol or anything else on your son; it's up to you what drug and dosage you are comfortable with."

We knew little about drug dosage but 0.5mg of anything sounded low. Dr. Sol leaned back comfortably, half closing his eyes, waiting. It must be the new psychiatry, patient-as-participant, a new '90s approach designed to put us at our ease. There was little choice, all the same. It was to be Haldol. "Oh, and make sure he wears dark glasses in bright sunlight, Mr. and Mrs. Orchard."

HALOPERIDOL (Haldol)

Introduced in the early 1960s, haloperidal is the most widely used of a group of drugs known as butyrophenomes . . . effective in reducing the violent, aggressive manifestations of mental illnesses such as schizophrenia, mania, dementia,
And other disorders where hallucinations are experienced.
Adverse Effects: Drowsiness, lethargy, weight gain, Parkinsonism, abnormal involuntary movements, stiffness of the face and limbs, muscle weakness or rigidity . . . Use of this drug for more than a few months may lead to tardive dyskinesia, i.e. abnormal, involuntary movements of the eyes, face, and tongue.

The Canadian Medical Association Guide to Prescription and Over-the-Counter Drugs.

"So you've put him on Haldol," said Dr. Bland, pleased.
He looked at me curiously. I had gone back on what I stood for;

the anti-medication teacher who had persuaded parents over the years not to put their kids on Ritalin now was putting her own son on a powerful anti-psychotic.

What was there to say? Dr. Bland was right. Things couldn't go on like this. So why did I feel dull anger, sadness?

Part Four

Julian with headphones on, at the
Listening Centre, Toronto, at age 14.

Twenty-four

A lec heard the interview with Annabel Stelhi on CBC Radio. Stelhi's eleven-year-old daughter, Georgie, had apparently been cured of her autism in a matter of weeks by something called "auditory training" developed by a Dr. Guy Berard, an ear, nose and throat specialist in France who had achieved success helping autistic children. Mrs. Stelhi had written a book about it. It was sold out in Toronto and I eventually found a copy in a bookstore in Oakville. We were full of excitement, hope: *The Sound of a Miracle.*

Diagnosed mentally retarded (I.Q. 75) and autistic, and deemed violent, dangerous, unteachable, and given to rage and foul language, Georgie had been placed at age six in a famous treatment center for autism in New York called Belleview. She was later transferred to Childville, another center where she was designated as suffering from "childhood schizophrenia" and put on anti-psychotic medications. After Dr. Berard's treatment, Georgie had emerged as a successful young woman who had just completed a fine arts degree with Honors.

I dwelled particularly on the epithets "dangerous," "unteachable," and "*psychotic.*"

Dr. Bland looked bemused in his usual way when we mentioned the possibility of auditory stimulation for Julian. There was a Listening Centre in Toronto directed by Paul Madaule that offered such a program. "Isn't it expensive, Mr. and Mrs. Orchard?"

"Three thousand dollars."

For a couple of hours' "Sound Stimulation" a day, over a three-week period, followed by a session a few months later.

Dr. Bland looked concerned. We were risking *three thousand dollars* on Julian Orchard on some way-out little recognized treatment called "Auditory/Sound Stimulation" just because one autistic little girl called Georgie in the United States had been supposedly "cured" by a similar technique? Dr. Bland stressed "supposedly."

He had, of course, read *The Sound of a Miracle* – he was always up on everything in the field. The accepted approach to remedial treatment of dysfunctional children in Canada and the United States still tended to focus on the child's visual-motor difficulties. Now every professional and parent, it seemed, was suddenly reading about this alternative treatment; the book was on everyone's lips. That an unassuming otorhinolaryngologist, not even a psychiatrist, in some small town in France had successfully treated Georgie's autism without the use of anti-psychotic drugs challenged the very concept of "psychosis," a fact not lost on Dr. Bland.

I was careful not to sound too hopeful and enthusiastic to Dr. Bland, or to Julian's new teachers at The Meadows. They regarded us with the same amazement and pity, that the Orchards were going to spend *three thousand dollars,* echoed in disbelief, on some false dream that Julian could be cured by some obviously quack "treatment that claimed to treat autism in sixty hours."

"Well, Dr. Bland, of course we don't expect it to *cure* Julian . . . "

I had difficulty controlling the enthusiasm and – yes – the hope in my voice and eyes. The money took up a lot of our savings, it was true, but if it only improved him a bit. If it only got him off Haldol and drugs altogether, it would be worth every penny spent.

Julian had not been fitting in as well as had been hoped at his new school, despite being on Haldol. "Maybe we should up the dose, Mrs. Orchard." A dose of 0.5 mg was supposed to keep the lid on things, mitigate the amount of dopamine that his brain apparently produced to excess, and keep Julian Orchard under control. But it didn't.

We scanned Jules' face anxiously each morning for signs and symptoms of the infamous side effects of the drug. Other than looking glassy-eyed, Julian remained as before, excitable, hyperactive, pacing around the house and the hallways of The Meadows, haranguing and hitting himself even as the anti-psychotic coursed his bloodstream. Yet, with a logic probably only logical to desperate parents of violent autistic children, we were secretly relieved that it was so, reasoning that the dose therefore must not be harming his brain We always dreaded that Jules would be turned into some mindless drugged robot. Yet we were always going to be caught in this dilemma, for at the same time, we sensed that agreeing to put Julian on an anti-psychotic was a useful lever for keeping him in this school — his last chance if he could but understand.

"Well, he *is* on medication," Alec and I would point out smoothly if things got too difficult. After all, we'd cooperated fully with the Board. But we longed for some other way out.

There had already been one serious outbreak in the very first week. *"Mrs. Orchard please come and get him immediately!"* It had been frustrating finding Jules locked up once again in a time-out room, two burly aides holding him down on a padded mat. Julian's arms were crossed under his chest in a turkey-grip. His head had swivelled sideways, his mouth catching for breath like some animal panting at bay, pinioned by keepers.

"It's so terrible!" Mr. Collie, the principal, had winced, perspiration clogging his dark curls. He was young and spoke with a soft brogue. "We wish it didn't have to be this way, Mrs. Orchard, believe me!" He wiped his brow.

Julian had looked blank when he caught a glimpse of my face at the observation window. How many windows in classroom doors had I peered through by now? "She's come to get you, Julian, 'cause you've been BAD. You won't get no trip to Pantages, Julian Orchard," he yelled, struggling.

Was that what all the bellowing was about? He wanted to go on the class trip to *The Phantom of the Opera* at the Pantages Theatre in Toronto with the rest of the class. The story of the phantom with his ugly visage, outcast from society, Julian would not know, it would be the lyrics he loved that he'd often heard Polly play in her bedroom. But Ms. Bryce, his new teaching assistant in Room 8, had felt it was safer to leave Julian Orchard behind in the day room, as teachers wouldn't want to risk a manic outburst from the mezzanine in the middle of the show.

"No *Angel-a-Music* for you 'UNLESS YOU SMARTEN UP, MY BOY!' " Jules wept, as the aides released him. A look of agony had passed over Mr. Collie's face.

"Ah!" went Mr. Collie sorrowfully. "Why do you do this to yourself, son?"

Our hope was that Listening Training, similar to Berard's Auditory Training, might provide some answers.

The Listening Centre was located on Markham Street in a browsy old neighborhood in the west end of Toronto. The dusty tree-lined street with its heavy mansions, now mainly rentals for new immigrants and students, was a favorite area of writers, artists and students. It bustled with quaint curiosity bookshops, fortunetellers, tealeaf readers and Italian bistros.

The Listening Centre was in the hub of everything. Yet the house was peaceful. Julian showed no dismay at the winding narrow staircase, and settled happily into the sunny front room upstairs which was a sort of play room where the "passive" phase of the therapy took place. He *stayed* sitting – if Dr. Bland and Ms. Bryce could but see – wearing a sponge on top of his head and headphones clamped over his ears as he listened to filtered Mozart. A pretty young assistant, Moira, snuggled next to him on the couch. Snow fell lightly against the large panes. It was near Christmas, just days away from his fifteenth birthday.

The Listening Training program used at The Listening Centre was based on the work of another French specialist in otorhino-laryngology (the medicine of the ear, nose and throat, ENT), Dr. Alfred Tomatis.

Both Dr. Berard and Dr. Tomatis believed that audiological problems were at the root of many behavioral and learning problems in children, including dyslexia, hyperactivity, and autism/PDD, explained Paul Madaule, the director, at our initial interview. Dr. Tomatis' early research with professional opera singers had led him to the realization that it was the ear that actually controlled voice production; in particular, listening to one's own voice, self-listening, *"to ourselves speaking."* Termed "the Tomatis Effect," it was an important aspect of the sound stimulation program and stressed the difference between mere passive "hearing" and active "listening" as the key to language and cognitive development.

We now learned more about this "sounding game" children played from infancy, the important babbling stage I knew Julian had missed. It was an exercise that attuned the ear, the body, the nervous system and the voice, and came before meaning. Young children could repeat the same words and phrases over and over out of context, with no intent of using them for communication, the private speech, or "magical language" termed by Piaget, that Julian was now doing – except that he was fourteen!

Both Dr. Berard and Dr. Tomatis also believed that confused *laterality*, being unable to distinguish from which direction sounds come (from the right, left, in front, behind, from above, or "from everywhere") was another cause of many behavioral and learning problems and was very much related to language development. Tomatis noted the lack of a "leading ear" in such children. Since language functions are mediated by the left brain and the majority of neural tracts serving the language area come from and go to the auditory and phonatory organs on the right side of the brain (right ear, right larynx), he deemed the right ear as best for this "leading."

In most children, the right ear becomes the leading listening ear. But sometimes the left ear becomes dominant or sometimes neither ear, resulting in no leading ear. Paul had found in his own clinical practice that children with deafness, Down's syndrome, and autism showed a higher incidence of "mixed dominance," resulting in mixed laterality.

To encourage and enable the ear to listen, Tomatis had devised an electronic ear. It consisted of a set of headphones, a microphone, certain filters and a bone conduction device which together were a working model of the human ear. The system enabled stimulation of the right ear by decreasing or filtering the volume of sound coming to the left ear. The filtered sound of music or the mother's taped voice also accentuated higher frequency sounds that stimulated the cortex. The music of Mozart was regarded as particularly effective, being rich in high-frequency sound.

Amazingly, Julian did not resist wearing the headphones. All this was regarded as quite controversial in the field. But remediating listening problems made sense to us. Like Dr. Berard, Dr. Tomatis noted that autistic individuals in particular tended to shut out sounds. He regarded autism as "the purest form of non-listening."

I looked back through Julian's old report cards from kindergarten up. Clue after clue became clear as I read teachers' comments over the years:

> *Julian's listening skills are poor and hence has difficulties following directions.*
> *In terms of oral language skills, Julian tends to be very quiet.*

By junior/intermediate grade, the warnings were more direct, if not ominous:

> *Julian often engages in inappropriate behavior. Adult intervention during these times works best when verbal input is kept to a minimum, and with low volume.*

The auditory stimulation program involved two intensive sessions of fifteen days each, given several months apart.

The initial listening test was obviously the key diagnostic tool crucial to the whole treatment, providing information as to exactly which sound frequencies were distorted in Julian's hearing. A listening test was given every thirty hours.

But the test itself depended on the accuracy of Julian's responses.

Paul Madaule was patient. Facing Julian across headphones and complex-looking electronic equipment buzzing with tiny lights, he smiled encouragingly. But, as we feared, Julian simply answered yes to everything.

"Julian, listen carefully now. Is this sound louder?"

"Yes."

"Is it louder than the one before?"

"Yes."

"Is it softer, quieter?"

"Yes."

"Is it *very* loud, Julian?"

"Yes."

After only five minutes of this, Paul quietly set aside the earphones, smiling gently.

"Good, Julian. Good try."

Julian was smiling to himself, quite unaware of what had been at stake. Nevertheless, Paul was sure that Julian could be helped. He did not feel that lack of response meant lack of understanding. He assured us there was always a percent of children unable to do the test. Julian could be given a limited, adapted, more general treatment program that would help, but not cure, his autism.

Julian was sitting cozily with an assistant, Jennifer, on a low sofa by the window. He was wearing the headphones clamped over his ears again with a sponge on top to cushion his head, as he listened to the weird scratchy filtered music of Mozart that was supposed to be "adjusting" his responsiveness to high and low frequencies. This was the passive phase of the program. The electronic ear alternated these frequencies to make his ear attend.

He was reading, making paper crafts, or playing snakes and ladders.

The evening sun streamed across his face, as Julian responded to his pretty young assistant. Sometimes from the parents' room adjoining the playroom I heard him singing to himself, immersed in painting. He had not painted for years. "Ah! Julien is merry today!" smiled Paul, pleased, popping his head round the door.

Why was this working? Was it the atmosphere of the comfortable old house? It was not as if he always had the same assistant, either. The three young therapists had the same quiet, soft-spoken approach. They requested Julian to do things, and were never confrontational.

In the active phase of his training, Julian submitted without protest to being taken off to a small room upstairs on the third floor. He hummed to Gregorian chants, chosen for their calming yet energizing rhythms. He then listened and responded verbally to prepared tapes of carefully designed instructions that were gradated from easy-to-follow, to difficult. I could hear his deep voice rumbling monotonously down the stairs giving the answer to: "Which one is different, Julian, *dog, cat, bird, banana, horse* . . . ?"

Would he say "banana"? Perhaps he wondered why I cheered from below.

"There's something different about Julian. He's looking at you more when you talk to him," observed Ma Christmas Day, after five days' auditory stimulation treatment. We were elated because this was in such marked contrast to the previous Christmas when my mother-in-law had actually had to ask us to take Julian home.

That previous Christmas Julian had grabbed fistfuls of potato salad before supper was even served. Diced eggs and potato had ended up splattered over the tablecloth and floor while he'd yelled at himself: "That's GREEDY!" He had started pacing the tiny kitchen, door to stove, trapped, digging his nails into his cheeks; blood had oozed, frightening the younger grandchildren.

"He's insane!' my father-in-law had bellowed, whisky and soda in hand, his face sagging in alarm, sensing for the first time Julian's abnormality: this was truly like insanity. Both Alec's parents had been frightened, trying to hide their fear so as not to upset their other little grandsons further.

Polly and I had tried saying soothing things to divert Julian's attention like "Let's look at the Christmas tree downstairs, Jules."

"He should bloody well clean up the mess first," grunted Father-in-Law, setting Julian off again.

"Shush, Pet," Mother-in-Law had been alarmed. "Best you leave, Alec," she'd whispered, and we'd left without even our presents.

Things were no better with my mother. She continued to insist it was time we seriously considered putting Julian away. She rarely came over to visit now, feeling she was too frail with her osteoporosis and bronchial asthma to deal with any rage attacks. "You and Alec should be thinking of your own health and safety too, Thelma."

Now when Ma asked Jules: "How are you enjoying your Christmas holidays, Julian?" he answered "Fine, Granma, thank you."

"He is getting to a point where he is ready to understand what a conversation is," said Paul, pleased. "We are having a conversation, Julian, you and I."

Meanwhile I was involved in taping sessions of my own, recording a song that was to be played to Julian.

The use of the mother's filtered voice was an important aspect of the child's language development. Unlike Dr. Berard's auditory integration training used with Georgie, the Tomatis Method had a psychological component to it.

I began reading *On The Tomatis Method*, and Paul's book, *When Listening Comes Alive*, to understand the approach. It seemed that Tomatis believed that individuals not only shut out sounds that were physically painful to them, as in Georgie's case, but also emotionally painful. That, in fact, the "desire to listen" began as a fetus, during pregnancy. Talking to the unborn child was critical in the fifth month of pregnancy when the inner ear and its connections with the brain were operational and the fetus "tuned in" to the sound of the mother's voice through bone conduction. A child whose mother talked and sang to it in the womb, for instance, and played "good" music, such as Mozart, would be more receptive and musical. I began to feel powerful rushes of guilt. I had sung and played the violin whilst carrying Polly, and Polly had turned out musical. But I had been working, too harassed and weary to bother while carrying Julian. The violin had lain untouched, its bridge collapsed in the furnace room.

But the fetus could also "pick up" negative charges and "turn off" the mother's voice and the "will to listen." Tomatis believed that the mother's voice, when filtered in a special way, recreated the dynamic of intra-uterine life and had a beneficial effect on children with learning difficulties. Paul had written only too convincingly: "A voice that carries joy, calmness, warmth, love, hope and fulfilment is more likely to 'invite' listening and the desire to communicate than a voice that carries anxiety, anger or sadness." I began to observe the quality of my voice — it didn't always carry love and hope. However, I decided that if the sound of my taped filtered voice singing *My Bonnie Lies Over the Ocean* was going to have a positive effect on Julian, make him aware of me as his mother in a more intimate way it would be worth it.

Paul had adapted the best of Tomatis over the years for his program, he explained. What he tried to accomplish with the mother's filtered voice in Listening Training was to reproduce the step-by-step development of the listening and language function before a child was born.

But the fact was a part of me wanted, needed, to believe, the part of me that secretly believed in miraculous transformation.

Paul's description in *Listening Comes Alive* of the moment when the child recognizes his mother's voice as from the womb had rivetted me. I had read it over and over in my corner of the divan in the parents' room, hoping for my own moment between Julian and me:

Children's reactions to their mother's voice can be extraordinary to watch, especially for the parents. The children become more affectionate. Those who tended to be distant took to their

*mother's lap, and started kissing, hugging, and embracing her.
What a delight for a mother of an autistic child!*

I still hoped for a similar change in Julian, even though Paul
had explained that this step was usually done only with very young
children.

"So . . . did anything happen when Julian heard my voice?" I
asked the assistant.

Katherine looked blank.

"You know, when you played the tape of me singing *My Bonnie
Lies Over the Ocean*." I was beginning to feel foolish.

My filtered voice must have surely sounded scratchy and unrec-
ognizable to Jules.

"Jules looks happy whenever he hears your voice, he's content."

The scratchy unfiltered voice he loved, perhaps?

Everything was going wonderfully well. They were doing Farley
Mowat's *Owls in the Family* with him now, as part of his "Active"
program!

"Do you think you should be reading that to him?" The book
was at least grade-six comprehension level, I hinted.

"But he *understands* the story, even though he may not be able
to read the words," insisted Katherine calmly. "He's enjoying it.
Come watch."

Katherine proceeded to demonstrate with Julian, keeping the
questions concrete.

"Where does Billy and his family live, Jules?"

"Skatchwan," said Julian.

"Yes, Saskatchewan, Jules. And what are the owls' names in the
story?"

"Wol 'n' Weeps." Gruffly.

"Who are Billy's friends? Can you say their names, Julian?"

"Murray 'n' Bruce."

"Who are your friends, Jules?" *Silence*. I felt anxious.

"Mr. Collie-dog, woof-woof."

"Oh, you have a dog, Jules?" Katherine looked surprised.

"Yep," said Julian before I could intercede. "Stanfield."

"Oh?"

Did Julian actually see the principal as a dog, or was calling Mr. Collie a dog a compliment, a clever pun supposedly beyond the linguistic capability of an autistic, which veered always to the concrete? It was a small but curious point.

Julian had done drawings of owls in his art folder. He had written some simple words and phrases about the story; some of the words were in cursive script, which he had begun to learn back in Lymewood school with Mrs. McDougall.

Naturally Alec and I hoped these skills would be transferred to school and home. Julian's teachers at The Meadows seemed to be making a special effort now to encourage him to participate in class, rather than turning to consequences of behavior modification right away. Ms. Bryce started giving Julian a daily schedule so that he could see the day's routine ahead of time and mitigate some of his anxiety. It was as if everyone was suddenly trying to justify the money we'd spent on him – still talked about at The Meadows in awe.

I recognized how hard it must be for Ms. Bryce to reproduce the lightsome intimacy of the assistants at The Listening Centre. Julian's teacher had to deal with ten demanding developmentally challenged students ranging in age from fourteen to nineteen. I was sure Ms. Bryce did her best to try to coax Jules into a quiet nook. Room 8 offered a good program of "functional academics" and also extra-curricular activities such as bowling, skating, choir, soccer. Mr. Collie himself led The Rovers soccer team decked out in a steel mask as goalie – Jules *had* to like it! It was all there for him if he would only avail himself of it.

The Meadows' Declaration on Mr. Collie's desk said that a student was to *"grow in knowledge, seek truth, assess values, develop physically, and find his/her place as a happy productive member of society."* But Julian did not seem to want to. It was so frustrating. He loved music, so why did he not participate in Mrs. Percival's choir?

I wondered whether so many programs were too much for Julian. He had been used to being in a core class most of the day at Lymewood School with the same teacher. The Meadows followed the secondary school model and had a constant – and perhaps for

Julian – a bewildering rotation of classes, teachers and teaching assistants. What he needed was a personal teaching assistant, preferably male, to provide some consistency to his new day. But out of twenty-eight teaching assistants, only two were male. This lack of male assistants, and consequent lack of male role models, was an ongoing concern due to budget cuts. There was Mr. Cameron, a big gentle black assistant Julian talked about a lot, but he was already working with another student in a different class.

It was all the more perplexing when one saw how successfully Julian adapted to the Summer Teen Program run by Community Living.

The summer program focused on outings: trips to Ontario Place, Wild Water Kingdom, mini-golf, bowling, swimming, walking everywhere to take public transit that even included the subway in downtown Toronto. Julian went along, participating fully, even on Movie Day.

Like the approach of The Listening Centre, I found myself asking why this worked with Julian. The young counselors, mostly university students working for the summer, had little idea that Julian was a serious "behavior problem" with a solid number of suspensions to his credit at school. Their training was intense but brief: one week of in-session training from Community Living. The workers certainly had expectations of behavior, with rules to be adhered to when taking public transit, or out in public places like malls and theaters. Yet we had little complaint about Julian. It wasn't as if he didn't pace around and talk to himself. He did.

I came to the conclusion that the success was due to the focus on outdoor activity, being in the community, and the small group size: four participants to two workers. The result was a camaraderie and closeness that Julian responded to – in his way, of course.

When he paced excessively, was over-anxious or verbalizing with an intensity that could not be ignored, Brad, the group leader that week, humored Julian along: "Hey, man, what you doing that for? It's Wild Water Kingdom today, Jules, let's go."

There were only two occasions over the summer that we were called to pick up Julian because he was out of control. One incident was when another boy teased him, calling him a "dung-head." Another was a day of excessive verbalizing and self-hitting for no apparent reason. The counselors could not "talk him out of it." I suspected the temperature: it was an excessively humid day, and Julian was sweating profusely. Back in the cool air-conditioned house he'd quickly settled down. On both occasions, Julian was welcomed back in to the program the next morning. It was encouraging, hopeful; Jules could do it.

These young men were role models for Julian all summer. He talked about Brad and Tom, but also others in his group. "Liz cried she didn't have no chocolate bar in her lunch-box today." I took photos of his groups, little knowing he was to spend long winter evenings over the years looking at them intently, talking and laughing to himself by the hour.

Back at school there was Julian's behavior once again to understand and contend with. I couldn't help but mention to the teachers at one of the many meetings how successful the summer program had been with Julian. Dedicated though I knew the teachers to be, educators could learn a lot from the active outdoors approach of Community Living.

The end result was a sort of compromise. Jules was more or less allowed to pace the halls for a certain part of the day talking to himself, until such time that the medication was "upped" – the implication being report card time. This approach at least used up his excess energy. But his self-imposed isolation became greater as everyone got used to it. "Julian the Wanderer" he was becoming known as in an affectionate if resigned way.

"Try to keep your words in your head, Julian," went the teachers with the best of intentions, trying to prevent what they saw as his negative non-stop talking-to-self.

This self-talk had become significant after the auditory stimulation. I wondered whether it might not be the process of "listening to oneself talking" posited by Dr. Tomatis as a necessary step in the language process, and therefore beneficial to Jules. Might not the self-talk be the baby-babble stage he had missed as an infant?

It was left to Ms. Bryce to provide some of the bonding Julian desperately needed in school, whenever she did manage to get him to settle down in class. Ms. Bryce rode a Harley-Davidson motor-

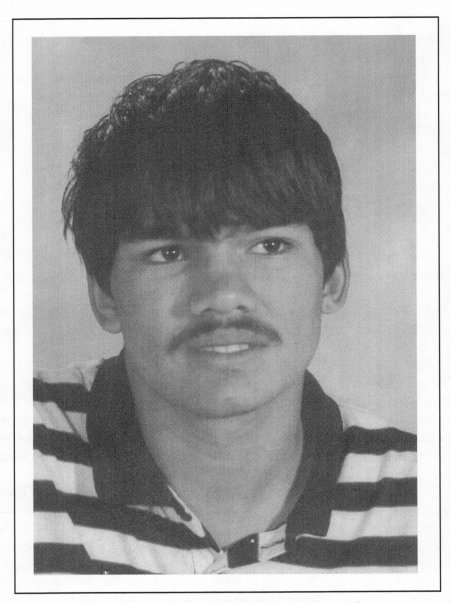

Julian at age 14, in 1991, during an unhappy phase.

bike and believed in tough love. There seemed to be a problem right at the start of each morning when Julian balked at Dancersize, the physical exercise routine that began the day. It consisted of slow-motion arm-waving movements followed by syncopated marching around the gym to staccato-like instructions firmly beat out by Ms. Bryce.

Dancersize was ideally suited perhaps to the overweight girls in the class, but questionable for thin hyperactive Julian who reportedly spent the time careening excitedly round the performers making high whirring noises, totally *out-of-control,* reported Ms. Bryce, frustration evident. (Everyone else in the class loved it.)

Admittedly, Julian did enough walking in the halls for a marathon, but couldn't he have a vigorous basketball session, instead of Dancersize, I hinted. Gradually, we began to get reports of him spending more time in class responding to the morning news, weather, and sharing-time. He was beginning to participate in rotary, the hands-on part of the programming: packaging, labelling, sleeving bottles.

One day Julian counted one hundred bottle tops with 99% accuracy, reported Ms. Bryce, not unpleased.

"Ms. Bryce goes like hell on that motorbike," said Jules.

Now where had he got *that* from?

There was nothing stopping me from working with Jules myself at home. Paul Madaule kept up an interest in Julian's progress, evaluating the effectiveness of auditory stimulation. We both knew Jules could do it!

But what did one give a functionally retarded, autistic fifteen year old to read with a reading vocabulary of "Look, Jane, look"? Add to that intermittent inattentiveness, hyperactivity, and spasmodic bursts of violence, and it seemed an unteachable situation for me no less than his teachers.

Yet there were the real successes of the therapists at the Listening Centre to build on. I still secretly tended to give as much credit to their approach in handling Julian as to the effects of filtered Mozart. I had to reproduce not just the technique, but the whole tone: keeping everything as quiet, soft, as possible, just Julian and myself, side by side, nothing too intrusive, on the sofa, like Vanessa and Moira and Katherine. And, like them, keeping my voice gentle, encouraging.

"Jan! Jan!"

I infused a suitable amount of excitement in my tone into the opening words of the famous grade one reader, *Mr. Mugs.* I realized I had to take Julian back to the beginning. There was so much he had lost over the past two years. But I just could not face *Dick and Jane* again. Was I really sitting here on the same sofa once again trying to teach Julian to read at this level?

Mr. Mugs, the big cuddly old English sheepdog beloved of the pre-primer children, at least related to Stanfield, who lay at our feet in a stupor, large mournful eyes blinking up at Julian, ears trailing over the carpet, stinking from his walk.

"Mommy! Daddy! Curt!"

Jules hesitated. Then, in a deep gruff bumbling voice, mumbled "Mommy! Daddy! Curt!"

It was never too late, I told myself, The Listening Centre had demonstrated that. If for nothing else, I was grateful to the Centre for revealing that obvious truth to me. At fifteen, Julian was beginning to read again, if only a sort of instant sight reading. He tended to glance at a page and at once memorize the words, repeating whole sentences by heart without necessarily understanding them. It was great to get him going, and I knew had to rely on it, but the phonic method, though much slower, was surer. Once it clicked with Julian that the sounds c-a-t "spelled" as they sounded, he understood how rat, fat, hat, mat worked. Moreover, it appealed to his autistic love of order! Soon Julian was sounding out most of the vocabulary of Mr. Mugs like any other regular six year old in first grade.

At the same time I made sure I read age-appropriate books aloud to him at the interest and comprehension level of *Owls in the Family*, trusting he understood enough to hold his attention.

One particular story, *Last One in is a Rotten Egg* truly got to him. It seemed to be "The Big Boys" at the swimming pool pushing the little helpless ones into the water that caught his attention at the outset. All the little kids at the pool, including Freddy the hero, feared The Big Boys. *Here come The Big Boys,* Jules," I read somnolently, not prepared for what was to come. Julian leaped off the sofa electrified, and began circling the room in agitation, swinging at the air with his fist. This wasn't supposed to happen. He was to enter imaginatively into the story, not live it!

"Big Boys!" he shouted defiantly, but frightened. His cheeks flushed with excitement. He swung his fists again, barely missing the hanging lamp. "Afraid of Big Boys!" a hidden darkness suddenly imploding, the old pain, whatever it was that had taken place with the "big boys" at Lymewood Public School, we would never know.

I wondered if this terrible unresolved intensity was what his psychosis was all about: helplessness. How could Haldol or any drug resolve that? That my task was to help him feel less helpless, build up whatever it was that was lacking in his brain and heart, and this might be a way.

"Ah, but here comes Tom — the good guy, the lifeguard," I go smoothly, carefully, cunningly now, the technique coming back to me, watching from the corner of my eye. Jules jerks back to reality. Tom! Tom, the "One in Charge." Julian so loves authority through a story, "the law being laid down."

Eagerly he bounds back to the sofa: Tom is going to order The Big Boys OUT OF THE POOL. The Big Boys are IN TROUBLE. He never tires of these big boys in trouble, squeezing his knees excitedly next to me. "Mr. Collie!" he shouts.

And so I learn what books to choose, what delights him; what draws him to me, relying on me to give this to him, stir him, give him pleasure, however brief, intermittent. Not since "little dollies" has he been so stirred. *Boys in Trouble at the Office with the Principal,* boys frightened of Big Boys ... I keep it going, week after week, it's essential, cleverly inserting word card games, picture bingo — "Join the letters that are the same sound, Jules" — that he so diligently applies himself to.

"Got all the S's, Mommy," he growls.

Keep him at it, keep the restlessness burned into *Last One in is a Rotten Egg,* the maniac laughter.

I am anxious, the anxiety that comes from needing to be cautious, control the rising excitement that this after all might be "it." Not a cure, exactly, he'll never be cured like Georgie, of course. We realize that, always have from the outset, keeping in mind Paul Madaule's cautionary "We can't promise any cure, Mr. and Mrs. Orchard." But this is the closest thing so far to real improvement, if he can but hold on, if whatever part of his brain that this is helping remains stimulated, and integrated.

Of course there were moments, many of them, when Julian for no explicable reason would jump up in the middle of a sentence and walk away round the coffee table. Useless to say "Now you ought to . . . " Or "You should . . . " You had to wait patiently to get him back into it again. What worked was acknowledging it: "Oh, you need to stretch your legs a minute, Jules?"

But there'd be the disastrous moment I'd forget, like when I said peevishly to Alec, "I don't know where the hell your glasses are; how the hell would I know?"

At which Julian would shoot up off the sofa, at once enraged, punching himself, snarling, *"How the hell should I know? How the hell?"* And then it was lost. Yet gradually a body of work was forming, his journal and the many language drills and exercises, drawings. Admittedly the handwriting was ill-formed, messy, showing stress, but there, proof I vaguely felt I had if needed in Julian's defense at the important upcoming mid-year Interim Report. That he could still progress. I so wanted to believe it was the auditory stimulation that was effecting this improvement, and not the Haldol.

Twenty-five

The most important thing was always to keep Julian involved with his peers, many of whom were high-functioning and highly verbal. So Alec and I were thrilled that Jules was to attend the school dance as any other student, even if all he might do was pace the evening away.

"Dance, Jules," I smiled encouragingly. "Meet lots of friends, teenagers like yourself." I stressed *teenager* and *fun*.

Students were attending not only from The Meadows but from all the D.C. satellite classes in the area. He might meet old friends like Lonny.

"Natcho chips and pop!"

I was going along as parent volunteer. "We think it might be a good idea, Mrs. Orchard . . . "

How was everyone else behaving, compared with Julian and Duncan, that is? Duncan was another autistic student who had turned up at the dance from a satellite class. He was much like Julian, thin, nervy, walking stiffly and tirelessly round the perimeter of the gym, skirting the dancers. The room seemed to rock and gyrate to explosions of rock music mainly from the '50s, like *Rock Around the Clock* with Bill Haley and his Comets. The gym was packed, couples shuffling intertwined round the floor for the slow ones, regardless of rhythm, others bopping in groups. Teachers supervised and joined in dancing with the students, everyone having a good time.

So it was all the more startling to see Julian and Duncan circulating in a rapid, identical, stereotypical autistic way, though they had never met and were from different backgrounds. Any attempt to get them to join in a dance with an actual female partner their age met with oblique resistance, much like horses shying at the bit: Julian running away at top speed, Duncan running in the opposite direction. Yet both claimed to be having "a great time"!

Duncan seemed higher functioning than Julian. He had the famous Asperger's syndrome I had so far only read about. His conversation between bouts of roving seemed directed, meaningful, impressive, at first.

"Hi there. You're Julian Orchard's mum aren't you?"

"Yes. And you're Duncan."

"Duncan McTavish. That's a Scottish name isn't it? You have an accent."

"Yes, I'm from Wales."

"It rains a lot there doesn't it? Now Julian," he went on, "he's a different color to you, Mrs. Orchard. How come?"

"Yes, well Duncan, that's because Mr. Orchard is from Sri Lanka."

"That's near India isn't it?"

"Yes, on the tip."

"They have monsoons there, don't they? It doesn't rain *all* the time. So how come Julian is a different color to you, Mrs. Orchard?"

"Well, that's how he turned out, more like his dad. Sometimes you're like your dad and sometimes like your mum."

"So when's your birthday, Mrs. Orchard?"

I regretted the moment I told him.

"That was a Sunday, wasn't it?"

"Was it?"

"And Julian's fifteen? That means you were thirty-five when you had him, Mrs. Orchard."

I was impressed by Duncan's powers of conversation and focus. Would Jules ever reach this level? But then he began all over again! "Does it rain a lot in . . . ?'

I recalled Tomatis' theory that we "listen with the whole body." Was Julian and Duncan's obvious need to be on the move and at the same time keep up constant "self-talk" connected, a "behavioral" problem?

"See how similar Julian and Duncan are. They haven't stopped circling and talking all night, yet they're both having a great time," I couldn't resist pointing out to Ms. Bryce.

Ms. Bryce frowned. She was faced with a syndrome for the first time because there were two of them, rather than Julian's individual rebellious behavior. It helped to see Julian in a new way, not just as one violent dangerous student needing constant discipline.

Participating in the dance had shown the importance of keeping Jules involved socially, of belonging in the community. Now he sometimes broke out into snatches of *"I'm your baby!"* as he paced around the house. So we made every effort to attend the school workshop for parents: "Sex and Your Developmentally Challenged Child," given by Ms. Handscombe, sex specialist in the field of mental retardation. We wanted to be part of the group.

Alec and I had doubts that Jules had any real sexual awareness, or ever would. He did not masturbate or show interest in his sexual parts as yet, for which we were so far thankful. He was still inclined to walk around naked after his shower regardless of who was present. Was that a sexual problem or a social problem? Either way, it had to be dealt with.

The important thing was to be seen sitting in the library with other concerned parents, sipping tea and nibbling seed cake that had been sawed in a desperate way by Ms. Bryce; that Jules was part of Room 8 despite Dr. Bland's affected "Oh-h, the Orchards are here. Well . . . welcome."

Alec was more relaxed about the sex curriculum than myself. He was prepared to enjoy discussion with other parents. "Let's face it, Thel, Jules has to be protected from himself. You can't let him be having children, they'd be dead of starvation in a week."

But what Ms. Handscombe had in mind was the exact opposite. She was for the right to sexual fulfillment of the mentally challenged. There was talk of "the pill" for the girls, teaching masturbation to both sexes as "a safety valve" – though how did she plan to *teach* that? Ms. Handscombe smiled hugely. The adolescents were also to learn how to say no, how to identify unwanted touching, and how to distinguish between normal, OK-touching (hugs from parents, reliable friends) and "wrong" touching.

Much of this was reasonable, necessary. Yet I felt uncomfortable about Julian attempting to process the actual sex act, sexual intercourse. Was he even ready for it, I queried?

There were six parents in the circle. The library lights glowed against the rows of books and our bowed heads. What was there to say about sex and the mentally retarded – our mentally retarded children – when sex was what had given them birth?

"No one is suggesting you all go out and put your girls on the pill tomorrow," Dr. Bland tried to smooth things over.

Alec wondered whether giving Julian details of sex, especially accompanied by explicit pictures and diagrams – a sex video was rumored – might encourage him to think, being autistic, that he was *supposed* to go out and have intercourse because Ms. Bryce had told him to. Dr. Bland laughed outright. Yet these were issues we all had to face – our children were becoming adults.

Julian seemed to burst in through the door after school. I'd never seen him so excited since the days of Little Dollies. He tossed down his tote bag and stood nervously in the middle of the living-room, giggling, with his hands on his hips: "Tentacles!"

"Tentacles?"

"Here!" He thrust his hips out; his sweat pants looked hot and soggy.

"This is your tentacles. And *this* – " with a flourish he clutched his navel, doubling over laughing, "is your peanuts!"

Well at least he had the idea, chuckled Alec. Mrs. Batcup and Ms. Bryce had obviously begun the sex education program endorsed by Ms. Handsombe, and the opening lesson must have been basic human anatomy. I could well imagine how serious Mrs. Batcup and no-nonsense Ms. Bryce would have taught the subject, using filmstrips, slides, overheads, word-cards.

"That's very good, Julian. Yes, your *penis,* and your *testicles.*"

"Poor old Jules, doesn't have a clue!" observed Alec later, affectionately.

It seemed Julian could have a mental grid of the greater Toronto area in his head and yet not be able to relate a picture of a penis to his own penis! He had been shown the same picture set as the others, assured Ms. Bryce stiffly when I brought it up. It wasn't her fault he didn't know where his testicles were. But it wasn't just the mix-up of words he'd heard wrongly – "tentacles" for "testicles" – close enough, just not accurate. It was the disconnectedness again, spatial and psychological, despite his auditory stimulation work.

In his book, Tomatis had noted a lack of connectedness with the body, problems with space and time, in dysfunctional children that he felt was part of the problem of "mixed lateral dominance."

Perhaps the failure of Julian's "leading" ear to lead, negatively affected his sense of where and how his body stood in space. When I brought this up with him, Paul Madaule agreed. In fact, he confided that he wished he had the resources to include a comprehensive program of occupational therapy to complement auditory stimulation. He felt strongly that integration of bodily movement was connected to speech and language stimulation.

Yet he felt the whole incident demonstrated a wonderful improvement in Julian's communication skills: look how he had *wanted* to tell us about the sex lesson! He's been excited over it, demanded our attention! It was true. I recalled Jules' shining eyes, his excited grin, and flushed cheeks, the way he'd been thrilled to name what he'd thought were his genitals, no matter that they were somewhat off the mark! He'd definitely been eager to share his new knowledge that he was aware he had acquired. We concluded he must have listened attentively, even though Ms. Bryce informed us he'd been pacing round the edge of the chairs throughout the lesson.

I knew now what was needed: "You're going to have to show him, Alec. Get in the shower with him, let him see your body, compare, know he's a male."

"What? Me shower with Julian?" Alec was alarmed.

"It'll help him see what he is, Al, in the flesh!"

It might even be part of his general confusion. Perhaps his new unfamiliar body confounded him and that was in part why he'd punch, slash, and dig his teeth into himself. It seemed all 0.5 mg Haldol did was blunt these feelings of confusion, "take the edge off things," as Dr. Sol had intimated. Maybe Julian needed bonding, imprinting, like the birds, I reasoned to Alec.

"What's imprinting?" asked Alec suspiciously.

"You know, the way a mother owl imprints on the new babies that they are owls — otherwise how would they know what they were? She makes sure the babies see only her in the nest, so they'll know what they are. That's how a bird knows it's a bird and not a cat."

"What d'you think I am, a ruddy owl?"

It was not Alec's traditional idea of father-son bonding that he had always anticipated. I had seen him looking out sadly over the garden at times, watching Julian under the willow lost in a cloud of pollen. Caught in the sunlight of the moment, Julian twiddling a twig delicately in his big new hands, over and over. The "talk" he had so wanted with his son, had so earnestly looked forward to, never to be. "You'll see," he had boasted once proudly, "I won't be like my father with my son. I'll sit down with him and tell him everything he needs to know."

Nevertheless, I could hear lots of excited giggling from Julian that evening in the bathroom as Alec reluctantly, gamely, undressed with him, keeping up a jovial patter of conversation as if it were perfectly usual to be sharing the shower in a cramped bathtub with a fifteen year old who towered over him.

"Alec and Julian in the shower — together!" I heard Julian's voice breaking.

I peeked round the curtain. He was flushed and happy, covered in soapsuds.

"No more baths from Mommy," I said firmly. "You're a big boy now, Jules, a teenager."

"Teenager."

"It's a good thing to be a teenager, Jules. All boys become teenagers. Mummy is very happy Julian is a teenager."

Alec slowly began to take over the task of helping Julian shower and dress, shave, trim his moustache, even wiping his behind. There were two types of autistic people, apparently, Alec had learned somewhere: the ones who obsessively wiped themselves ten times a day, and those who walked away from the toilet without as much as a backward glance at their behinds. Julian was the latter. No matter how often Alec demonstrated, sitting plop on the toilet, going through the motion patently step by step, Julian was not attentive. He seemed incapable of forming the necessary mental picture, was not aware he had a behind or where his feces came from, and didn't care. "You see, you put the paper *between* the cheeks of your behind, Jules, like Dad. Watch Dad." Alec bent over.

"If your OAC students could see you now," I grinned from the doorway.

"It's a hell of a life," grumbled Alec. "How many fathers my age have to go through this?"

It was Alec now who also helped Julian with bed routine, changing into his pajamas that they began calling "PJs' — "Put your PJs on, Jules" — an intimate short-hand language developing between them from which I was necessarily excluded.

Alec who now touched Julian's body intimately, that physical bonding usually between mother and child, now extending abnormally into adolescence, fostering a continuing security, a trust.

You'd hear them laughing together behind the closed door, the slap of soap, the howls and giggles, a new language, the language of relationship. "Dad!" said Julian more often now, with a glow. "Dad in the shower with Julian."

Alec even succumbed to Martha Welch's "holding" therapy; he'd watched the video on TV one night.

"Martha Welch says to hug your autistic son whether he wants it or not!" reported Alec heavily.

So each evening we began hugging therapy, taking Julian by surprise, at first, forcing him to submit to being hugged by each of us. A shy grin crossed Julian's face when Alec first opened his arms in the living room and said: "Hug Dad."

Julian remained stiff and unyielding, rigid as a pole, but did comply, bending graciously, if somewhat on sufferance, down to each of us in turn – we were both shorter than he. "Here they go again!" he seemed to be thinking as the nightly automaton-like hugs carried on.

Now it was Alec who also had his Saturday mornings disrupted, his sleep-in disturbed after a long hard week at school. Mothers could not use the women's changing rooms at the pool to change their disabled sons once they reached a certain age, so the fathers had to take over the showering, changing, dressing, though from the sound of it I wasn't exactly sure who was taking over in there, father or son.

We mothers stood in a stolid row outside the men's locker room, waiting and wondering what the heck was going on inside. We could hear shrieks, the thud of feet, and slapping sounds.

"It's like a madhouse in there!" gasped one father, emerging. It was Mr. Reynolds, a thin, bespectacled, harassed-looking man running after his sixteen-year-old son, Seymour, who had Asperger's Syndrome and was given to touching every Ford – only Fords – in the parking lot.

Alec staggered out next with a definitely disheveled Julian dragging his towel, but glowing with a happiness I hadn't seen in years.

"That Reynolds is a nice chap . . . but, Thelma, you just don't *know*, what it's like in there," said Alec.

More fathers staggered out into the sunlight. I had to laugh. We mothers waiting in line gloomily for our sons had always been so long-suffering, you'd never catch any one of us saying something like, *"God, he pisses me right off!"*

I didn't always see this thing in Julian, something wonderful emerging inside him. Everyone was always concentrating so hard on what he was *not* doing, I didn't get it at first when I saw him with old Mr. Phiz, the school caretaker at The Meadows.

"Julian watches for me," Mr. Phiz smiled at me shyly, moving the broom aside as I clumped up the hall for yet another consultation with staff concerning Julian and his pesky new problem of constantly shaking everyone's hand.

"He's like a son to me," assured Mr. Collie softly, as we came out of his office. "We are not so unalike, Julian and I, believe me, Mrs. Orchard."

Julian walked rapidly towards us, abandoning Mr. Phiz. He grasped Mr. Collie's hand in a jolly, if disconcerting, way. "Mr. Collie-dog, woof woof!"

Silly old Julian singling him out. The office staff noticed: "Well, Julian likes you, Mr. Collie!"

Mr. Collie was pleased, as was Dr. Bland, when Jules shook his hand vigorously too. *Dr. Bland?!* Julian couldn't possibly like Dr. Bland, but he did. And Dr. Bland liked him, too.

It was a delicate issue. His affection for people kept growing, and we didn't want to discourage him. Yet surely we had to warn him that many people were not necessarily thrilled at having their hands continually pumped and squeezed in Julian's big hot sweaty one.

It sounded so crazy: social niceties, social etiquette, yet so essential for getting along with people. And, Jules took absolutely no notice either at school or at home, as he bound eagerly out of the car in Granpa's driveway for the dreaded monthly visit.

"Maybe we should make it six-monthly," said Alec dourly, it was becoming stressful watching out for Julian all the time. We try to forestall episodes by choosing my father-in-law's naptime for our visits, and by warning Julian ahead of time to shake hands "only once" if he had to.

"GRANPA!"

Alec's father was agog in the kitchen, Scotch in hand, leaning against the sink, "What the bloody. . ?"

Jules grasped his hand, then forced a cardboard hug on his grandfather. We were still into Martha Welch's holding therapy.

"Rascal!" shouted my father-in-law, his jowls quivering, though not unpleased.

"There, pet," soothed Ma, pleased. "See, he likes you!"

Well, who would have thought? Jules and Granpa. Jules had developed a mystifying sudden interest, obsessive in a way, in his granpa. Throughout childhood Julian had barely acknowledged his existence, much like his relationship with our dog, Stanfield. Now Jules was suddenly aware of both.

Jules was happy as Granpa shouted at him. He shouted back, mimicing: "Rascal! Don't tease Granpa, he's your *grandfather*, Julian."

Father-in-Law's eyes boggled. Time for his afternoon nap, his siesta, ritual of another era in time, colonial time, the British colonial era on a faraway tea estate in old Ceylon, up in the tea hills of Kandy. On the wall of the frowzy old bedroom was a sepia print of Kandy temple and the lake, like a jewel. On another wall, a faded print of the Sri Lanka tea-planters' cricket team before the war: Mr. Orchard leaning on a willow bat dressed in whites and an alpaca hat, slim, colonial, in the long hot tropical time of privilege and wealth.

"Sh-sh-sh, Granpa's *sleeping*," Julian whispered loudly, loving this part, tiptoeing gently, carefully, down the hall, and peering through the open bedroom door at Granpa.

Soon Granpa was awake: "Pet! pet! Stop that bloody racket and bring me a beer!"

With a sigh, Ma lifted her fingers off *Abide With Me* and closed the organ. Soon he was in the garden, slumped in the deck chair under the apple tree, snoring again over a Molson's Golden. Julian seemed to love that image of his grandfather as he circled the tree and the deck chair.

"Sh-sh-sh!" he whispered again, giggling. "Granpa's sleeping!"

Julian kept circling, longing for him to awaken, yet fascinated at the snores that shook Granpa's belly.

It was as if he wanted Granpa to wake up: "Talk to me, Granpa, shout at me, get red in the face and scowl! Call me *rascal*, again and again, Granpa!"

"What's he laughing at like that, like an imbecile?" grunted Father-in-Law, waking with a start. Sun streamed across the raspberry canes, and he blinked against the sudden glare. He looks up, open-mouthed, his vest soaked with perspiration, his watery eyes alarmed at Julian – the beautiful unreasonable boy he could not accept as retarded, insisting always there was nothing wrong with him.

The scent of rice and *brinjal* wafts through the window.

Julian wanted his grandfather to talk to him, tease him, love him, but he couldn't. Not until his last moments in the hospital.

We decided to take him with Polly and us. He was interested in the idea of Granpa's impending death.

"Granpa's *sick*," he whispered loudly down the long dim hall of the cardiac wing, shushed by death.

Everyone stood with bowed heads in sadness round the bed, Ma stoic, saying the rosary, curtains pulled round for extra privacy.

"Kidney failure," murmered the young intern outside the curtain. "Prepare yourselves . . . "

"Very very *sick*, Julian. You have to be *quiet*, Granpa's near *death*."

"What the hell d'you mean, you rascal? I'm not bloody well anywhere near death!"

Recklessly Father-in-Law pulled out the I.V., setting off monitors in the nursing station.

"Now you must keep the needle in place, Mr. Orchard," the young nurse clucks reprovingly, "Otherwise you won't be going home."

"Damn bloody nurses!"

"Damn bloody nurses," chanted Julian, pulling down the sides of his mouth like Granpa.

Time passed, how much later I couldn't tell. Father-in-Law turned his head on the pillow, and extended a hand towards Julian, the most difficult of his grandsons, the most elusive and volatile, the most like himself.

"Ah, rascal . . . " he murmered, his full eyes softened on Jules now, the only time he'd ever really looked at him. "Poor boy . . . my rascal!"

Then, he was gone. Months later Julian was still tiptoeing past the bedroom. We'd been concerned how much he'd miss his granpa, an important male figure in his life.

"Sh-sh-sh!" I heard Jules in Father-in-Law's bedroom. He was lying straight down on the chenille coverlet on Granpa's side of the bed, looking up at the ceiling and murmuring, "Granpa's *sleeping.*"

The author working with Julian, age 15, in the "kishen."

Twenty-six

Father-in-Law had been an indomitable, quixotic character in the family, important to Julian. His passing left us feeling insecure, vulnerable, especially when Alec himself had a heart attack. It happened the day before his forty-ninth birthday.

Alec had thought it was an allergy attack. He hadn't experienced the infamous chest pains of heart attack, just a tightening in his jaws and funny shooting pains down his arm. Now he was slated for an angioplasty at Toronto General Hospital.

We still couldn't believe it and our instinct was to downplay the problem. Our concern still focused on Julian, to keep everything routine for him as much as possible, which meant going to school as usual, and bath and bedtime routines.

"Make sure he doesn't pour the shampoo all over his body, Thel, he tends to do that," Alec's eyes filled with tears. He lay against the hospital pillow, plastic see-through tubes snaking out of his arm and nostrils.

But there were deeper, legal implications concerning Julian's future now that Alec had heart problems. I attended a seminar given by Community Living for parents on residential placement and future planning for their special needs children; the tacit understanding had been that Alec and I would keep Julian with us for as long as possible. We would have an associate home under the aegis of Community Living, with worker support, into our old age – Julian need never leave home.

"But I don't know, Thel, if I want to have our own group home anymore . . . "

Dr. Bland wasted no time pointing out the absolute necessity of reviewing Julian's "meds" in the light of this new stress on our lives.

"Why *wouldn't* Mr. Orchard have got a heart attack, trying to keep a difficult autistic psychotic at home on minimum medication?'

The alternative, should we be unable to cope with Julian any longer, could mean his placement in a residential youth treatment facility, he hinted, or possibly, if they'd take him, a private group home. Community Living homes were slated to be "frozen" due to imminent cuts in government funding. Dr. Bland seized the moment: Auditory Training might have been all very well for Georgie Stelhi, but Julian needed more than that to stay on track. Point five mg of Haldol was a ridiculously low dosage, given the circumstances, he insisted.

We hesitated and pointed out that Julian's "boost" was coming up soon at The Listening Centre — our last hope. The boost was a three-to-five day follow-up session of auditory stimulation that would give Julian's hearing a "tune-up." The electronic ear would massage his inner ear with the high-frequency sound waves he so obviously needed, I explained.

Dr. Bland snorted. "Do you want Mr. Orchard to have another heart attack?"

But we didn't want to up the Haldol. Once we started upping the dosage a bit, then we'd probably have to up it again and again until he was dependent on it – there would be no turning back.

But there was little choice.

Dr. Sol, ever non-adversarial, was cautious about the benefits of auditory stimulation.

"If it's helped Julian somewhat, that is good. But he still might be in need of something to keep him under control." He went over other options if we were uncomfortable with increasing the Haldol: drugs such as beta-blockers, about which not too much was yet known, and even Prozac, which he said was usually used as an anti-depressant, but was also known to provide some possible relief from obsessive-compulsive disorder.

Obsessive-compulsive certainly fit Julian, we had to admit.

"And of course, there is always lithium . . . "

Dr. Sol favored lithium, had many patients on it. He said he was "comfortable" with the drug. We tensed.

Wasn't lithium for manic-depressives? Julian was at that moment pacing up and down the Child and Family Clinic yelling and hitting the wall with his fists and his head. An outbreak was happening again after a relatively long peaceful spate of time, which was the main reason we were in Dr. Sol's office. Soft-voiced, likeable Dr. Sol lolling in his armchair, surveyed us as from a distance, cautiously. We were the new generation of parents who were better informed. Dr. Sol knew this. Yet still we had to put trust in him: we needed his professional expertise. It was his job to know what drug and dosage to advise — especially dosage.

"Isn't lithium dangerous?' asked Alec finally. "Doesn't it affect the kidneys?'

"Well, you do have to be monitored on it, yes, Mr. Orchard. It would involve regular blood work, but it's a safe drug when used properly."

It made no difference to him, it was our choice, he intimated, careful to stress the point.

Julian was chanting down the hallway, "He's gonna be on *lithium*, for God's sake!" He picked up everything.

"You could try Ativan," Dr. Sol suggested. We were eager to put our trust in Dr. Sol, so it came down to Ativan (lorazepam), another drug. It was a different class of drug from lithium or Haldol, one of the benzodiazepines, an anti-anxiety drug.

Right away I didn't like that word *benzodiazepines* because there was a whole slew of them, and which was the right one for Julian? Yet we felt anything would be better than anti-psychotics — "psychotics" always sounded so insane. "Anti-anxiety" sounded reasonable. Dr. Sol was reasonable. He was teddy-bear-like, wearing an open-neck shirt, old grey socks peeking under his rumpled pants. He had an armchair, we had armchairs. So Ativan it was. Now about dosage.

"Well, I know you always like to start low, Mr. and Mrs. Orchard . . . "

Of course we would opt to start Julian on minimum dose, 2mg/day. But we had the feeling that if we had said "Maximum dose, Dr. Sol — as high as can be humanly tolerated, something that will knock Julian out for good at home and school," Dr. Sol would have agreed to that, too. Yet at least he was open, allowing options. He respected our fears.

"You're gonna be on Ativan, Julian!" Julian was speaking in a new low lilting familiar way. It was Dr. Sol's tone of voice. "Look, Julian. It's gonna be minimum dose to start!" He listened in to everything.

"You have to have help!"

Dr. Bland raised his head, his deep crimson face once again sweating with concern. "You don't even have a worker and Julian is fifteen!"

It was true. It was a foreign idea to us to hand Julian over to some stranger. But we had to admit that we did need help.

Dr. Bland quietly, quickly, used his influence and connections with Community Living and some residential agency called "Kerry's Place" to get us help. We were surprised and grateful. After years of altercations and conflict, Dr. Bland was pulling through for us. Suddenly we had a "worker," a student from the University of Toronto called Fred who would "do things" with Julian six hours a week. Suddenly we were one of thousands of families in Ontario who received this service paid for by Special Services At Home (SSAH), funded by the Ministry of Community and Social Services, COMSOC.

Alec and I had fought for these social services in the past, and now had to receive them ourselves.

Fred was a big cheerful happy-natured student just out of university. He was not sure what direction he wanted to go in life, yet, but he was veering towards social work; working with Julian would be excellent experience for him.

We were doubtful. But he was tall, big, affable, and gentle in speech — a good role model for Julian. Alec and I were grateful to Fred, eager for him to feel secure with Julian. We warned him that Julian could be difficult and suggested swimming at the indoor pool with hot tub, and a hamburger at McDonald's afterwards, Julian's two favorite activities.

"So how did it go, then?"

We tried to sound casual, as if we expected everything to have gone smoothly — a nice young student out with an autistic teenager who needed some help with social niceties.

"Oh, fine!" enthused Fred. He was just a bit excited in the changing room. His friend Seymour Reynolds was there with his dad, and they were flicking towels — weren't you, Jules? — that sort of thing."

Fred shrugged easily, typical teenagers razzing was how he miraculously saw it.

"And that was it?"

"Well, Julian didn't really want to put his clothes back on, he was gonna walk out naked as a babe!" chuckled Fred.

"Oh! Well, some autistic kids tend to be like that. Seymour Reynolds had once pulled off all his clothes in Instant Car-Wash and lain naked on the car-wash tracks, demanding: 'Wash me!' to the absolute shock of the attendants.'"

"Ugh-huh, no! Mrs. Orchard! You mean — Seymour Reynolds actually lay naked on the floor of a car wash and asked for a wash? Wow! Hey, that's weird, man, I mean, really weird. D'you think he thought he was a car? A Camaro, or something?"

The house reverberated with Fred's hearty laughter, and we couldn't help but join in, realizing how little we actually laughed now. Poor Seymour, and poor Mr. Reynolds, harried and over-wrought, arriving in a police cruiser. "Seymour, get the hell out of there!"

Since things were going so well with Fred, Dr. Bland suggested we might like to try out Kerry's Place, a group home that specialized in autistic adolescents, said Dr. Bland. It would give us some needed respite, he added. We were meeting again to discuss our family crisis after Alec's heart attack.

Once again Dr. Bland was putting himself out for us, sharing his expertise gained from his involvement with the Autism Society, an organization that so far had been irrelevant to our lives as it did not offer practical services. We thanked Dr. Bland as graciously as possible, promising to look into it.

Kerry's Place turned out to be a big old turn-of-the-century Ontario farmhouse with gracious front doors, double-fronted large windows, gardens, fields and a barn. It was located in the village of Maple, about a forty-five minute drive north of Toronto.

The surrounding countryside of Maple was gentle, the rolling hills washed in the evening light as we'd approached the avenue of maples that curved round the front of the house. At once we imagined Julian tending to the chickens and horses.

"So you're in charge?" we asked Rolph Schellenberg, the

director. He wore faded jeans and T-shirt but seemed about our age, we noted with relief. We were anxious whether young workers were capable of coping with rage attacks should they arise. It was reassuring to find an older person with experience to rely on.

"Am I in charge?" Rolph mused gently. "I guess so. Sometimes I don't feel in charge of myself, let alone others."

He showed us around the grounds and the atmosphere was relaxed and comforting everywhere. We learned that this group home had originally been designated for autistic/PDD children and adolescents, but now was shifting its mandate to the care of adults as the original residents got older. It was one of several in the greater Toronto area and surrounding small towns, and each was named after a particular resident. Parents had played a major role in founding the first group home and continued to have strong representation on the board of Kerry's Place Autism Services. Kerry's Place was government funded, explained Rolph, but parents also raised a great deal of money yearly in volunteer fund-raising activities.

Julian had already gone off to feed the horses behind the barn with Jem, one of the workers who seemed a gentle kind young man. Chickens pecked at seeds through the sparse hot grass, a large cat lay curled in the shadow of the porch; vast sweeps of sunlight lit up the fields beyond the barn. It all seemed ideal, yet we were cautious, asking lots of questions around medication, our prime concern. Rolph was patient. He assured us the workers were well-versed in "meds," and regularly received updates in their training. There was a medication schedule to administer everyone's drugs, and the worker on duty had to sign a logbook, which he showed us.

It was the beginning of many happy weekends at Kerry's Place for Julian. We were allowed three weekends a year and one week in the summer, that we paid for privately. Soon Julian was coming home talking about Mark and Jem and David. He was particularly fond of Rolph, whom he always called by his full name: "Rolph Schellenberg, don't-tease-him-Julian," followed by immediate chuckles.

We were thrilled at the relationship developing between the male workers and Julian, similar to that with the Summer Teen counselors. They had a wonderful influence on Julian. He seemed to love and respond to this new male camaraderie in his life, despite the few weekends really he spent there. We wondered whether Julian's constant urge to escape to the hallways at The Meadows, where he loved to tease old Mr. Phiz, the caretaker, sloshing his mop along the floors, was an instinctive seeking out of more male bonding that he needed like any other teenage boy.

Knowing of no other group homes, we weren't yet aware of how lucky we were to have the high proportion of male workers that Kerry's Place offered. Kerry's Place itself housed only male residents in their late teens and early twenties, some of them strapping youths.

We received no reports of "bad" behavior at Kerry's Place, no violent outbreaks or self-abuse. Julian still paced a great deal and talked to himself; that was acceptable and Julian was encouraged to do it outside in the yard. The workers and Rolph had difficulty associating the Julian they knew with the one we described at home and at school. Maybe it was the combination of outside activities, jobs in the barn and feeding the horses, fresh air and sunshine, or being allowed to walk off his inner tensions — or was it the fact he was only there for short spates of time? And away from us? What was it we must be doing wrong? We mulled over it, feeling frustrated, self-accusatory.

The counselors and Rolph even had a good laugh in an affectionate way at Julian's idiosyncracies. They didn't often come across functional echolalia since most of the residents were non-verbal. Julian was so funny, they cried.

"He has each one of us pegged! He's such a character! Come back again, Julian!"

"There isn't a mean bone in his body."

Those words stayed with us a long long time. How we had needed to hear them. *Gentle Julian. Not a mean bone in his body.* I wept.

Twenty-seven

Despite Jules' occasional successful weekends at Kerry's place, tension, subtle, invidious, continued to simmer in June. It would flare up in violent outbursts.

Something else seemed to be at the root of his disturbance; some other, as yet unsolved mysterious response within the brain that neither the drugs we'd tried so far nor auditory stimulation could allay.

It seemed to start up again shortly after his first trip to Kerry's Place, when Julian went for his six-month boost at The Listening Centre. It was supposed to last three to five days involving the same procedures as before: Jules wearing headphones and listening to filtered music that would tune up his auditory faculties. But on the first day of treatment, we'd barely been in the place five minutes when Julian became loud and agitated. He was pacing in a frightening maniacal way up and down the stairs, punching himself and threatening to smash his head through the window, alarming the children and even Paul – the electronic equipment was expensive. Paul had not seen Julian's outbursts and he was shocked and concerned for him as well as anxious about the other children in the room.

Reluctantly Paul asked us to leave. Julian obviously needed "specialized" treatment, possibly psychiatric, beyond what auditory stimulation could now offer – the programming could only do so much. We had to accept this. Yet we never doubted that the Tomatis Method had been the best thing for Julian so far. Auditory Stimulation therapy had been worth it, if only for alleviating part of Julian's suffering. It had shown us a way when everything else had failed.

Dr. Bland smiled at my loyalty when I discussed it with him at the next opportunity. "Ah, Mrs. Orchard! You know the consensus in the field is that Georgie Stelhi very likely wasn't autistic in the first place."

I tensed indignantly. It was just this sort of professional skepticism that had infuriated Stelhi. It seemed many professionals in the field of autism were unwilling to approach any kind of alternative treatment with a skepticism that often ruled out the alternative before it was even given a chance. Stelhi's difficulties included not only being excluded from her child's treatment, but being accused of being "schizophrenic" herself, and the cause of Georgie's problems: "I felt as if I were being told that what I could give her, which was my best, wasn't good enough," recalled Stelhi bitterly.

Ultimately, her experience with professionals, she realized, had been one of *"totally self-abnegating, slavish obedience to doctor's orders"* — until she'd taken the risk to try alternative treatment, and followed her own judgement.

A young couple with a six-year-old autistic boy named Jacob had moved into our neighborhood. Jacob's mother, Beth, was fascinated with the way Julian talked to himself, while I was fascinated with Jacob, with his large dark eyes like Julian's glancing sideways. I noted that he barely talked. He had been diagnosed at age four by none other than Dr. Rakka. I was amazed that Dr. Rakka was still in service, she'd seemed old in 1981.

Nothing much seemed to have changed over the years, especially the diagnosis at the magical age of four. Beth confided that Dr. Rakka had recommended she "put Jacob away." One wondered where Dr. Rakka intended to put Jacob? Thistletown Regional Centre was slated for closure by the New Democratic Party government, and Huronia Regional Centre in Orillia had been in the process of de-institutionalization since the '70s. Beth had an idea that Dr. Rakka might have placed him in "foster care," but, wouldn't it be obvious that if foster parents could raise him so could Beth and her husband?

Dr. Rakka's logic seemed so untenable, yet she was obviously still convinced of the rightness of her approach, part of a whole mind-set that once again stirred up deep issues I mistakenly thought had been resolved long ago. I wanted to examine this, the whole drama of putting children away "for their own good," and by what authority, and lay it to rest in my mind.

I went back to the Gerstein Library and the Archives of Ontario to seek out original documents, tracts, papers, and histories on institutionalization in Ontario.

"But Thelma, what does it *matter?*" echoed Alec, eyeing *Reports for the Feebleminded in Ontario 1905–35, Reports of The Inspector of Prisons, Asylums and Public Charities* littering the table. "It's almost a century ago!"

Alec said he felt sorry for me wasting my precious summer holidays for nothing while Jules was at Teen Camp.

But vital issues concerning Julian had been confronted and battled as far back as 1911! "Putting children away," I was discovering, involved a complex process of institutionalization that had evolved slowly, even innocently at first.

As far back as the nineteenth century, in Britain and Europe, kindly individuals, often poor clergymen, had begun to share their own homes in a simple way with a few destitute retarded children. These early group homes gradually gave way to small institutions. In Canada, the inspector of asylums, prisons, and public charities, Dr. Langmuir, impressed by the success rate of the British training schools, urged the government of Ontario for similar facilities for the feebleminded population.

In 1878, the old insane institution in Orillia, Ontario, was converted to an "asylum for idiots"; it was to be the only one of its kind in Canada for thirty years. Institutionalizing the feebleminded altered the way mentally challenged people were treated, and the laws devised to handle them. Gradually, the power of parents to decide for themselves whether to place their children into homes and institutions or keep them in the public school system gradually shifted under governmemt control. Furthermore, the treatment of the mentally challenged fell more and more under the domain of medicine and the Department of Health, rather than education. Mentally challenged children were no longer allowed to attend regular classes in public school, and the only alternative was institutionalization where some skills were provided.

By 1955, the number of inmates at Orillia had reached nearly three thousand; most had been placed by parents who had believed they had no other choice.

Sun seeped through the potted plants fretting the floor of the Archives of Ontario. Other researchers moved like ghosts with their files and boxes. Please be quiet. Please use pencils. I moved on to the psychotic children of Orillia, the autistic, childhood schizophrenics, as I neared the end of my toil that would bring me closer to Julian and Dr. Rakka.

Pierre Berton's article exposed the "atrocities going on in Ontario Hospital School in Orillia" in a January 1960 edition of the *Toronto Daily Star.*

The Willard Report, published in 1976, the year Julian was born, was an investigation into these abuses. It cited, amongst other things, concern about the future placement of the "autistic children" in the autistic unit, "Sunrise." These children, ranging in age from nine to eighteen, were schizophrenic, violent, "behaviorally disturbed," and had been receiving "experimental" treatment for five years.

The Report helped dissolve the program. In 1978, when Julian was two, the schizophrenic and autistic children were "transferred," but no one seemed to know what exactly happened to them.

I was beginning to understand how attractive, suitable and *justifiable,* a group home in a small institution like Thistletown Regional Centre must have seemed to Dr. Rakka in 1981. But small group homes, I now discovered, had not been created without resistance. The idea had been in part influenced by the work of John Brown, a social worker and the director of Warrendale in the 1950s. He'd insisted that the homes of Warrendale be in an ordinary residential neighborhood. Psychiatrists at Thistletown had not been overly supportive. (Brown had once called psychiatry "the most vicious profession," and accused the Department of Mental Health of running a "children's services mafia" through the "Toronto children's pipeline.") Brown believed in "unconditional love," and "unconditional care" and parental involvement in decision-making. By the 1970s, the administrators of Thistletown, influenced partly by Brown's success, began to move the resident autistic children out of the big main building into small group homes in the grounds, one of which Dr. Rakka had recommended for Julian.

I seemed to have come full circle in my research, in my need to believe the best in Dr. Rakka, keep trust in her, reach a point of final understanding and reconciliation. Yet, from this long strange saga it was evident that committal to some institution or other would have been Julian's ultimate fate had it not been for one little old grandmother in Toronto, whose action was to change the course of history for the "feebleminded" in this country, forever.

On September 29, 1948, Mrs. Victoria Glover submitted an unsigned letter to the editor of *The Toronto Daily Star* that electrified its readers:

> *Sir: May I say a few words on behalf of our backward children, and their bewildered mothers. There is no school for such children, no place where they could get a little training to be of some use in the world, only Orillia which is always full. If these children can be taught something at Orillia, why cannot a day school be put at their disposal? I am sure their mothers would gladly pay for their transportation to and from school. After all, they are paying taxes for other more fortunate children's schooling. I think it is time something was done for parents who from a sense of faith and hope in a merciful providence want to keep them at home living a normal life. These are real parents, only asking a little aid and encouragement to shoulder their own heavy burden. God bless them, and may the Ontario government help them and their children who might still be made something of, living a normal life and with the perfect love, understanding and guidance of such parents."*

The challenge swept across Ontario in an unprecedented way! The whole point was that Victoria Glover's grandson had an I.Q. below 50 – he was supposed to be up in Orillia.

Inspired by Mrs. Glover's letter and the issues she had raised, parents soon found out the identity of the letter-writer and together they formed a delegation and presented a brief to the Minister of Education requesting classes for all retarded children regardless of I.Q. The minister responded that it was illegal for a local Board of Education to teach children with below 50 I.Q., Section 11 of the Public School Act. So the parents began to organize their own classes!

By 1953 a school was opened on Beverley Street, Toronto, funded by parents. The Department of Education revised the Education Act to support classes run by the Association for Retarded Children, providing $25 per month per pupil. The medical profession still believed that institutions were best for children with an I.Q. below 50. This conviction changed little over the decades even when de-institutionalization began to take place in the '70s.

Parents had become aware of their power of choice: whether to have their children serviced by the old system under mental health authorities or by the education system. They realized that to accept services from Mental Health would mean continuing the same old segregation from the mainstream, however well-intentioned and good the department's programs might be.

Now parents began their long fight for the inclusion of all disabled children, regardless of I.Q., into the public and Catholic school system – no more institutionalization for life. Eventually their struggle bore fruit: the inclusion of all disabled children regardless of I.Q. into the public and separate school system itself . . .

On December 2, 1980, Bill 82, passed by the conservative government of Ontario, granted that all children, regardless of ability, I.Q., or handicap, were entitled to an education in the public school system.

And Julian had been able to be part of that inheritance.

I felt myself tingle. Once again I had somehow come full circle in my long labored research into institutionalization, realizing a deep need I'd had to understand events. Choosing to keep Julian had saved him from much that I'd had little knowledge of that July day in 1981. But I also recognized the courageous parents who had gone before me, and had labored unsung to enable that choice, and something deeper and more subtle – the realization that a mother's self-image was often the key to the success of an outcome.

I closed my files. I put away Dr. MacMurchy's *Reports on the Feebleminded in Ontario* . . . and her endearing cry, "They have gifts!" In a sense my research was over. Only one set of documents remained, the ones I'd always wanted to see, that now miraculously came into my hands . . .

In 1992 a landmark decision had been made – *McInery v. MacDonald* – after a patient in New Brunswick had challenged the courts for full access to her medical records which had been denied her, and won. A new bill enacted by parliament now granted everyone in Canada the fundamental right to personal medical and social information, including information transferred from one doctor or psychiatrist to another. It meant that at last we could read not only the speech and language pathologist's report to Dr. Geene from 1980, but more importantly, Dr. Rakka's . . .

More than eleven years had passed since Julian's diagnosis and Mr. Corsen's interview. I was nervous and excited. The memory of Dr. Rakka, in particular, returned, stirring, enigmatic in her power.

Yet Mrs. Crump hesitated at the rows of files extending from ceiling to floor behind her in Dr. Geene's office, medical records going back decades yellowed with age, locked away. Reluctantly she handed over the reports, glancing at a bold black statement of Dr. Rakka's stamped on the front:

THIS IS A CONFIDENTIAL CASE SUMMARY
AND UNDER NO CIRCUMSTANCES IS TO BE SHOWN
OR READ TO ANY MEMBER OF THE FAMILY
WITHOUT OUR CONSENT.

Twenty-eight

I decided to read Mr. Corsen's report first as his had been the first vital observations of Julian at age three, so long ago now. It turned out to be a mere page, but a telling one: " . . . deviant language . . . serious delay . . . autistic tendencies."

What we had suspected was here: Mr. Corsen had indeed recognized, as had Dr. Geene, that Julian was autistic, but had chosen not to tell us. "Thank you for this very interesting referral," went the friendly confidential words, one professional thanking another for the commission.

I realized it was another instance of having to let things go as part of a past that could not be changed or even challenged, circumstances that had been influenced by the belief that it was not necessarily in a parent's best interest to have medical information divulged to them. I turned to Dr. Rakka's report, trembling.

Naturally, I wanted to know Dr. Rakka's opinion of Julian, of us all, that July day in 1981. But that word "confidential" stamped on the cover made me feel as if I were peering into someone's private papers, as if I had no right. It was a slim document, divided into headings: Family, Results of Examination, and the final diagnosis of "Developmental Delay, Mild to Moderate; Language Delay, Moderate to Severe. Autism."

At first glance, the report seemed much like any other document; after all, I had read in my students' Ontario School Records which contained similar documents. Dr. Rakka stated the usual information about Alec and me: our backgrounds, education, professions, and how long we'd been married. There were expected facts relayed about Julian's development, his birth weight, feeding and constipation problems, and his limited language skills.

Yet I was surprised to also read how he "presented," in the lingo of the profession, as: "a handsome, lithe, racially mixed child with synophrys and widow's hood."

I could see the necessity for describing Julian's appearance from a medical viewpoint (whether he bore any physical stigmata of mental retardation) but this comment on his racial features, his curved eyes, was surely fatuous especially alongside her next comment that Polly was "a good student and behaviourally normal. Her features are fully Caucasian . . . " I decided that this told me more about Dr. Rakka than about the children.

I began to feel anxious. Many professionals, including Dr. Bland and Julian's principals and teachers, would have had access to this document over the years. I read on: "Polly was given the responsibility to look after and discipline Julian and indeed she was much more efficient than either parent in doing so."

To me, this sounded as if in Dr. Rakka's opinion, Alec and I had not been good parents, often shifting the onus for disciplining Julian on to Polly.

In a flash I saw the struggle once again in Dr. Rakka's office: Dr. Rakka's eyes peering through the darkness on the other side of the two-way mirror as we'd tussled with Julian in the brightly lit room, illuminated for her to watch our pain and difficulties as Julian tore his teeth into us, resisting us as we tried to remove his clothes. She saw how we had enveigled Polly's help so we wouldn't look so bad in front of the doctor. But didn't children, even autistic ones, respond better with other children, as he had?

I was shocked to read further, under "Family," that not only were Alec and I apparently not good disciplinarians, we also had poor emotional relationships with Julian. Julian, she noted, "ignored" his father and "avoided" me, his mother ; I was described as "intrusive." Dr. Rakka's report began to focus exclusively on me. She observed I had a "symbiotic" relationship with Julian, that he related to me in an "infantile way" and that I was no less infantile. Had it been so obvious then that I hadn't been able to cope? It must have — but infantile? Helplessness waved over me . . . I read the words again: *"He tends to relate in an infantile way to his mother and I do not feel that she can relate to him in any other level either."*

The words burned on the page: *"I feel he avoids the mother who is verbally very intrusive . . ."*

The painful implication was that somehow my behavior around Julian had contributed to his autism, though my common sense and knowledge from my research helped me recognize this as the "psychogenic" approach, the current thinking of that time. It was "blame the mother," something that Annabel Stelhi had experienced only too well.

Then the pain returned, because now Dr. Rakka observed that little Julian, four and a half, could only combine "two, at most three words." It was so true and so sad.

Julian, she noted, was a "bizarre, idiosyncratic, resistive child, explosive, unpredictable, ritualistic, smelling objects or holding objects in his hands and staring at them closely." She recorded his language delay as "severe."

We had been told Julian was "retarded, with autism," but we hadn't been told his language delay was "severe." We hadn't been told the extent of his autism. Instead, Dr. Rakka continued to suggest we put him away in a treatment center.

Of course, this communication had never been meant for me, I reminded myself. I couldn't help but see it as "pipeline" information, meant for treatment centers like The Creche and the Regional Centre. They would need to know the level of severity, were entitled to know. We'd just been expected to follow course. And we hadn't. At the six-month parent follow-up, I recalled remarking drily to Dr. Rakka as she continued to push the Thistletown and Creche placements on us that professionals' main concern seemed to be ensuring business for each other.

I had actually said those words, had implied that Julian was somehow an object to be passed between these "treatment" places.

Dr. Rakka had almost catapulted from her seat at the intrusive words, for such they must have been. Her lips tightened, her eyes glassy with anger as I'd inadvertently criticized one professional to another. As if I had the right to say what I thought, to make my own observations. As if I'd forgotten momentarily that I was the patient.

"What do you mean?" she had glared.

Alec and I had simply been struggling to express something about the whole process, trying to see the reason in a decision we did not feel was right for Julian.

It took us a long time to get it.

This diagnosis belonged to the past when I had been young and inexperienced. I decided to look at it in this more fulminating light and move on. I was now in my fifties, no longer that younger woman who had confronted Dr. Rakka in one desperate intense moment in time, though it had shaped me for the struggle.

Alec agreed. "You're caught," he mused. "Best to forget it. Who really gives a shit, anyway? That was the '80s, that was the way it was; it wouldn't happen with the rules and guidelines of today. Besides, we've got enough on our plate right now with Julian again."

Twenty-nine

Perhaps Dr. Rakka was proven right after all, as things were turning out, for we were barely holding on again as it became more obvious each day that Jules was slipping back into that dread phase we knew so well.

That last summer, that long hot summer before the end, hurtling us along towards some terrible finale. Julian was sixteen, taller than us, lean and handsome with small flashing white teeth, dusky lips and dark glossy hair. One thought: *What a lovely boy, so handsome, so gentle.* How could we know what was to come that summer, "the summer from hell" — the "Holiday From Hell," marooned with Julian in Cape Cod, Massachusetts, in Whispering Pines Family Motel.

The motel was close to The Strip and the John F. Kennedy Memorial Alec had set his heart on. There was a laundromat, a string of fast food take-outs, a Tibetan shop and long hot blinding sands strewn with seaweeds we never got to walk along in any sunset. We were trapped in the motel room with two queen-size beds with beige chenille coverlets because Julian refused to come out of the bathroom, frightened of the curtains.

"They're just lilac, plastic shower curtains, Jules, like the ones at home, nothing to be afraid of. We're on *holiday*, Jules, we're in *Cape Cod*, a famous, famous place where the Kennedys have their famous summer family compound we want to see. There's a JFK memorial Dad wants to photograph in the park, a famous memorial."

But they were not the white plastic curtains at home back in Canada, in Port Credit.

"You don't want to be in Port Credit, Jules; you want to be by the *ocean*, with *waves*." The vast, blinding, relentless ocean that rises through space with that huge, relentless, beating sky—an American sky, endlessly blue, he was not used to it, nor the strange seaweed the ocean tossed skyward mysteriously out into space onto the sands. "No-o!" howled Jules, backing up against the shower stall.

Instead we were holed up for the day in the Olympic-sized indoor swimming pool which Julian refused to leave after breakfast, possibly because it was the closest familiar thing to special needs swimming at home up in Canada. Flanked by middle-aged American grandmothers stretched out on chaise-lounges..

Julian would not leave the pool until ten at night, except for the meals at the one same restaurant as for breakfast. We were forced to sit watching Julian anxiously doing the crawl up and down the pool, and we were exhausted from lack of sleep. A delinquent teenage group from the Bronx, on therapeutic holiday with their "counselors," had screamed foul expletives through the thin wall of our motel room next door all night long, listened to attentively by Julian.

"Fucking asshole!" we had heard, followed by girls' screams and water spraying in the shower stall.

"Fucking asshole!" Jules had repeated, pausing, head cocked in the dark.

"Is that what they're saying, Mommy, Daddy? Are they bad kids in the wall? They're bad, aren't they?"

"No, they're disturbed, Jules, that means . . . " I had sighed against the pillow, struggling for words he could comprehend, that would not worsen the situation. I was so tired of all this, of Cape Cod, of being on holiday. "It means sometimes they get suspended from school, but basically they're good."

Was it any wonder Julian was as he was, growled Alec, lying prone and exhausted across the bed, fanning his brow. We were supposed to have visited Martha's Vineyard that day. What kind of double-talk was that to be giving him? No wonder Dr. Rakka had called me symbiotic, he snarled, unfairly. I keeled over on the bed and wept.

"Aw, c'mon," said Alec gruffly. "What the hell does this 'symbiotic' mean anyway?"

"It means . . . it means stuck together, like as if you're one person," I gulped foolishly between sobs into the pillow. "Like Siamese twins."

Alec grinned, in moments doubled over laughing. "Christ! I can't believe we take this crap seriously!"

The next morning we drove non-stop back along super freeway 87 to Toronto, grim and exhausted after only three days' holiday, Julian punching himself intermittently all the way until we reached home, and the familiar white-lined shower curtains.

Yet this was the same Julian who only months before had done so well at Kerry's Place.

"Julian's changed so much . . . He's not the same kid. There's something seriously wrong with him," said Dave Perriman, the coach of the weekly Special Needs Summer Baseball program run by Community Living Association.

My only hope was that Julian not be banned from the Bombers. The Bombers team was all he had to get him – and us – through the rest of the summer. Bombers versus Sluggers Friday nights at the ballpark.

But Julian was having difficulty staying in the dugout with the rest of the team. He was running around restlessly, shaking hands eagerly with people over and over again. It was becoming a real problem.

It was the championship game this particular Friday evening – Hell's Angels versus Sluggers. It was my job ostensibly to help with helmets, fasten the strap under each player's chin, but in reality keep an eye on Julian, that he *stay put* like everyone else on the team. But Julian just is not going to sit with the Bombers on the bench like the rest of the team, quietly and obediently awaiting his turn. I knew how difficult, impossible, that was for my restless son wired up differently.

Inexplicably, Julian began ranting about "Ricky Morris" – this hallucinatory Ricky Morris was back in Julian's mind. Except, as it turned out, "Ricky Morris" was real, a real live grown-up Ricky, tall, fair, angelic, playing first stop for his team, Hell's Angels. Everyone seemed to know about Ricky Morris and his pluck.

I had little recollection of Ricky Morris.

But Julian did. Something clicked back twelve years in his brain whenever this Ricky Morris appeared. He recognized Ricky as the little five-year-old child he'd known in childhood, the frailest one in Special Needs swimming, wearing a metal brace and leg irons. Now about eighteen, he was healed and strong after many operations.

"Ricky Morris can't walk!" exploded Julian from the dugout. He began to mimic Ricky's old handicap, crooking his arm and dragging

his leg. I sensed something would happen any minute. *Somebody help me, please.* But no one understood; Julian Orchard was my responsibility.

It was blazing hot in the dugout. The mothers in the bleachers, far away, white baseball caps cocked at cheerful angles, clapped, confused, everyone trying to carry on as if Julian Orchard was not dragging himself up and down the diamond.

One mother's look of dislike was undeniable, a dark wave striking across the bleachers. It was Mrs. Morris.

"Ricky Morris can't walk."

"Get back in here, Jules! Get in the dugout!" I called out. But Julian continued, locked away in this unreal fantasy, *this* psychotic dream, of a little five-year-old Ricky who was no more.

"Ricky Morris can't walk!" he persisted, his voice bellowing across the bases. He began to drag his leg again, before the horrified parents; his arm cuddled to his side at the same angle as Ricky's years ago. I saw the flash of pain on Ricky's face, his scowl as he shuddered on first base.

"Ricky Morris . . . " chanted Julian as I ran over to try to put a stop to it. Julian laughed jubilantly, enjoying himself, unaware of the embarrassment and shame for Ricky, and for himself. The mothers in the bleachers flushed for Ricky, pained for Julian, perturbed for me, and watched in silence.

"I hate Julian Orchard!" yelled Ricky.

The terrible words cut across the diamond. Ricky gritted his teeth, tears squeezing angrily down his cheeks; there was a tight shocked silence of sympathy. I felt pain for Julian, still chuckling to himself, so obliviously unaware he was making everyone resent him, and for Ricky, for his shame and hatred.

"Julian can't help it. It's so hard to make him understand. But he is on medication!" I heard myself adding wildly as a sort of defense: that we were trying to do something about this, he was on Ativan 2mg twice daily. But it didn't solve this, make it stop. Action was what counted.

"Julian stop it. Enough!" I strode firmly across the diamond tried to whisper this closely to his face, not appear agitated myself, absolutely essential. But my voice was quivering. I was quivering. It seemed hours since the game began. His mood shifted swiftly, dangerously. *Oh, where was Alec?* At home having a beer.

"That's BAD, Julian, you're BAD BAD BAD!" he howled. "You shouldn't make fun of Ricky Morris," he wailed as I began to try to pull him by the arm away from the play. Pitching had stopped.

"Play ball! Play ball!" called the coach desperately.

"Think of his mother!" Julian was going, full-rate now, his voice bellowing across the bleachers. Mrs. Morris looked pained. This was such a farce, but it was real. I dragged at Julian. He began to realize we were heading in the direction of the parking lot not the dugout.

"Are we going home, Mom? Am I a bad boy? Yes you are, Julian! You're BAD BAD BAD."

Thud, thud.

"Oh-h went the crowd, Oh-h-h . . . !"

Julian, in another shift of mood, cackled uproariously, he had glimpsed Ricky Morris back on base. Between laughter and sobs he suddenly beat his face against the wire mesh of the dugout. "Bad Bad Bad!"

Would it ever stop?

"D'you want help, Thelma?"

Lorraine was an old lady of seventy with a special needs daughter of her own. She tried to offer to help. But there was no helping this situation.

"What's wrong with him?" she asked kindly, offering me a tissue.

"I don't know," I gulped; the nearest I could come to honesty. Poor Jules was slamming his teeth against the wire mesh.

"He's been like this for a while," I tried to make it sound reasonable, not too alarming. "He's on some medication; it's supposed to help for now. I think it's his age. You know, adolescence."

"Won't he hurt himself?" Lorraine looked pityingly at Julian, at his forehead smeared with blood. I was blotting it with the tissue. By now, her daughter, Betsy, was tearing off her Sluggers shirt and shredding it to bits, and Lorraine had to go.

I managed to coax Julian into the car.

"Oh my God, I'm so sorry for you," gasped Lorraine, pushing Julian's mitt through the window, Julian sobbing in the rear seat. Her face was filled with concern and fear.

I wanted to lean out, call back to her, to all of them, as I drove off slowly home into the sunset, not to be afraid of Julian.

There was no let-up back home. Julian continued storming through the rooms beating himself, yelling for hours. Darkness loomed, a long desolate night.

"You're BAD, JULIAN ORCHARD — Git back in that dugout!"

"What the hell's this now . . . ?" Alec turned off the TV.

"STUPID!" screamed Julian, the incoherent insane-sounding rush of words — the pacing — flashes out of a darkness obliterating the room like fireworks to such a point that he gripped my throat: "KILL MOMMY! I'm gonna kill Mommy, fucking ass-hole! Fuck you!"

He threw me against the kitchen wall, and everything came crashing down off the fridge, bottles of herbs toppling off shelves. I heard more crashings from the other room as I staggered across the kitchen to the phone. But Pino and Francesca weren't at home. Now I knew I must do it quickly while I was able. I heard Alec panting and his wails of pain: "Can't hold him, Thel!"

I dialed 911. "Send someone quickly, please, right away." A few minutes later, there were three police officers in our living-room, their muscles flexing under their uniforms. Alec sank into the corner and wept, and we heard the dull thud of the officers trying to hold Julian down on the floor.

One officer had a radio in hand, another a billyclub and pepper spray. Two were holding Julian down in the corner of the living room.

"Think we should call for more help, he's strong, man!"

"Just don't hurt him!" I cried, covering my face with my hands as Julian groaned. It was so frightening, I wished we'd never called them, but we couldn't have lasted it this time. Alec sat in the corner, his head in his hands. His chest hurt from the pounding he'd received from Julian; he was trembling as if he were having another heart attack, yet he called to the police, "Don't hurt him!"

"Look mister, you stay out of this! We're in charge now, you get over there out of the way." The officer pointed to the dining-room table with its swinging Tiffany lamp.

"Don't you order me around in my own house!" Alec struggled to his feet.

"Don't antagonize them," I whispered to Alec.

"He's not really dangerous," I kept calling from the fireplace, weeping.

This was more terrible than anything. The room rocked, things were getting nasty, and I was terrified the officers were overreacting.

"Can't hold him down," I heard one groan. "He's strong, man!"

Suddenly Julian lunged at me: "I'm gonna kill Mommy! Don't you kill your mother, Julian, you witch's tit!"

The officers grabbed him back and there was another sickening thud.

"Think we should use the pepper spray?" asked the youngest officer.

The other two were locking Julian's arms into handcuffs.

"Oh not too tight, please officers! He's just upset. He's not schizophrenic!" I pleaded.

"Well he's damn dangerous, get back there, lady, you're interfering with the law!"

There was a rush of spray, and in seconds everyone was coughing out of the door. The officers were staggering round the lawn, coughing and gasping for breath before a silent row of neighbors. They'd pepper-sprayed themselves as well as Jules. Julian sagged in his handcuffs, sinking to his knees. I ran across the grass and grabbed a wet towel someone gave me. I mopped Julian's face, which was now pressed against the back of the cruiser, his arms shackled behind him.

A ring of neighbors in pajamas and robes stood back in silence.

"Oh what are they doing to poor old Julian?" whispered old Mr. Craddock, trembling in his night clothes, starting to come forward.

"Mommy! Mommy is this what it was like when I was a baby? When I was a baby!" Jules sobbed unbelievably. What was he talking about? "Am I a baby again, Mommy? Am I? Am I?" He was confused yet very alert.

I couldn't stand him being strapped down like an animal at bay. Yet there's no other way right now.

When the ambulance arrived, the attendants surveyed the scene grimly as I quickly explained to them that Julian was retarded and autistic. I stress "retarded," to convey what I meant, that he wasn't a criminal. They nodded.

"He'll be safe in the ambulance."

We seemed to burst upon the waiting area of the hospital. Julian was still yelling, his hands still shackled behind his back, his face and nose swollen and bloodied. He was flanked by two officers and an ambulance attendant, Alec and I had followed the ambulance and police cruisers all the way, going through two red lights.

"I'M GONNA KILL MOMMY RIGHT NOW."

The usual sort of people in the waiting area with sprained feet and broken arms, asthma attacks and bee stings, stared numbly, their eyes on Julian.

I shoved Julian's health card through the slot at the reception desk, anxious about Jules.

"IS MOMMY AN ASSHOLE? WHAT'S A COCK-SUCKING MOTHER-FUCKING IDIOT, MOMMY? IS THAT BAD LIKE FART?"

The officers tightened their grip on Julian and pushed him towards the wall, not without a smirk. Doctors and orderlies came out of emergency rooms—What was going on? A nurse hurried down and whispered urgently that there was no bed available. "Then make one!" came the curt voice of the attending doctor.

Julian was still trying to swing at the officers in spite of the shackles. I longed to go to him. "Hey, boys, go easy on the young fella there, he's just a kid, remember!" tutted the receptionist, Mrs. Judd, through the slot. She was middle-aged with tight grey curls and round glasses.

Even the big burly officer hesitated at Mrs. Judd's words. She was this sudden blessing – there always was one, I marveled, grateful.

An old gentleman with tubes coming out of every orifice was being wheeled out of cubicle 6 to make room for Julian, his eyes round and startled as Julian was dragged past. "In there, kid!" the officer said, as another blocked the doorway.

"I want to be with my son!"

"No one goes in 'til we say, lady!"

"You have no right!" cried Alec.

"You wanna be arrested?"

"Arrest me, officer, for wanting to be with my son!"

"ARE THEY ARRESTING ALEC?" yelled Julian from the room inside. He was being put in restraints.

"I think we're all upset – let's cool it, boys," said Nurse Moira. She had the needle ready. "Just a touch, darling," she crooned, patting Julian's thigh.

But it was more than just a touch, it was a powerful shot of Valium, but I didn't care. I was thankful for any drug, as Julian twisted and struggled against the restraints on the gurney. "It'll stop him hurting himself, we have to, dear, until the psychiatrist comes. We'll need his expertise," she sighed.

"Am I a bad boy, Mommy?"

Dr. Chizick was an old grey-haired fatherly-looking sort dressed in a pinstriped suit under his long white lab coat. He observed Julian for a moment in an expert sort of way, sizing up the situation: Jules' bright hot face, bruised and bloody, the bright eyes glowing weirdly as he jerked against the restraints.

"So what's your name, son?"

"Ricky Morris."

"Well, Ricky — "

"No, his name's Julian. Julian Orchard."

"So what's the problem here?" Dr. Chizick leaned sternly over Julian.

Julian stared back up: "Are you a fathead?'

Dr. Chizick frowned. "Schizophrenic?"

"It's a bad word, isn't it, Mommy?" Julian jerked anxiously. We explained that Julian was autistic and had had a bad breakout, that he seemed to be under tension from the baseball game.

"Age?"

"Sixteen and a half."

"Sixteen and a half! Yes, you're sixteen *and a half*, Julian, you're old enough to know better!" said Julian.

"This will tide him over," says Dr. Chizick brusquely, giving Julian a sharp glance. It was a prescription for Valium.

"He's on Ativan, 4mg a day, Doctor."

Dr. Chizick snorted. He had thin grey hairs spouting from his nostrils, and a slick of hair swept sideways across his forehead.

"That's just candy for someone like him! Might as well be giving him colored water! This boy needs something strong, much stronger, an anti-psychotic, to get him under control. Here, if you need to see me again." He pressed a small white business card in my hand. "My private office." The card said: "Frank Chizick, M.D. (Psych)."

Julian during the "psychotic" stage (1989–1996).
This photo is at age 16.

Thirty

D r. Chizick tossed the bottle of Ativan into the garbage. He
had on the same stiff suit and knotted silk burgundy tie. His
hair was slicked back apropos the '50s era; his eyes glinted under
bushy brows.

"That stuff is rubbish. Useless for a boy like him, as I told you,
colored candy!"

We sat opposite Dr. Chizick across a large desk full of important
papers. We'd had our doubts about returning to this psychiatrist,
but what was the alternative? The final weeks of August still
stretched ahead long, intense, and dangerous, and kindly Dr. Sol was
away on vacation.

We tensed, anxious about maybe being forced into accepting
some unknown drugs we didn't want. If this Dr. Chizick could only
give Julian something, not an anti-psychotic – not Haldol – to get
him by, a stopgap until Dr. Sol returned, we'd be relieved. It was
obvious the Ativan was not the answer we'd hoped for.

Dr. Chizick's office was large and formal with grey walls, grey
drapes, grey rows of filing cabinets, a grey sky beyond the window.
There were two adjoining rooms, one for reception, and one for Dr.
Chizick's office. Everything was in its place: a copy of DSM on the
desk next to a brass penholder, papers, and a prescription pad.

"You only have to look at him!"

Julian was pacing as usual round the room, touching things
restlessly and smelling them, muttering to himself.

Dr. Chizick gave Julian a cursory glance. We had been stressing
Julian's abilities, that he could read and write and sing, and had
been doing fairly well after the Listening Centre sessions until this
recent outbreak. After all, I urged, he had managed to stay in the

209

Sluggers all summer; he was still in the Special Needs Summer Teen Programme.

"Of course, it can get pretty difficult," conceded Alec. "That's the problem. When he explodes. Right now it's over the slightest thing. Usually, to do with my wife. If she gets upset, he just over-reacts, can't seem to take it." Alec glanced apologetically my way, he wasn't blaming me.

"Is he suicidal?"

"Well, he bites at his arteries at times, yes he does," Alec hesitated again.

Could a mentally handicapped child reasonably think out the concept of suicide? Suicide implied intentional despair. Julian was more on a constant energy high.

Was that suicide? For that matter, was smashing his head through the front window or tearing his nails down his face and throat suicidal?

Dr. Chizick briskly swept his pen over a prescription pad.

"Perphenazine, 16mg a day, taken in two doses, morning and evening. And 2mg of Cogentin. Be sure to give the Cogentin.

"Get in touch with me in a week or so, to see how it goes."

"But this isn't an anti-psychotic, is it?"

Dr. Chizick frowned. "Perhenazine is one of the major tranquilizers used to treat psychosis. It's one of our most commonly prescribed medications. If you wish to use the term 'anti-psychotic', yes it is used in that sense. After all, your son *is* psychotic, Mr. and Mrs. Orchard, whether you want to face it or not."

"But anti-psychotics are dangerous! They have serious side effects!" I couldn't recall anything about this drug "perphenazine" — I'd only ever heard of Haldol and Mellaril (thioridazine). Perhaps it was a milder version, but Dr. Chizick did not seem the kind to recommend anything mild.

"At the dosage he's on there is little chance of side effects. Some effects show after being on these drugs for many years, but even then they are carefully monitored. Just be sure to give the Cogentin," he insisted.

"Well, why, if there's no chance of side effects?"

Dr. Chizick looked nasty.

"I mean, what exactly is Cogentin? Why do we have to give two drugs?"

"Just give the Cogentin, Mrs. Orchard," said Dr. Chizick, visibly irritated. "It will keep him relaxed. You can even continue the Ativan as well if you want," he seemed amused. "It's about as good as sugared water, and as much use!"

"You must understand, Doctor, we love our son. Naturally we're concerned," said Alec.

"It's just that 16mg seems high! He was only on 0.5mg of Haldol before. We don't want him over-drugged," I added.

"Mr. and Mrs. Orchard, I have patients on 35mg and higher, this is nothing! Just make sure he gets the Cogentin."

We still had little idea of the real function of Cogentin, but it was obviously very important to Dr. Chizick.

Thirty-one

J ulian woke up dazed, his pupils enlarged, his eyes looking distorted. Something was wrong.

Normally he would have kicked up a fuss at missing Wild Water Kingdom, but on this day he was mute when we said he'd better stay home. He sat in a dull way, obediently, on the sofa, staring ahead. Was this what we wanted? What were we doing to our son?

We watched him anxiously all day, noting every symptom for Dr. Chizick: strange, uneven gait, shoulder muscles twitching, spaced out; he hardly recognized us.

Unhappily we gave 8mg perphenazine and 1mg Cogentin as directed at bedtime.

The next morning Julian wanted to go back to Summer Day Camp. Was he a bad boy? he kept asking. It seemed a good sign, that he was alert; perhaps he was adjusting to the drug so we let him go. We determined to go back to Dr. Chizick that morning and ask if the dosage could be lowered by half: 8mg of perphenazine total and no Cogentin.

Once again, we faced Dr. Chizick in his inner office. He did not hide his annoyance, insisting that 16mg was a perfectly acceptable dose for Julian. Reluctantly, Dr. Chizick finally agreed to compromise and drop the dose to 12mg perphenazine in total and 1mg of Cogentin, "against his better judgment."

But it was already too late. At that very moment, Julian was undergoing a severe drug reaction. His group was bowling at Prime Bowlerama that morning. The counselors later informed me that at about 11:15 Julian began complaining of pain in his neck and head.

Suddenly his head began to twist sideways in a gruesome spasm, frightening everyone, including himself. It locked sideways at ninety degrees on his shoulder. He kept trying to swivel it back, crying out in pain. His legs began to shake, giving way several times. A makeshift "bed" was set up on the floor and a sweater wrapped around his neck. The head of the program, Alice Cheng, was called.

Annie Cheng's report later verified what exactly had happened.

Community Living Summer Teen Programme
August 4, 1993.

Dear Mrs. Orchard:

In response to the incident that took place concerning Julian on Thursday, July 29h, 1993, I have written this report in summary of my observations.

I was contacted by Joe Pasquali (Support Worker) to come to Prime Bowl because Julian Orchard was acting strangely and was in a lot of pain. I hurried to Prime Bowl and approached Julian who by then was holding his neck, which was twisted around, and repeatedly saying "It hurts." I asked him to sit down, but he kept leaning on the counter and placing his head on the counter. I then called his home and since I was unable to contact Mrs. Orchard, I then contacted Mrs. MacPhail, the Emergency Contact. She agreed to pick him up and take him to her home so that he could lie down. During the wait Julian asked me to "touch" his neck and so I massaged it; during this time he was in obvious pain and was crying. He started to walk around again and soon became very weak in the legs and needed to lie down on the floor. This lasted about an hour, until Mrs. MacPhail arrived to take him home. I left a message for Mrs. Orchard so that she would know what had happened and where Julian would be when she arrived to pick him up.

Sincerely yours,
Alice Cheng.
Supervisor, Summer Teen Day Programme

Seeing it written out objectively in some succinct order clarified the issue for us — No one had thought to call an ambulance. When I asked why they hadn't, the counselors, all young university students, said they hadn't understood what was happening and expected the spasm to pass. They'd thought it might be an epileptic seizure which they'd been trained to cope with: lie the patient on his side, put nothing in the mouth, wait it out and in the meanwhile call the parents.

Julian's head remained twisted and this was how I found him at 4:30 P.M. when I finally arrived at Mrs. McPhail's house, our emergency contact person where Julian had been taken.

"Mommy!" he cried as soon as I stepped into the living-room. I tried not to react. His head had been at that angle all afternoon, for six hours total, admitted Mrs. McPhail. She also had not called an ambulance; she had expected Julian's head to right itself. She was a single parent with a developmentally challenged boy of her own; she'd done what she could. I thanked her, but there was no time to lose, it was essential to get Julian to Dr. Chizick for help. I wanted Dr. Chizick to see the effects of the drug for himself before it was too late.

I drove straight to Dr. Chizick's office with Julian lying across the back seat moaning and holding his neck.

"Good God . . . what the?" Dr. Chizick half rose from his chair in the inner office as we burst in. "Do you realize I have a *client* in progress, Mrs. Orchard?"

The client, a middle-aged woman dabbing at her eyes, gaped in horror as Julian advanced faceless, grotesque, arms in motion above his head — the moment transfixed in time. I was frightened myself.

I'd expected Dr. Chizick to drop everything to attend to him. What I got was a rush of dismissives: the spasm was a mere side effect; a temporary dystonic reaction; it looked more alarming than it really was; these things happen, just give extra 2mg Cogentin; there was no need to overreact — such as coming into his office unannounced, "without appointment." I wondered if Dr. Chizick would be so complacent if his own head were twisted sideways for six hours? I was confused, amazed that Dr. Chizick was not surprised and shocked at the drug reaction. He wanted us out of his office. Out! Out! Out!

"A tradition of patient care" read the logo on the letterhead. The letter was from Dr. Hook, Chief Psychiatrist at the hospital, to whom we had decided to turn for help. But he seemed no less surprised about Julian's drug reaction than Dr. Chizick.

August 30, 1993.
Dear Mr. & Mrs..Orchard:

> *I am pleased to be able to tell you that I have now met with Dr. Chizick and have also received his written report concerning his treatment of your son, Julian. While, of course, I do appreciate the concerns that you have expressed in your letter of August 2, 1993, and while I regret the distress that your son Julian experienced, it is my opinion, following thorough investigation, that Dr. Chizick's treatment of your son was appropriate, and in no way negligent . . .*
>
> *The use of Perphenazine, an anti-psychotic medication, to assist in the control of behavioural symptoms in patients with autism is quite standard medical practice. The dose suggested by Dr. Chizick, 16mg per 24 hours, is well within the acceptable therapeutic range, being large enough to control symptomatology, but not too large as to cause excessive sedation. Unfortunately Perphenazine, as with any other phenothiazine drug, carries the risk of extra-pyramidal side-effects. These side-effects are most commonly either prevented or controlled by the prescription of the anti-parkinsonian drug, Cogentin.*
>
> *I can only express my regrets that your son did experience a not too uncommon side-effect of the drug Perphenazine.*

The conclusion he came to was that Dr. Chizick's choice of dosage was *"quite standard medical practice."* It was signed: Dr.. Cecil Hook. M.B., B.S., F.R.C. (Psych.).

Well. That certainly put everything in perspective. Anyone who got his head twisted backwards for six hours from treatment with drugs was simply suffering from "a not too uncommon side effect." Case closed.

And that essentially was how it remained despite a subsequent interview with Dr. Hook himself and an appeal to the College of Physicians & Surgeons of Ontario, which promised to look into the matter — *"Protecting the public . . . guiding the profession."*

"You mean you actually reported Dr. Chizick to the College of Physicians and Surgeons?" asked Polly, excited. "Mom, what's going on?"

"For once in your life you're showing guts!" e-mailed Elsie.

But it was Jules' unnecessary suffering that had spurred me. It was soon evident that we were but parents pitting ourselves against the expertise of professionals, with only the *Compendium of Pharmaceuticals & Specialties* (CPS) from the local drug store to back us up. But the CPS *did* cite the recommended dose, a point I stressed in my letter to Dr. Hook and the College:

> *We feel that Dr. Chizick failed to assess our son's needs individually — we feel that 16mg was far too high a starting dose, causing our son to suffer unnecessarily. C.P.S. and The Canadian Medical Association's Guide to Prescription Drugs states that the maximum adult dose recommended is 24mg.*

A well-crafted letter of apology from Dr. Chizick followed forwarded by the Public Complaints & Investigations Department of the College. It gave us a sense of just how nebulous and indeterminate the issue of dosage could be . . .

"*Dosage was a problem,*" wrote Dr. Chizick, "*and in my experience a low dosage might have caused agitation and a slightly higher dosage might cause spasm which although distressing would quickly respond in a short time to Cogentin.*"

But how high was a "slightly higher" dosage – 10mg? 16mg? He added: "*I sincerely apologise for the misunderstanding and the discomfort to your son.*"

I could sense the danger of the real issue being bypassed, that of individualizing treatment to the needs of the patient. The complaint was filed away for "future reference," assured the patient representative; we had to settle for that. After all, Dr. Chizick hadn't deliberately set out to torture our son, etc, etc. It was so exhausting.

"Look, why don't you see Dr. Huggins, Joe Huggins?" said Rolph Schellenberg at Kerry's Place.

We were dropping Julian off for our third and last respite weekend of the year. Julian would be back at school in a week.

Rolph had listened to the story of Julian's summer, smiling in his kindly way at "the summer from hell."

"Dr. Huggins will put Jules right in no time, he's done wonders with the kids here," Rolph urged.

He meant well, but we weren't keen on seeing yet another psychiatrist.

"Oh, but Dr. Huggins isn't a psychiatrist," said Rolph. "He's just an ordinary doctor – except he's not ordinary."

Part Five

Dr. Joseph Huggins

Thirty-two

D r. Huggins was a graduate of University of Toronto Medical School. He turned out to be a short, stocky, intensely sincere-looking man, middle-aged, with a bristly black crew cut and twinkling eyes. He was from Trinidad, of Chinese origin, and spoke with a rich West Indian lilt.

"Man, just listen to that language," he observed. "Is he ever high-functioning!"

Julian was darting in and out of the tiny office, very excited.

"Huggins, Huggins," Julian was going, twirling a tongue depressor. "Now don't be *touching* things, Julian, you know Dr. Huggins won't like it, people don't *like* it . . . You have to be persponsible."

"I guess you must have already heard him outside," we were apologetic.

Dr. Huggins shared offices with four other physicians in the Medical Arts building located in Don Mills, a suburb of Toronto. Julian had been pacing up and down the reception area, laughing and talking to himself, waving his arms to the interest of the packed waiting room. But besides being a family doctor with his own practice, Dr. Huggins was medical consultant for Kerry's Place Autism Services in the greater Toronto area; he had a great deal of experience helping autistic individuals.

"Oh, he did come in here a couple of times checking me out. I'm not sure the patient appreciated it though," Dr. Huggins chuckled.

He had been bent over a computer when we walked in. The screen was filled with weird-looking lines and squiggles. A diagram on the wall had the same weird convoluted look. "An algorithm," explained Dr. Huggins; a flowchart he was working on, a universal diagnostic and treatment tool to control abnormal rage behaviors in autism. He aimed to make it applicable to any autistic individual. We told Dr. Huggins about Julian's latest outbreak smashing his head through the big front picture window at home. One false move and his neck would have been severed – only it hadn't. He'd pulled it back through the jagged raw glass with barely a scratch and punched himself instead, both victim and torturer, Jules, our son!

On and on we went suddenly unable to stop, the list was endless, the litany of pain, of sufferance, of Jules' desperate anguish, agony of spirit. Alec held out a letter we'd received that very week from Mr. Collie and Dr. Bland. It suggested we try Julian in CPRI, the Children's Psychiatric Research Institute, a treatment facility in London, Ontario. Dr. Bland favored a short stint in Phoenix for Julian in the fall, "get a handle on Julian Orchard before the school year got underway" sort of thing. The enclosed brochure said: *Residential Assessment and Treatment.* "Phoenix" was a dual-diagnosis unit for adolescents through seventeen years of age with a developmental disability and "severe psychiatric and/or behavioral disorder." But CPRI was tertiary care. "Tertiary" meant "end of the line," last resort. When everything else had failed. And how short was "a short stint"? What was Dr. Bland trying to tell us? *"I think what we're trying to say here, Mrs. Orchard, is that we've pretty much exhausted our options concerning Julian . . . "* The address said: 600 Sanitarium Road.

Dr. Huggins nodded patiently. He had heard it all before, experienced much of it himself first-hand with his own autistic son, Jonathan, who at fourteen had once spent an entire weekend desperately sawing down a pine tree doing a costly amount of damage in the garden. Nothing could stop him, Dr. Huggins recalled. His home had been regularly "under siege," he added wryly.

Dr. Huggins stroked Julian's hand, and Julian let him. "That's good, Julian, good."

"Dr. Huggins wears glasses."

What Dr. Huggins really wanted to know was whether Julian's face flushed a lot when he "paced." How often were his hands, his palms, sweaty like today? All the time? Most of the time? Some of the time? How rapid was his cycling? Dr. Huggins was asking questions no one had ever broached with us.

"Cycling?"

"Shift in mood," explained Dr. Huggins. "Shift in behavior,

personality, too, A Dr. Jekyll and Mr. Hyde sort of thing. Sometimes manageable, calm, then changing, maybe the same day, the same hour, in some clients even moment to moment. Lots of pacing, talking out. Labile. Like Julian now. . . . "

Labile was one of those psychiatric terms.

"Arising from an over-reactive adrenaline system," went on Dr. Huggins.

Most autistic individuals had an immature unstable adrenaline system that was in a constant state of arousal, he explained. Surges of adrenalin flooded the body culminating in violent unpredictable rage behavior and the phenomenal strength that went with it, which was why three police officers had trouble holding Julian down.

Dr. Huggins had found that anti-psychotic drugs used mainly as a major tranquilizer tended to be ineffective in controlling rage behaviors in autism. He had taken a more physiological approach, and found the use of beta-blockers like Inderal (also known by its generic name of propranolol) to be often more effective in controlling behaviors like Julian's. The drug worked by stabilizing the adrenalin part of the autonomic nervous system, preventing it from being over-activated, keeping the individual calm. The only caution was for clients suffering from broncospasm, bronchial asthma, or sinus bradycardia. Since Julian suffered from none of these ailments, Dr. Huggins felt he would benefit from being on a low dose of the drug.

Julian exhibited adrenalin-related "beta" rage symptoms. Most juvenile autistics tended to be this type, which was more out-of-the-blue and very explosive but of short duration. We'd always thought rage was just rage, but it seemed there were two types, "beta" and "alpha." Alpha rage, driven primarily by noradrenaline, was the more deadly variety and often without remorse: cold, premeditated, *targeted* and locked-on in its violence. Dr. Huggins did not feel from his own observation and our description of Julian that Julian was an "alpha." After all, he didn't *plan* to kill me — or did I want to see it that way?

I pushed back a sudden twinge of doubt: what proof was there of any of this substantially, as compared, for instance, with Alec's heart attack, verifiable on an EEG and angiogram: verifiable, X-ray-able, tangible, actual. Dr. Huggins was still going on observed behaviors. But that was all anyone ever had to go on, he pointed out. There was no disease, "rage," inside Julian. There was, and always would be, only observable "symptoms" and "behaviors." And it was the behaviors you had to get under control when all was said and done, said Dr. Huggins pragmatically. "I'm not claiming to *cure* anything, I'm not Jesus Christ."

He recommended starting Julian on 20mg propranolol twice daily, given Julian's age and size. Meanwhile he wanted to give Julian a thorough medical check-up, starting with taking his pulse before putting him on medication.

Of everything about Dr. Huggins — his warmth, his kindness, and his openness — this impressed us the most. Dr. Huggins was ordering a full range of tests that included a thyroid check and blood sugar test. The lab form was soon criss-crossed with ticks for CBC, platelet count, BUN, creatinine, alkaline, phosphatase, SGOT, SGPT. This Dr. Huggins was nothing if not thorough!

"Well Julian, let's take your pulse."

Once again Julian allowed Dr. Huggins to hold his wrist without taking off, enjoying the attention. He giggled as Dr. Huggins counted rapidly, "One, two, . . . "

"Ugh-huh, so high you can barely get it -140 plus!" he exclaimed moments later, not surprised. "When that comes down, you won't know him. He's gonna be a pussycat!"

Dr. Huggins was not one to push. He suggested we read his article, *"Managing Rage Behaviours in Autism, Taking a Different Approach,"* before making up our minds. It had just been published in the June issue of *Ontario Medicine*, 1993. We read:

> *The explosive violence, intensity and energy expended by an autistic patient during a rage attack simply has to be witnessed to be believed.*
> *The day-to-day management of an autistic individual exhibiting chronic adrenergic over-arousal and rage behaviors represents a parent's worst nightmare and a treating physician's dilemma . . .*

Dr. Huggins explained that something had had to be done, and it had been left to physicians like himself to come up with some sort of treatment. *"Many family doctors are 'forced' to treat autism in their own practices."*

Dr. Huggins estimated that by the time an autistic patient ended up in his office he'd likely already been through a whole range of psychotropic drugs that included benzodiazepines, thioridazine, Haldol (haloperidol), fenfluramine, clomipramine, fluoxetine (Prozac), buspirone (Buspar), methylphenidate, desipramine, carbamazepine (Tegretol), and lithium, to name but a few. The high dosage often recommended for neuroleptic drugs increased the risk of irreversible tardive dyskenesia, the dreaded "TD," particularly dangerous for autistic children, he noted, since its early symptoms were virtually indistinguishable from the many bizarre and idiosyncratic behaviors of autistic children. In selected cases, he had found the best initial success so far was with the use of beta-blockers. But the use of propranolol for this indication was not an officially approved indication by Health and Welfare Canada. Beta-blockers were normally recommended to lower blood pressure in heart patients, which meant Dr. Huggins was using them "off label," a not uncommon practice in psychiatry, especially when dealing with autistic/PDD patients. Doctors and psychiatrists using this management option would have to do so at their own risk after carefully weighing up the benefits versus side effect profile with the full knowledge of the parent or guardian.

Polly was now at the University of Toronto working toward a degree in exceptionality and human learning. She had been doing some research of her own for a paper on medications and autism. "Mom!" she cried excitedly on seeing Dr. Huggins' article, "There's these guys R. Ankermann and John Ratey with all this research on this very topic!"

Ankermann had already drawn attention to the two types of rage in autism that Huggins himself had observed. Ankerman pointed out that epinephrine in the body stimulated beta adrenaline receptors causing "beta adrenergic rage." Norepinephrine stimulated alpha adrenaline receptors resulting in "alpha adrenergic rage."

In 1989, researchers John Ratey, D.J. Luchins and D. Dojka had found that the use of beta-blockers like propranolol decreased aggression by soothing the over-reactive adrenaline system. Ratey concluded in 1987 that hyperarousal actually caused the sensimotor rituals! But it had been left to someone like Dr. Huggins to organize this research and put it into actual practice.

However, you wondered if the significance of having his work portrayed as alternative, outside the mainstream, outside the DSM, would affect acceptance of his methodology. The editor of *Medicine Today*, Elizabeth Watson, had noted that Dr. Huggins had "moved from more conventional treatment modes to more 'desperate' methods."

Yet Dr. Huggins was obviously eager to consult with his peers. There was something surely open-hearted, a trust in human goodness, in the Parting Comments of his article:

"I would be happy to hear from any doctor who may have any comments, suggestions or experience in dealing with this most difficult area of medical management."

We began Julian on 20mg of propranolol twice daily on September 2, 1993, and anxiously awaited the next morning . . .

Thirty-three

J ulian strolled, unbelievably casual, into the kitchen dressed for
school.

"Mommy cooking breakfast." He peered into the frying pan.

"Eggs 'n bacons," he smiled. "Julian have eggs 'n bacons. And
toast," he added, looking at me. That was what was different. Alec
put down his coffee.

It was stunning how immediate was the effect of the drug.
Julian was so calm, smiling, relaxed. He remained that way for the
next few days, unprotesting at the new shoes, new pants for school,
new class, new teacher. We were fascinated, tense. How long would
it last? We watched cautiously, unable to grasp it, like stillness after
torrents . . . calm after shattering storm.

We took his pulse daily as Dr. Huggins had shown us, and
recorded it. Surprisingly Julian had submitted without protest to my
taking his pulse. At first it was well above 140. A normal pulse was
80! Over the next few weeks, it fluctuated between 68 and 64, a big
drop from the original 140+. Taking the pulse was an essential part
of the medication protocol. It formed the base line before medication was started with which to compare later, giving us insight into
Julian's physiological — and therefore his mental — state as never
before. For more than three years Julian had been running around
with an elevated pulse. Who knew exactly what it had been!
Gradually the medication stabilized at 120mg daily, still a low
dosage considering that the maximum was 240mg per day for
Julian.

The propranolol worked successfully for a year and a half, until Julian was nearly eighteen. There were times we wished there were another way, that we did not have to use drugs at all. You had that unhappy feeling each time you handed over the small green pill, and watched Jules swallow it so innocently, guilelessly. "Your pill, Jules," he mumbled to himself. "Dr. Huggins said you have to take your pill like a good boy."

The pill so small, so pale, green, deceptive . . . a compound of chemicals pressed together into a tablet by some drug manufacturer somewhere responsible for this transformation in Jules, our loved one. There was no denying it.

Yet we were proud and excited, it was only natural to want everyone to see the difference in Jules – and they did. "What happened to Julian?" "What happened to your son?" cried teachers at The Meadows.

Jules sitting in his desk for the first time in how long, not since his success with auditory integration at The Listening Centre. Jules doing operations on his calculator again, + − % x. Jules filling up the pop machine outside Room 8 with Cokes and Sprites, putting in the change, slamming the door and clicking it locked, with minimum supervision. Here were binders full of cogent work for the first time since "it" had taken over. His science folder contained the Rules of Health: Poison Signs and Labels of Household Cleaners and Detergents. "Never, never swallow Lysol, Dr. Huggins," said Julian.

Though Jules could not seem to grasp fractions, you knew he knew the difference between a half a chicken order and a quarter at Swiss Chalet by his wails!

And maybe he never would be able to get "Deadly Differences:" *"Here lies the body of Jill: she died when she saw her credit card bill."*

"See, that's funny, Jules."

Blank response.

"Jill *died.*"

But his work contract was now regularly stamped with stars and happy faces: math, writing, reading, listening, painting, puppets. Jules was part of the group, part of The Meadows! His report card for 1994 stated: "Julian has made positive progress in social functions. He now participates in assemblies, eats in the school café, attends school outings. His self-awareness and self-esteem have increased."

He carried his behavior contract everywhere with him, even to the toilet.

My Contract

1. Coming off the bus well.
2. Coming in the classroom at 8:50.
3. Write down daily plan.
4. Good behavior at break.
5. Listen to instructions from all staff.
6. Good behavior at lunch.
7. Good behavior at afternoon break.
8. Not talking or yelling excessively.
9. Did not wander the halls at will.

Yet Jules still needed us, perhaps always would; someone to be the signpost, the "shadow self" Dr. Cantor had described in *The Schizophrenic Child* so long ago, steering him through ordinary everyday life that most people didn't have to think about.

"People don't like it, Jules, they don't like you touching things, smelling their Colgate."

We were in aisle two, "Personal Care," at Hoppers Pharmacy amongst the mouthwashes.

You can touch *some* things, you concede. Newspapers, magazines. You can even pick up bottles of shampoo, Jules, just don't unscrew them.

We switch over to malls, to large community stores like K-Mart and Zellers with their long, anonymous, mainly deserted aisles where every Saturday Julian could wander at will sampling the samples, his favorites being Allure perfume and after-shave lotion. Who knew how many bottles of Old English Leather bought by unsuspecting customers had been sniffed by Julian.

Once I caught a glimpse of him down an aisle lightly swinging a bag of bath salts in his hands in silence. The bag moved hypnotically back and forth in a lilting motion, Julian with that dreamy fixed expression on his face so like the little boy he had once been, the autism still pushing through his consciousness despite the drugs.

We took up journal writing again. The orange exercise books showed his daily doings. They included the strange weird rows of self-portraits that had never changed over the years: arms and legs emerging from his head colored vigorous green, enormous pointed ears, a thatch of hair, and an intense daubed moustache. "That's a nice moustache, Jules," I commented encouragingly. "Very nice."

Jules smiled, pleased, fingering his moustache. "Mommy the cat," he went affectionately looking at me, stroking my chin as you would a cat, our cat.

I was now expected to say in a giggly way, "Don't Jules, it tickles!"

To which he chuckled, "Julian tickling Mommy," returning to his drawings.

Once again it was hard to find reading material for a seventeen-year-old autistic young man with a grade one reading vocabulary, but you thought, "I must take advantage of this while it lasts." For who knew really how long it would last? So back to Port Credit Library and the section of "high interest/low vocabulary" young adult books put out by East End Literacy Press in Toronto again, something familiar.

But in the face of such progress, I hadn't taken into account Julian's autism. We had the new novels and some teen magazines of cars and sports laid out on the table. I'd planned for him to cut out familiar pictures of baseball and swimming, activities he enjoyed, and make an album when he suddenly jumped up, agitated.

"Where's Mr. Mugs, Mom? I want Mr. Mugs!"

"You said you didn't like Mr. Mugs!" I kept my voice even; yet I was curious. Did Julian remember the rage, his passionate words that time? Usually he passed through rage attacks like an amnesia.

"I do like Mr. Mugs! I do! I do!"

Was this the signal for an attack? Julian rushed anxiously to the music room cupboard and amazingly pulled out the worn copy of Mr. Mugs from its exact old place on the second shelf.

"Aren't you too old for Mr. Mugs now, Jules?" I hinted, you had to go carefully, this could go either way; this was one of those moments.

The idea seemed to bemuse him.

"Yes, you're old, Julian."

He seemed to take satisfaction in this, this was corroborated: he was a different Julian now, he was older, had a moustache, had a man's fanny pack round his waist to carry his popsicle money and bus tokens in. "You're too old for Mr. Mugs!"

Nevertheless it remained an option resting on the table next to the jam-pot. Big, fluffy, old English sheepdog Mugs bounding happily forever after his ball. Just being there keeping some link open, some fusing he needed.

But the most dramatic noticeable improvement that everyone was talking about, was still the change in Julian at school. So it wasn't a flash in the pan. *"Julian has had the courage to take part in all activities offered in his school curriculum,"* went his report card again. He had received a Student of the Week Award, his photo on the display in the school hall. He'd even participated in school cricket!

His work "Towards Independence" in the Work Experience Programme cited Julian doing light assembly work two days a week, using a time-card to clock in and out of work. He'd worked on the computer keyboard. He learned to use the telephone in emergency (did he know what that meant though?) to call 911 for: Fire, Ambulance, Police!

He had been promoted to washing and polishing cars in CarWash, using the jig counting nails and screws for Canadian Tire.

"What do you do in Work Experience, Julian?" asked Dr. Huggins at one check-up.

"Nails, nails, nails."

For the first time he began walking close to us on our evening walks, instead of pounding the pavement half a mile ahead. He stopped talking out loud in an urgent voice as he walked along, stopped berating himself so much in public, and gesticulating like a maniac. People stopped looking at us wherever we went.

He sat with us at the table now at McDonald's, enjoying our company, instead of pacing restlessly up and down the aisles or back and forth to the washroom. His face was relaxed, the flush gone. His hands stopped sweating profusely. There were still moments, such as the time Alec noticed Julian with a wad of gum in his mouth coming out of the washroom at McDonald's.

"Julian, where did you get that gum from? Thelma, did you give him gum?"

"No."

Alec looked queazy, "Oh no!" He dashed into the washroom, emerging looking greenish. "It's gone!"

"What's gone?"

"The gum stuck to the urinal. Julian did you get the gum from where you do pee-pee in the toilet?"

Julian threw out the gum. "Julian took it, Dad! Julian's a bad boy! I won't do that no more! I promise me, Dad! I promise me!"

"Daddy's not angry! But that is a very . . . very dirty, dangerous thing to do, Julian. Never, never, *never* take someone else's gum, especially out of a toilet. Been in someone else's mouth and pee-pee! Very very dirty, make Julian sick! Very sick!"

Dr. Huggins was remarkably stoic. He had long since come to the conclusion autistic children were protected by Heaven. "Yes, you and I might get sick if we chewed gum from a urinal in McDonald's! But not them. God is looking out for them, that's the only conclusion you can come to!"

So we were shocked — indignant — to receive a suspension letter concerning Julian from Mr. Collie:

"This will serve to notify you . . . suspension made under the authority of the Education Act, Section 23 (1) . . . moral tone of the school . . .", etc.

"Man, they sure are throwing the book at you," grinned Dr. Huggins.

But the propranolol was working, he insisted, handing back the letter. "He *is* blocked." There was certainly no need to up the dose. Whatever the incident had been at school — the letter cited "unco-operative resistive behavior" — Julian was already over it: his palms were dry, his pulse normal.

The last paragraph said: *"You have the right to appeal this suspension. . ."* something we had never presumed to act upon. But for the first time a suspension struck us as unfair especially when you considered that it was the school system that had pressured us to put our son on medication. That very fact changed the focus somehow.

A few phone calls to other boards revealed crisis intervention teams in place to deal with rage behavior, special time-out rooms, staff specially trained to calm the situation, strong parent-teacher committees with input from parents on discipline . . .

Suddenly on our side with support was Mrs. Boopsingh and a Mrs. Clement, whose daughter Amelia was a spitter. Amelia could shoot spitballs a distance of ten feet! And, yes, it was disconcerting and infuriating for staff. But between us we counted more than fifty suspensions over a three-year period! That was to be the mainstay of our appeal to the next Special Education Advisory Committee meeting at the Board of Education: that suspensions only punished parents who surely had more than enough punishment to bear.

"Way to go, Mrs. Orchard!" exulted Mrs. Boopsingh, twitching her sari. Mrs. Boopsingh had turned out to be no informidable opponent herself. "Instead of concentrating on what the kids *can't* do why don't they program for what they *can!*" she fired. Dr. Bland flushed pink. Scribbling furiously on a piece of paper as he sat on committee, he looked disconcerted, even reproachful. What was happening here? In the tizzy that followed he was heard to insinuate about "teachers who bite the hand that feeds them . . . "

It was a criticism I was to hear often in the days to come. But wasn't I *improving* the hand that fed me? Suspensions of developmentally challenged students began to drop dramatically. A Parents' -Teacher Council now met monthly in the school café. There was a new time-out room, and not just your regular Time-Out but a "Snoezelen" Room, specially designed to "provide pleasurable sensory stimulation and recreation for people with profound or multiple disabilities." The idea was to catch Julian's outbreaks before they happened. Soothing psychedelic womb-like lighting wavering across walls and ceilings. Fluffy cuddly carpeting, soft chairs and couches, soothing Nature music of waterfalls or melodies from happy musicals . . Now at the slightest provocation Julian was whisked into the Snoezelen Room, the Snooze Room as he called it, to sink into a puffed beanbag chair and listen to the somnolent strains of ocean waves lapping the shore.

So Jules was still a success. At eighteen he was transferred to a satellite class – at last! – The class encouraged more academics, integration with regular "normal" high school students in a peer-tutoring program, and meant that Julian was, well, in high school! "I'm going to Polly's school," said Julian. "Mr. Sully is my teacher and

Ms. Bryce came as well because she loves me so much." Ms. Bryce had opted to accompany Julian to his new school so that he would have a familiar face to relate to.

"That's nice you have Ms. Bryce, Jules, she must like you a lot. And you like your new class?"

"Yep."

It was a struggle to find more words that weren't in the inevitable Socratic question mode that was conversation with Julian.

"So tell me the names of the kids, your new friends."

Jules' face cleared.

"Robbie Ramsay, Francesco di Amaricchio, Amar Singh, Betsy Pollack, Meena El Mohammed, Caroline Farquar," he responded happily. How like Jules to give the exact full names.

Mr. Sully noted that Julian had "adjusted very quickly, quietly, and with dignity." Jules was making "great strides" he informed us in his academic skills, and was learning cursive writing.

We were particularly thrilled at his success in integration with regular high school students in the Peer Tutoring Programme. Julian had participated in ping-pong, swimming, and basketball, wowing everyone by being the highest scorer and M.V.P. – and without even *looking* at the net, the students marveled. Even Dr. Bland was impressed.

Of course CPRI was now a thing of the past, thanks to propranolol. I thought it might be helpful to other parents if I wrote an article about Julian's success on Dr. Huggins' protocol for *Rendezvous*, the newsletter put out by Autism Society Canada. A photo of Julian reading peacefully at home on the sofa subsequently appeared on the front page. The accompanying blurb said:

> *A tranquil activity such as reading is now among Julian Orchard's many pleasures since innovative use of a medication calmed his autistic rage behaviors . . .*

The article circulated to branches across Canada. There was an unexpected spate of letters in response, one from a mother isolated out in the frozen vastness of Labrador-Newfoundland whose autistic teenager ransacked the fridge in rage attacks . . . they had ended up bolting it to the sundeck outside. It was a cry out of a darkness only too real and intense.

I wondered if I should send the article to various treatment centers and hospitals around Ontario. Professionals might be interested in Julian's case that showed how a prospective client was able to be managed successfully on a regimen without being on antipsychotic drugs, who in fact no longer needed their services, I enthused to Dr. Bland.

"Well, well, we're getting to be quite the little expert on medication aren't we, Mrs. Orchard?"

Dr. Bland wasn't sure that psychiatrists would take kindly to a parent proffering advice.

I had a sudden image of myself passionately displaying photocopied pages from the *Compendium of Pharmaceuticals & Specialties* before the Chief of Psychiatry that time, citing page and line of dosage concerning perphenazine, my proof from CPS itself in the dispute over Dr. Chizick's use of medication. Dr. Hook's lip had curled. He had had a long lean face and aquiline nose, thin lips drawn in a thin line. "Actually, I'm afraid we could wish at times, Mrs. Orchard, that the general public did not always have access to CPS. Does more harm than good . . . "

Dr. Bland was observing me curiously.

"You know these alternate therapies, these so-called miracle cures never really work. Swimming with porpoises in the ocean, swallowing snake venom . . . and now this drug protocol of Dr. Huggins, 'the propranolol Doctor,' " Dr. Bland chuckled. He had made a point of reading Dr. Huggins' article in *Ontario Medicine* and had even attended his workshop at the Geneva Centre on "Managing Rage Behaviours." He liked to keep up with any development in the field but took a "wait-and-see" attitude.

"Of course, you mean well, but the fact is, Mrs. Orchard, we always have to come back to *proven* medication, I'm afraid."

I posted off the article anyway. There was little response. A child psychiatrist from one hospital in southwestern Ontario did ring to thank me for the information. She was familiar, she said, with Dr. Huggins' work with propranolol, which she admired, and agreed that propranolol could "alleviate anxiety" in autistic children. Others were more reserved: propranolol had not been tested in "double-blind, placebo-controlled, cross-over trials," the "gold standard" of research.

Case studies and anecdotal testimony of parents was deemed "the lowest form of research," and did not count for much.

Thirty-four

D r. Huggins was seated as usual in front of the computer working on an algorithm. Other doctors were beginning to close their offices and leave for the night. Outside the window the setting sun gleamed across the courtyard flagged by trees, soft ashes and maples. The Medical Arts building was tall, of pale concrete and glass on Don Mills Road, opposite the Science Centre.

The grey paving stones had been pinkish in the evening light as we'd steered Julian across the parking lot. As usual, we were the last family on the waiting list. The secretary always booked us the closing appointment so that Dr. Huggins could spend more time with us; we were often still talking together at ten o'clock, sometimes later, who knew when Dr. Huggins himself finished up. By the time we left the other offices were usually long vacated, eerily so. Gleaming footrests of the examining tables looked oddly grotesque in the emptiness as we'd walked down the hall, glittering instruments hung up for the night on hooks. Empty corridors echoed with the clank of night staff, cleaners' mops swishing the floors. Dr. Huggins, with dark-encircled eyes, turned towards us with interest.

"You won't get no stickers!" Julian was yelling. He had pushed his way in and stuck his face right up to Dr. Huggins' nose. "You'll have to go straight into the gross motor room where you belong, Julian Orchard, with Amelia Quentin!" he snarled. "Amelia Quentin is a spitter!" he added by way of explanation.

Oh Jules, there was so little we could do for you, driven like this, I thought: the madman anguished yet again. He was eighteen.

"So who's this Amelia Quentin?"

"Well that's the point, Dr. Huggins. She's not even in The Meadows any more, she graduated last year. They haven't been in the same class for four years!"

But Julian had been going on about her for weeks. There was no violence yet just this non-stop excitation day and night, Julian pacing the living-room until five in the morning sighed Alec, his nerves frayed. Going without sleep was worse in its way than dealing with an all-out rage attack.

Dr. Huggins had already put Julian on an extra drug called clonidine (Dixarit), 0.025mg/day, the lowest dose available in Canada, earlier that year. Julian had begun to have a few serious "breakouts" despite the propranolol – sudden short intense rage attacks – the "alpha" rage we had often suspected and feared. The pharmacist's eyebrow had raised when she'd read the prescription – for Julian. "This is usually prescribed for menopausal women," she'd muttered.

It had been disappointing that propranolol alone had not been enough to control Julian after nearly two years of success, but it wasn't unusual for this to happen, Dr. Huggins had explained. As someone like Julian matured, adrenaline-driven over-reactivity often shifted to a more "noradrenaline-driven" alpha-type dyscontrol, with the result that an attack becomes more focused and intense. Julian was now classified as *"beta-alpha"* rage combination, "mixed rage."

Like the propranolol, the clonidine (Dixarit) had worked wonders at first. Rage attacks had stopped. Julian's life had resumed its round of school, special olympics one evening a week, Saturday morning swimming lessons with Fred, occasional respite weekends at Kerry's Place; there'd be the occasional burst of restless behavior but nothing unmanageable – until now, August. He was about to start his final years at school, which would signify the end of his time forever at The Meadows, did he understand that? Or was it anxiety once again that summer was coming to an end, no more shorts and sandals he loved so much?

"If we could only book them into the Caribbean for life, half their problems would be solved!" sighed Dr. Huggins. He tended to believe in the influence of climate on autistic individuals. He'd noticed far less rage outbreaks in summer. Fall and early spring, on the other hand, always seemed to be "difficult" times for the autistic population, seasons of change.

The sudden pacing, verbalizing and mood shifts that we were witnessing in Julian again was something Dr. Huggins explained was *"atypical rapid cycling bipolar mood instability,'* an important component of dysfunctional behavior that tended to be overlooked. It had to be managed separately. With another drug. We tensed.

Dr. Huggins recommended a low dose of Epival (valproic acid, Depakene in the U.S.). Epival was usually used as an anti-convulsant, but it was known also to control mood cycling. He wanted Julian to start on 250mg twice daily.

"I know three drugs seems a lot." Dr. Huggins hesitated, noting the dismay on our faces — *When would this ever end?*

"We've talked about Julian's rapid mood cycling before. In fact, I feel it is linked to Julian's alpha rage."

"But bipolar?"

To us that meant manic-depressive. But Julian was never depressed!

"He doesn't have to be depressed. This form of mood modulation instability can involve rapid shifts with only the 'manic' side coming to the fore." Dr. Huggins hesitated again, noting the weary expression on my face. He wanted us to understand the necessity for several drugs. Julian was so close to the edge, to all-out violence. A sedative action from "mega-dosing," a favorite gripe of his, in his opinion did not represent good quality control.

"It's better for Julian to be on two or three indicated medications at appropriate dosage levels than on a massive dose of a single neuroleptic drug."

I nodded, recalling how the anti-psychotic drug perphenazine had slammed through Julian's brain.

"Another drug!" exclaimed Elsie. She'd phoned to see how Julian was doing, if he was any better now. So she *did* care, then. Elsie always seemed so distant, far away out there in Kitchener-Waterloo at the foot of Chicopee Hill.

"D'you think this guy knows what he's doing, Thel?"

"Well, if he doesn't, no one does."

I tried to explain the meaning of "proactive," sort of controlling a behavior before it happened. "Ugh-h," went Else, "what is he, psychic or something?" The complexity of manic cycling and its terrors, that eternal edge of sorrow and darkness was something that Elsie perhaps could never comprehend but that Dr. Huggins knew, oh so well.

But Elsie wasn't really listening. She was suddenly full of Brett: Brett going off backpacking in British Columbia with a couple of pals, Brett who had just finished high school with a grade-twelve diploma. He sported a wispy goatee, all the rage right then, and a stud through each ear; eager to explore the world on his own, cried Elsie excitedly – and I do share her delight, I do I do. But a stab goes right through me, the old sharp tight pain. Brett grown and gradu-ated, wanting to be off out West like any adventurous young man, while Jules . . . .

But following Dr. Huggins' protocol was going to enable Jules to go backpacking too! Not independently, of course, there must always be protective companions looking out for him, but definitely tenting overnight with friends and workers from Kerry's Place, sleeping in a sleeping bag, hiking, canoeing, *roasting* marshmallows over a campfire, fun fun fun.

And he did. We were packing his bags for the upcoming trip to Inisfil Beach.

"Mom, my creams! Don't forget my creams," said Julian.

"Creams?"

"My sun cream, my shave cream, my bug cream."

"Yes, you'll need lots of mosquito repellant up there, especially in the evening."

I still thrilled at having these precious little dialogues with Julian, which were getting longer over time and more interactional and focused. As Paul Madaule would say: "We are having a conver-sation."

Carefully I zipped his plastic dosa-pack of medication for the week into the toiletry bag; three sets of drugs three times daily, propranolol, clonidine, and now Epival, the most important item in his baggage.

"So what are you going to do up there, Jules, with Phil and Len?"

Julian paused, perplexed, his eyes rolling upwards thoughtfully. He still had difficulty answering such a general question that demanded he relate past incidents to the future.

"Um . . . um. Swim. We swim. We walk. And we get to eat."

Thirty-five

B y now Dr. Huggins was medical consultant for Kerry's Place Autism Services and had the largest primary care and consultative autistic practice of any physician in Canada. Many clients also had other medical and psychiatric diagnoses such as diabetes, hypoglaecemia, hyperthyroidism, ADHD, Tourette's syndrome and schizophrenia in addition to rage behaviors that had to be taken into account. As the editor of *Ontario Medicine* had noted, in 1993, he was regarded as "something of an authority on medication and autism."

Dr. Huggins felt it was time to publish his findings. He first brought out a photocopied handout in 1995, *"The D&T (Diagnostic & Treatment) Model for Managing Self-Injurious Behaviours, Rage & Other Hyperadrenergic Behaviours in the Autistic/PDD/DD Populations."* He had always admired Alec's meticulous record keeping of Julian's pulse and blood pressure readings, and he now incorporated them into Julian's case study in this early version.

Julian was featured as "O.J." to protect his identity. We weren't sure we exactly liked the acronym! He was Case Study #1, "Uncomplicated Mixed Rage:" 1AB2a. Was that really our son, in one neat formula? Apparently "uncomplicated" meant that he had no other comorbid medical or psychiatric disorders; but if Julian was uncomplicated, Alec wanted to know what "complicated" looked like. As we studied the other cases we soon found out. There were worse scenarios than Julian's. One critical component of rage behavior was the added complication of epilepsy that occurred in the autistic/PDD population as high as 25% to 33%, often arising in adolescence. The appearance of a seizure disorder would generate many new variables in drug management that Julian seemed to have been spared so far. Dr. Huggins could only declare, *"One should hope and pray that it does not develop!"*

Julian's "case" included charts delineating his mood patterns and dysfunctional behaviors and response data charts showing his improvement on propranolol and clonidine. Dr. Huggins noted how an excess of both adrenaline and noradrenaline in Julian's sensitive system had given rise to violent dysfunctional behaviors that had needed both a beta-blocker and an alpha a-2 agonist blocking agent, clonidine, to get him under control.

Reading Julian's case study afforded us wonderful insight into how Dr. Huggins actually deduced a client's "behavior sub-type," as well as a pertinent and at times poignant reminder:

> *O.J. was assessed at my office in August, 1993. He was extremely restless and fidgety. He paced around the Clinic's passageways constantly. He was continuously vocal with many echolalic utterances. His face was flushed, his hands were hot and sweaty with a resting tremor and a labile rapid pulse. No rage episodes were witnessed.*

From these observations and checks, Dr. Huggins had assigned an initial diagnostic behavior subtype, using his Behaviour Model Flowchart: *"1A2B (Autistic/Normal/Atypical Rapid Cycling Bipolar/Peripheral-B)."*

Dr. Huggins continued:

> *Beginning in October, 1994, O.J. again began to exhibit worsening hyperadrenergic symptoms. Self-injurious behavior, Free Floating Anxiety and episodic Rage reappeared . . . At this point, O.J.'s parents were introduced to the concept of Multiple Superimposed Behaviour Subtypes. I explained to them that O.J.'s dominant subtype was fully controlled on the 120mg/day of Propranolol, but there was now a second superimposed seasonal subtype needing treatment. Since the undesirable behaviors were more focussed, intense and locked-on, the most likely secondary subtype was Peripheral "Alpha" rage:*
> "1A2a (Autistic/Normal/Atypical Rapid Cycling Bipolar/ Peripheral-a)."

On January 31, 1995, O.J. was started on a low dose a-2 Agonist-Dixarit (Clonidine) 0.025mg/tid with a dramatic improvement in all undesirable behaviors. Propranolol remained unchanged.

In retrospect, based on accurate charting and feedback from O.J.'s parents, O.J. appears to have two extra rough periods annually. The first tends to occur in the late Fall-early Winter and the second in the late winter-early Spring. Many other autistic clients at Kerry's Place appear to exhibit similar seasonal variations.

Dr. Huggins concluded:

With continued observation and accurate charting, the minimal medication requirements for optimal behavior control of O.J. can be achieved.

We realized how lucky we were to have been able to place Julian in Dr. Huggins' practice when we had. Dr. Sol had been supportive of our switch over to Dr. Huggins. Though he was familiar with the use of beta-blockers for behavior control, he did not have the same expertise and know-how as Dr. Huggins to work out such a drug regimen himself. Other parents were reporting great difficulty in getting their family practitioners to implement this management option. Julian would be equally vulnerable should anything happen to Dr. Huggins. We had a sudden dread of him having heart failure – or veering over the rails of the Don Valley Parkway.

Somewhat amused, Dr. Huggins assured everyone that there was more than enough clinical evidence deposited away in the National Library of Canada for his methodology to survive his "eventual earthly demise."

"Well, just watch you don't get struck by flying wheels off a truck, Dr. Huggins," said Alec gloomily.

So when Dr. Huggins published out *The Reference Management Handbook (Diagnostic & Treatment Model – Universal PDD/ADHD/DD)* in 1996 we felt a certain relief. A book was lasting testimony, something tangible for medical professionals to consult for the future.

Getting published had not been easy. Financial aid in the form of grants from leading research and drug companies had been disappointing. Dr. Huggins noted that anything not following "established standard of practice" was held suspect. On the other hand it had meant he'd been free to develop a methodology in his own way – sponsorship would have limited his approach, in fact would have killed it outright, he mused. The book was eventually published by Bitemarks Publication Inc.

The Reference Handbook was a powerful diagnostic tool that even a lay person could grasp once the terminology was understood. Dr. Huggins had used what he termed an evidence-based approach. The very early approach of this methodology utilized a patient's symptoms and behaviors to identify, target and prioritize individual neurotransmitters for control instead of the customary "principal diagnosis-target symptom" approach, which targeted individual symptoms for management. Dr. Huggins was careful to stress this. A "behavior subtype" defined differing degrees of neurotransmitter dysfunction. Dr. Huggins had provided an amazing number – one hundred thirty-seven, meticulously tabulated into a table.

The manual also provided step-by-step procedures for conducting a D&T model "single consultation." A Behaviour Analysis Chart was provided that had been specially developed by Dr. Soula Homatidis, the clinical psychologist who had joined Dr. Huggins' team at Kerry's Place Autism Services. Parents' testimony was valued as part of the process. "It requires considerable observation, feedback, involvement and cooperation with Parents, Siblings, Teachers and Physicians to allocate an accurate behavior subtype," he had written in the early version. This was what ensured an accurate choice of medication. But it was essential for caregivers to be totally honest and specific about symptoms, he warned, otherwise parents could end up "with a whole mess of medications."

He encouraged parents to bring videos of their child at home with them to a consultation, warning: *"There's no magic in medicine."*

But it was Case Study #5, "M.L.," A Mixed Central & Peripheral Rage," that gripped you in the Case Studies section.

It seemed that "M.L." had one of the most "refractory of rage behaviors to manage," noted Dr. Huggins. The unfortunate client had been given "massive" doses of Mellaril – up to 600mg/day, and Buspar, 30mg/day, yet *still* had to be strapped down to four bedposts in a treatment center in Toronto. Under Dr. Huggins' protocol, these drugs were slowly discontinued until the Mellaril had dropped to 125mg/day and the Buspar completely eliminated. 40mg bid propranolol was started instead, eventually optimized at 160mg.a day. Epival was also introduced to provide mood modulation control. "M.L." eventually reached some sort of plateau and gained a life, no longer strapped to bedposts. It brought back the absolute seriousness of any rage behavior, and how truly terrifying it was. What parent could ever forget the opening words of the handbook, not recognize their darkest truth:

> *Unless one has been personally touched it is not possible to fully comprehend the anguish, the terror, or the suffering that exist in a household with a family member inflicted with uncontrollable rage behavior. Time stops, and life is put on hold for years at a time . . .*

Dr. Huggins was invited to present the D&T Model at The 1996 International Symposium on Autism in Toronto, and to The American & Canadian Psychiatric Associations at the Joint Convention of Child & Adolescent Psychiatry the following year. We followed his career with enthusiasm, enjoying the fact that he was a bit of a maverick. Awards and honors followed – The Kerry's Place Autism Services Award, The Gerry Bloomfield Award for "outstanding professional contributions in the field of autism" from Autism Society Ontario, induction into *Who's Who of Professionals* in 1996, and the Ontario Association on Developmental Disabilities 2002 Professional Recognition Award with the inscription . . "whose professional interaction with individuals with developmental disabilities has contributed significantly to their quality of life."

"Dr. Huggins, you're gonna win the Nobel Prize one day!" we teased.

Presenting at the symposium was important. The International Symposium for Autism organized by The Geneva Centre for Autism in Toronto took place every two years in the Metro Convention Centre. It was attended by hundreds of professionals in the field of autism as well as many parents. Being a speaker meant that Dr. Huggins' work was beginning to be recognized on a par with other leading professionals, such as Dr. Tony Atwood, and Dr. Margaret Bauman.

Yet Dr. Huggins was always first and foremost a general practitioner, a family doctor. His approach was based on twenty-five years' hands-on practical experience out of which had evolved this new "evidence-based/outcome-based" management paradigm. He had found himself challenging the old psychiatric medical model as too restrictive for defining the complex symptoms of autistic rage behavior. In particular, he'd found that the traditional "Principal Diagnosis-Target Symptom" approach "just did not work." He'd tried it, and found that it "failed miserably."

In contrast, Dr. Huggins stressed the importance of recognizing and treating the neorotransmitter components generating and sustaining rage behaviors. In addition, "rapid mood cycling" that he had observed in so many autistic/PDD patients, if excessive, also needed to be managed. He cited his experience with Julian:

> *Many case studies, such as O.J. consistently show that it is not enough to simply block all comorbid neurological, psychiatric, and peripheral causes. Good quality and predictable behavior control can only be achieved when the 'Mood Cycling Disorders' are brought under control.*

He was also concerned with how unaware practitioners often kept drug dosage "fixed" at the dosage the client had needed during an episodic outbreak. Dr. Huggins had realized that a client's drug could be lowered back to the dosage it had been before the episode, once the neurotransmitter dysfunction and instability subsided. Mistakenly keeping the dosage at the new higher level once an attack had passed, meant it became "excessive," creating the potential for drug toxicity and generating abnormal brain chemistry, the Jekyll and Hyde scenario all too common in many autistic clients.

Once again Dr. Huggins seemed to be the maverick – his approach was not usual standard medical practice. Yet psychologists, social workers and other service providers were highly supportive, quickly recognizing its practicality, perhaps because they worked hands on with their clients. Medical professionals tended to be cautious, claiming that it could not be done and citing once again the lack of formal double-blind, placebo-controlled drug trials. A D&T consultation was also costly. It involved extra of a physician's time for which the provincial HMOs do not give adequate remuneration.

But Dr. Huggins was too enthused with the work to be discouraged. He decided to post up information on the D&T Model on his new website, *www.bitemarks.com,* to reach a wider public.

We had by now reconciled ourselves to Julian being on three medications for as long as the rage attacks and mood cycling continued, possibly for life. There was still the odd manic outbreak from time to time, when we'd end up at an all-night donut shop at three in the morning. "Might as well munch our way through a chocolate crueller," Alec grumbled as we surveyed with dismay a fresh-faced, intense Julian pacing the deserted aisles of Tim Horton's. Where did all the energy come from? At the same time we felt anguished by Julian's helplessness before the force that drove him, that kept him wired day and night. Based on the previously determined safe and effective dosage range for Julian, we increased the dosage of Epival temporarily to 1500mg/day. At the end of the breakout, which could last from a few days to a week, we would return to the "base-line" dosage when the mania had subsided, as Dr. Huggins had taught us. Eventually we got so adept at assessing a situation we could adjust the dosage ourselves "as well as any doctor!" Dr. Huggins observed, not without pride.

We realized Dr. Huggins was validating us and the same time de-mystifying medication. It was possible, indeed, for lay people to have a comprehensive understanding of the workings of medications, and we appreciated the time Dr. Huggins invested in us. A check-up sometimes lasted two hours and the doors of the medical suite had to be unlocked to let us out! We went home glowing with our newly acquired knowledge. I began to appreciate how complex and delicate as well as vital was the issue of medication and dosage, and that psychiatrists were often dealing with an unknown factor in clients, one that Dr. Huggins himself struggled with daily, he admitted. *"Listen, there are no easy answers in medicine!"*

Thirty-six

A snowball landed splash at our feet as Julian and I strolled out of Mr. Sun's Variety Store in the village. We'd just bought Julian a popsicle. At age twenty he still loved this treat, even in the middle of winter. There was giggling from somewhere, just kids playing around I thought.

But then another snowball, this time a sharp crack of icy snow hit Julian's cheek. *"Retard!"*

"Maaa!" Jules was frightened; he knew this was bad, there was some bad kid, and sure enough some little ten or eleven year old with rough blond hair darted from a doorway pulling his mouth wide in a grimace.

"Retard! Retard!" he went and there was no stopping Julian. For the fun was watching this big guy howl for his mommy and hitting his face.

"It's OK Jules. Don't take any notice, they're just kids."

"Retard! Ape-head!"

Before I could stop him Julian was swinging at himself, punching his face and then swinging at them. "Retard!" he snarled at himself.

His popsicle broke into pieces in the snow; they laughed — "Hey watch this guy crying!"

"Oh Mommy!" Julian sobbed, getting down on his hands and knees and struggling to put it back on the stick together again.

"But it's ice, Jules, it's gone, you can never put it back together."

Another splash of snow over Julian's bent neck, he was still grappling on the ground for his pink crushed ice, sobbing. "Retard!" he hit himself fiercely, the old words as fierce as ever.

"Am I retarded, Mommy? Am I an ape? Yes you are, Julian,

you're an ape, you know that!" To howls of delight from the kids. They were getting more brazen. The one with yellow thatch hair, Micky, ran lightly up to us, grinning at Julian without fear. With a howl of rage, Julian swung at him, and missed, but that was the new game, and I couldn't stop it. "Leave him alone, you guys!" was meaningless. This was fun!

Rows of commuters stood in line at the bus station, dazed, uninvolved.

"Help me! Help me, please, someone." Julian bounded in yelps of frustration and fury after the boys this way and that. Lumbering drugged Julian stumbling after them, running into the branch of a tree and knocking his eye, swinging round confused.

I grabbed the blond kid and actually shook him. "You can't touch me, you *bitch!*" he snarled. Was he ten, eleven, twelve maybe?

"So what you going to do about it? Call the cops? Why don't you?" I shook his shoulders, yes, I wanted to shake that smirk right off his face. "Yeah, why don't you?" I took a wild guess, there was only one of two schools around, "Riverlea School, eh? You touch my son again and you'll . . . you'll . . . "

"You'll what?"

What was I doing?

I dropped his arms.

Police cruisers had arrived; someone from the Go-Train must have called 911. The officers jumped out with their holsters, and the children were gone like little ferrets burrowing back into the maze of apartment complexes towering round, except for the thatch-haired one who wanted to stay for the real fun: Julian getting handcuffed, hustled to the ground, whistles blown, messages radioed for extra help: "He's strong, man!" Julian pushed weeping into the back of the cruiser. I jumped in with him. Julian beat himself over and over, wailing "My popsicle, Mommy!" The kid grinned past the window as the siren went off.

"There's nothing we can really do, lady," Constable Spikes sighed not unsympathetically, later, in Police Local Division 2. They were underage, protected by the Young Offenders Act from prosecution.

"It's a waste of our time even taking them to court," he had added wearily.

But what about notifying their parents, the schools? Getting everyone together to discuss it. I didn't want to take them to court; what good would that do?

It was so frustrating to be left to deal with it alone. Julian was the one attacked, put in handcuffs, hustled into a police car and driven away like a criminal. Now I would have to go into the donut shop, the teen hang-out, and try to reach out to that blond kid, try talking to him, help him see what he was doing, but how? Put on "Dawn of The Dreads," his music, and buy him a Coke? There was "Dawn of The Dreads" on the '50s juke-box in the corner, *Fishin For Religion, Serial Killer.*

Constable Sykes shook his head. Julian had been handcuffed for his own protection to prevent things escalating, which meant: Julian harming the boys, hurting them in some way. "If he ever caught them, ma'am, he's strong . . . "

"You mean, he's not allowed to defend himself if attacked by a gang?"

"If he hurt one of them, I'm afraid we'd have to arrest him. That's the law."

The fact is normal twenty-year-old men did not go around retaliating against kids' teasing. It was like an animal, Constable Spikes had pursued: if a dog was deliberately provoked by kids to the point that he ended up killing one of them, he still had to be destroyed, even though it was not his fault. Because he might kill again.

It was all so unfair, Alec cried to Dr. Huggins, relating the incident. Julian had gotten out of control, but this time we did not feel the medications were not working. We felt that Julian's rage had been justified for his mental age. "He reacted as any normal person would under the same circumstances, Dr. Huggins."

"Ah, but that's just it," said Dr. Huggins. "Unfortunately for our kids, in law their chronological age and size will always go against them. The officer is right. Julian has to be protected from himself, however justified his rage may seem to us." He added sympathetically: "Julian doesn't know his own strength. His rage has to be kept under control proactively — before it happens."

This word "proactive" was for us a novel disturbing concept — the idea of using medication to prevent a behavior "before it happened." But then, what was the alternative? "Do you want to take the risk of more all-out rage attacks?" reasoned Dr. Huggins.

We knew that Dr. Huggins had been puzzling for years over the problem of psychotic-like breakouts that still took place in certain autistic clients like Julian. Now he actually wanted to try Julian on Risperdal (risperidone), a new anti-psychotic drug on the market that Dr. Huggins felt was beginning to show promise. We tensed, pained.

"But Dr. Huggins, we always thought you were against anti-psychotics!"

"Yes, I know it's pretty ironic we seem to have come full circle back to the use of anti-psychotic medication. But Risperdal is not your regular anti-psychotic drug, it's atypical." Dr. Huggins stressed "atypical," in that it meant it had a lower risk of the dreaded "EPS," extra-pyramidal neuromuscular side effects.

"But — what about Haldol? Isn't it a bad drug?"

I could feel myself resisting, holding on to my bias and prejudice. I so wanted to believe Haldol — and by extension perphenazine and any other anti-psychotic drug on the market, typical or "atypical" — was "bad."

"Thelma, there are no 'good' or 'bad' drugs, only the way they're used. I've never been against anti-psychotic drugs *per se*, only against their indiscriminate use on autistic/PDD patients as a panacea for all and every abnormal behavior in the book! There's a difference."

"So you're not against Haldol, then?"

Dr. Huggins hesitated.

"Haldol has its uses."

He went on to explain that Haldol was a perfectly good drug, when indicated and administered correctly. The older neuroleptics like Haldol, Thioradizine, chlorpromazine, were useful for controlling the "positive" dopamine-driven symptoms of schizophrenia such as hallucinations and delusions. They worked by blocking what was believed to be an excess of dopamine neoroceptors in the brain. But they were ineffective against the kind of symptoms Julian and other autistic people like him had: anxiety, rage, panic, obsessive-compulsive disorders, symptoms that appeared to be mainly noradrenaline and serotonin driven.

It was the first time Dr. Huggins had drawn attention to the importance of other neurotransmitters like dopamine, noradrenaline, and serotonin. Julian did not require excessive dopamine blocade, which explained why he had not done well on Haldol or perphenazine or any of the older anti-psychotic drugs.

"But how do you know which neurotransmitters Julian produces to excess?" After all, even Dr. Huggins could not see inside Julian's brain.

"By his symptoms and behaviors. The behaviors reveal what is likely going on in the brain. For example, hallucinations, paranoia, delusions such as believing you are Jesus Christ and can walk on water, indicate "positive" symptoms of schizophrenia and a likely excess of dopamine dysfunction. On the other hand, obsessive-compulsive disorders, panic, agitation, anxiety, etc., indicate a noradrenaline and serotonin dysfunction." It was not difficult to distinguish which Julian exhibited at any given time once you recognized the abnormal signs and symptoms.

In his typical way, Dr. Huggins had meticulously examined the published neurotransmitter-neoroceptor binding properties of Risperdal. He'd quickly recognized that the advantage of Risperdal was that it possessed the capability of down-regulating, or blocking, noradrenaline, serotonin and dopamine-driven dysfunction at a low dosage range (0.25-1mg/day) — but only where the noradrenaline and serotonin-driven dyscontrol exceeded the dopamine-driven component. This meant that Risperdal was suitable for Julian, and would eliminate the need for other drugs, enthused Dr. Huggins.

He wanted us to try Julian on .5mg./day initially, to an optimal dose of 1mg/day.

It was tempting. Only one drug. Yet again we hesitated. We were still somewhat shocked and confused. For Dr. Huggins, the advent of Risperdal on the market was turning everything in the D&T Model upside down in a wonderful way since it provided a major control capability not otherwise available, but for us it was so much to grasp in one session: the change-over in drugs, in protocols, in Dr. Huggins' entire methodology. In the past he had tended to down-play the psychosis component in autistic rage behaviors since this form of psychiatric labeling justified the use of neuroleptic drugs at high-dosage levels with poor long-term outcome. It was clear that the largely dopamine-driven psychosis component needed to be redefined and integrated with the other neurotransmitters: adrenaline, noradrenaline and serotonin. He was very excited about further refining the D&T Model Management Paradigm for choosing the right medication. It was why he called 1997 "the pivotal year."

But we could think only of Julian.

"So Julian *is* psychotic, then?"

It was strange to be discussing this psychiatric term with Dr. Huggins of all people.

"Well, it all depends on how you look at psychosis," said Dr. Huggins evenly. That terror word.

Like most people we still tended to see it in terms of schizophrenia according to the Positive and Negative Symptom scale of Schizophrenia, "P-A-N-S-S." But Dr. Huggins had always been disatisfied with the PANSS terminology, which he felt focussed on symptoms and not on the neurotransmitters that generated and sustained them. "The most PANSS can tell you is whether you're schizophrenic – or not!" was his somewhat droll comment.

What he sought was a clinical methodology that helped "ongoing daily management," because it was the actual *management* of symptoms that counted, especially when you were having your home torpedoed every night, he added drily.

What was needed, he felt, was a universal neurotransmitter-neuroceptor-based model that would identify, quantify, and prioritize one or more neurotransmitters to be targeted for precise degrees of down-regulation or up-regulation, much like pressing the brakes or the gas on your car – "and it makes a hell of a difference which one," he chuckled. For Dr. Huggins recognized the volatile nature of abnormal symptoms, a fluctuating mental state that autistic individuals like Julian exhibited, which did not stay stable, but would "come and go."

Correctly identifying and managing one neurotransmitter would control a very wide variety of abnormal symptoms. This was in sharp contrast to the conventional "principal diagnosis/target symptom" approach, which resulted in using several different medications for managing the same scenario. It all seemed so simple: once the client's neurotransmitter/neuroceptor control requirements were determined, the most appropriate drug could then be chosen based on its published neuroceptor binding properties.

In fact, a working knowledge of the comparative neurotransmitter binding properties for the various neuroleptic drugs was essential to achieving this kind of control.

Important and fascinating though all this information was, our concern naturally was the "mental state" Julian exhibited.

"So Julian's not schizophrenic then, Dr. Huggins, not psychotic?"

"Not as a major psychiatric diagnosis, no. In management terms he exhibits a transient abnormal mental state."

It was true. Julian was not always "nuts." He intermittently *went* "nuts."

"Of course, that's not to say the episodic behaviors are any less difficult to control. They aren't!" Dr. Huggins assured us.

Seasonal, episodic behavior, he reminded us, superimposed on top of the predominant behavior pattern was what produced the terrifying, vivid autistic *"child from hell!"*

But at least Jules was not a schizophrenic. Years of anxiety and anguish seemed to lift as we realized this at long last – a small blessing perhaps, but one for which we were deeply relieved. We felt grateful to Dr. Huggins for taking time to give these explanations. We realized he was validating us by sharing and entrusting us with knowledge and know-how. It was possible for lay people to have a comprehensive understanding of the mysteries of medication and a share in decision-making. I began to appreciate how complex and delicate was the issue of medication and dosage, and that psychiatrists and doctors were often dealing with an unknown factor in any client, one that Dr. Huggins was intent on eliminating as much as possible, while acknowledging there were "no easy answers in medicine."

So Julian was to start on .5mg Risperdal that February day, (.25mg twice daily). The other three drugs were to be slowly eliminated over the next year or two, starting immediately with the clonidine. "He just won't need that anymore. Risperdal is a more comprehensive alpha (noradrenaline) blocker than clonidine."

Yet we were nervous. Risperdal was still relatively unknown. Just one small white pill to do so much.

But we were hardly paying close attention. Our concern was all for Polly right then, for the first time in Julian's life. Polly, our little Pollywogs, now twenty-four, had felt a strange serious pain in her shoulders and chest just weeks before leaving for Queen's University for her teachers training year. A huge "something" had been seen in an x-ray of her chest, under the thymus.

Non-Hodgkins Lymphoma was diagnosed. That moment, that hour, fell heavily on us all, but how gently, how kindly, the attending surgeon broke the news. Polly had had to have treatment immediately. Her teachers' training year was canceled at Queen's, everything put on hold for at least a year. Polly, always so loving, thoughtful, had helped us so much over the years, was now suddenly seriously struck like this. I took a leave of absence from teaching at once to be with her through the year-long treatment. Kerry's Place generously, we could never thank them enough, took Julian in one week a month during Polly's monthly chemotherapy and later radiation treatments. My mother-in-law and Alec's sister took a pilgrimage to Martyrs Shrine in Midland, Ontario, and made intercessions for Polly, lit candles, sprinkled holy water.

"Oh Granma!" Polly had smiled as Granma handed her holy water in a tiny bottle from Lourdes she ordered yearly from some monks.

"Sprinkle it on your chest before the biopsy," urged Ma.

"Hey, whatever works!" said the oncologist, surprisingly open about it. "I'm not against holy anything in this field," he added.

Even Mother, in Wales — old and much frailer now — had villagers praying there. The village church in Port Credit included Polly in their intercessions. We felt the dark sickness of heart as we struggled through, not noticing at first how jealous Julian was becoming. Normally, we would have been overjoyed at his finally displaying an emotion like jealousy — *"I'm gonna kill Polly!"* — but it was too vulnerable a time; Polly had to be protected at all costs. There was a deep incision across her chest, and the slightest blow would split it open; she was so fragile now — the entire family was. We started the Risperdal on Julian. Its effect was immediate as Dr. Huggins had predicted. Julian became calmer, in a dulled sort of way since he was now on four drugs until we could start reducing the clonidine and propranolol gradually. But there was little time to think about that.

Anxiously I picked up the phone one morning. A gruff familiar voice I yet couldn't quite place spoke. It was Dr. Bland!

"It's . . . Victor, Victor Bland, Mrs. Orchard. I heard about your daughter, Polly, and . . . uh . . . I want you to know how deeply sorry I am and . . . I'm thinking of you and Alec."

At once years of tension seemed to melt away at the words. I seemed to swim in confusion and the sudden rush of gratitude, realization of past indebtednesses swarming — for had it not been Dr. Bland who had placed Julian into respite at Kerry's Place, found us a worker, told us about funding, found us kindly Dr. Sol?

"I — we — both thank you, Dr. Bland, and thanks for everything else you've done for us over the years, especially for Kerry's Place."

"Oh-h, well, yes. Well, one never knows, of course, how these things turn out. You make recommendations but you never know . . . " There was an awkward pause.

"It was the best thing that ever happened for Julian, Dr. Bland." Other than meeting Dr. Huggins. It occurred to me that indirectly we owed that to Dr. Bland as well, for was it not he who had also finessed our meeting with Rolph Schellenberg who in turn had recommended Dr. Huggins?

He's not letting go. There's a muffled sound, and : "How is Julian coping . . . ?"

"Not too well."

I'm surprised how honest I can be now about this, honest and open. No, Julian is not doing well, but it's only natural.

"It must be hard for him . . . for you all."

There was a trenchant pause. " . . . You have always done your best for Julian."

"Thanks. Oh thanks!"

" . . . will call again some time . . . meanwhile . . . I'll be thinking of you."

We saw Polly off to Queen's the following fall in remission, recovered we believe and Polly believes. Life resumed its old pace people sighed in relief, though could it ever, really? Some other darkness entered me somewhere, something so fragile, what I had thought was surety, our healthy beautiful daughter I would never have suspected to be the one, so precious; it seemed life itself, all love, would tighten in me as to its darker hidden dimensions, that it was never to be taken for granted again. "Not the least flower, Mom . . . "

Thirty-seven

We finally turned our attention back to Julian in the summer, 1997, horrified to realize he was now on 1250mg of Epival, 160mg of propranolol, and 0.150mg of clonidine – plus 1mg of Risperdal daily.

He was also FAT! Over 200 lbs. It had happened gradually. Propranolol, Epival, and clonidine tended to cause the body to hold water and salt. But there was also something odd about his hands.

"He's over-drugged," observed Dr. Huggins quietly, noting a standing tremor, that telltale trembling Julian could not stop in his hands.

It was an awkward moment, a shock. Yet we respected Dr. Huggins' honesty and integrity.

"Too much Epival." He checked Julian's chart. "He doesn't need that extra 250mg anymore. It can be eliminated right away." He frowned. "Get rid of the clonidine too, right away. He didn't need that once he started on Risperdal," he reminded us. But we'd been afraid to eliminate it completely because of the potential danger of any aggression on Polly. We felt guilty: we'd kept Julian heavily dosed for her sake, but it had seemed the right choice at the time. This was now the first task. We began cutting it out at once. It took five weeks. Next we began reducing the propranolol. It took nearly a year to remove it from Julian's system. Epival would be the last to go.

There was no doubt in Dr. Huggins' mind that it was the imbalance of two important neurotransmitters, noradrenaline and serotonin, and to a much lesser extent, dopamine, that put the autistic individual "off-line" for cognitive control, and was responsible for much of the violence and dyscontrol.

He had now come to the conclusion that these behaviors of autistic individuals were not largely dopamine-driven, as generally assumed, but primarily noradrenaline and serotonin-driven or a mixture of all three along with excessive adrenaline function. The best management option to date employed the use of propranolol for adrenaline dysfunction, and Risperdal at a very low variable dosage (1-3mg). But the manufacturer, Janssen Pharmaceutical's recommendation of high dosage levels (3–12mg) for managing psychosis actually had the opposite effect on autistic/PDD individuals, Dr. Huggins had discovered. Which meant, he added drily, that both these drugs were being used "off-label."

We tried to grasp that it was important to make these distinctions in classifying symptoms because *this was the key to good long-term management,* stressed Dr. Huggins.

But Dr. Huggins was starting to get really technical!

He was actually drawing a diagram of a *neuron* in the brain, showing something called the pre-synaptic and post-synaptic ends that he expected me to understand! "But I'm an English major, Dr. Huggins, my brain just can't grasp this neurotransmitter stuff."

"Nonsense!"

For the neurons *do not touch,* they transmit one to the other through chemicals that are the neurotransmitters. For the nerves speak to each other through these, and the synapse is the space where it happens, where it all happens; tiny, invisible, neurotransmitters coursing through the filaments of his brain, of all our brains, lightning sparks illuminating, sometimes blanking out, their secret silent messages of pre-synaptic, post-synaptic fire . . . and Dr. Huggins was going to block and downgrade some of the receptor sites – but only some.

"You block just enough to lessen the anxiety, to mitigate the rage, to normalize Julian. Thelma, you are no dummy, you can get this – other parents have!"

"Hey," says Alec suddenly, "Students in high school learn about this synapse stuff in health!"

"Exactly."

Dr. Huggins is glowing. The office is small and hot, intense. Sparks are flying from Dr. Huggins' brain, his zillions of neurotransmitters working overtime to the nth degree, his eyes like coals.

For among the atypical neuroleptic drugs Risperdal was special in a quite wonderful and unique way, for not only did it have this noradrenaline and serotonin-blocking ability but the dopamine and serotonin blocking actions of Risperdal happened *at different dosage levels*, enabling the physician to selectively and differentially target the noradrenaline, serotonin, and dopamine neuroceptors.

Risperdal was only effective at controlling rage behaviors if used off label at *low dosage levels*, (.5 to 1.5mg/day) stressed Dr. Huggins. At this dose, optimum noradrenaline and serotonin blocking had been observed to occur. This beneficial effect actually appeared to be lost at higher dosage levels greater than 2mg/day for autistic/PDD individuals. For the majority of autistic/PDD individuals experiencing anxiety, agitation, panic, or rage, the most beneficial effect of Risperdal was for its noradrenaline and serotonin blocking properties and to a much lesser extent for its dopamine blocking effects, reiterated Dr. Huggins. The optimum dosage for Julian was determined to be 1mg/day administered in two doses of .5mg.

"More is NOT necessarily better when it comes to medication!" urged Dr. Huggins.

There was now a two-year waiting list for Dr. Huggins' personal consultations – his secretary could barely cope with all the incoming calls and faxes, some from New Zealand, Hong Kong, and even Turkey! (One pediatrician once drove up from Texas through a January snowstorm to hear Dr. Huggins present his methodology at The Aurora Golf & Country Club, north of Toronto.) Speaking engagements at international symposiums abroad followed. He gave the keynote presentation on Phase Two of his methodology at the International Conference on "Enabling & Empowering Adults with Social Disabilities," in 1998 in Dublin, Ireland. While there he assessed a very difficult violent young man with Asperger's Syndrome. We were surprised to hear of this. Individuals with Asperger's were regarded as the highest functioning in the autistic spectrum. "Oh, they can also be the most intractable and violent," Dr. Huggins grimaced. "Their very intelligence makes the aggression more complex and focused. It was quite an experience!"

Back in Canada, he gave another presentation in 2000 in Kamloops, B.C. Dr. Temple Grandin, another guest speaker at

Kamloops, observed to Dr. Huggins at this time, that she felt his methodology would gain greater acceptance in the United States which was more open to innovative approaches in medicine.

Many of Dr. Huggins' peers recognized his brilliant diagnostic acumen. Psychiatrists at The Clarke Institute of Psychiatry (now The Centre for Mental Health & Addiction) in Toronto often sent Dr. Huggins their worst cases with a challenging — *"Hey, Joe, see if you can solve this one!"*

But they were sending him more and more cases.

Thirty-seven

Julian graduated from The Meadows in 1997, and was out in the workforce. "You're an ADULT, Julian!" he warned himself.

He went to three job placements in the community accompanied by his Worker, Jai. Julian was very proud, and so were we, of his work in a business store in Port Credit called Options, his job in Port Credit Library, and in Andy's Toy-Shop in the local mall. He had all his meals planned out for each day of the week: Tuesdays, submarine sandwich; Wednesdays, chop suey at Food Court in the mall; Fridays the current menu at The Meadows café, often chicken fajitas or "poutine" on french fries, he enthused.

"The last thing you need is poutine!" teased Dr. Huggins.

"I'm retired now, Dr. Huggins."

Dr. Huggins now wanted to try titrating Julian's medication. It was what he called "working the therapeutic window" with variable dosage protocols, as opposed to the old fixed dosage method for administering medications. "I think Julian is ready for it, he's doing so well."

The most important wonderful aspect of Risperdal was that it possessed neurotransmitter-neuroceptor binding properties, which allowed us to titrate dosage in this way, explained Dr. Huggins. We would be able to adjust Julian's dosage of Risperdal even lower than 1mg by employing what was called a *proactive variable dosing protocol* while minimizing the risk of inducing an excessive amount of *new abnormal brain chemistry.* For example, continued Dr. Huggins, Julian was now completely stabilized on 1mg/day of Risperdal. When he was in a good cycle, his baseline dose could be reduced by .25mg to .75mg/day without any significant loss of control. After about 48–72 hours, the blocked neuroceptors in

Julian's brain would then readapt to his .75mg/day baseline dosage level. Should there ever be a breakthrough in rage or other abnormal behavior, a .75mg PRN (as needed) dose of Risperdal could be given at any point in time *without increasing his baseline dosage of Risperdal back to 1mg/day or higher.*

The use of PRN in this way was helpful in indicating how low or high Julian's baseline dosage needed to be. If, for instance, the .25mg PRN dosage was being administered more than three times/week, then this would indicate that Julian's baseline dose was too low and should be increased back to 1mg/day. If, on the other hand, the .25mg PRN dose was rarely needed, then Julian's baseline dose was too high and could be further reduced to 0.5mg/day.

Dr. Huggins often brought up the issue of achieving control without generating an excessive amount of *new abnormal brain chemistry* when using any of the neuroleptic class of drugs. Although this was most likely to occur with the predominantly dopamine-blocking older antipsychotic drugs, it could also occur with the newer atypical neuroleptic drugs – something that the brain certainly did not need.

Dr. Huggins had noted for some time that older autistic clients, those now approaching their late twenties and thirties, were becoming quieter, their beta-adrenergic systems settling down. This was important, but it did not appear to occur if a client was on strong doses of older anti-psychotics. The older neuroleptics did not allow for this natural maturation process to take place since they induced an unbalanced proliferation of a variety of neuroceptors that again actually created *new abnormal brain chemistry.* The result was an ever-spiralling increase in the dosage of the neuroleptic drug, the infamous vicious circle in the desperate effort always to play catch up.

"Dyscontrol breeds dyscontrol," commented Dr. Huggins, "often with disastrous results." He maintained his stance always against mega-dosing with psychotropic drugs.

Though this was all very technical for us to grasp, it answered the instinctual fear we had always harbored of Jules being "overdosed."

Alternatively, Julian could be weaned off even the 1mg of Risperdal in a year or so, assured Dr. Huggins. Dr. Huggins was already getting excellent results with autistic clients including his own son, Jonathan, whose drugs had now been reduced to only

Tegretol for seizures. Many young men who had once been violent and self-abusive, unmanageable, wreaking devastation for themselves and their families, were now drug-free, on only Risperdal PRN – as needed. And Jules might be, too, one day, hinted Dr. Huggins.

"PRN . . . *As needed!*" Surely the most blessed words any parent of a violent out-of-control autistic child could ever hear.

Except that Janssen Pharmaceutica (Janssen-Ortho Inc.) seemed unaware of the unique property of Risperdal: the gem of a drug they had created.

Originally developed to treat schizophrenia and other major psychotic disorders, Janssen had never intended Risperdal to be used for the purpose of managing rage behaviors in autistic/PDD/ADD clients. The company was interested in promoting and supporting their official indication for Risperdal, 3–15mg/day for its combined dopamine D2 and serotonin 5–H/2 antagonism in the management of a major psychotic disorder in persons eighteen years and older. The manufacturer's approved usage for Risperdal was in keeping with a uniform and complementary neurotransmitter blockade throughout the recommended therapeutic dosage range. (A more recent official indication has been obtained by the manufacturer for the use of low-dose Risperdal in a 0.5–2mg/day dosage range for managing "Behavioural Disturbances in Severe Dementia" in the elderly population.) This incidentally was the same dosage range used in managing autistic dyscontrol, observed Dr. Huggins, not without frustration.

Yet there were already some interesting studies on the benefits of low-dose Risperdal for PDD behavior disorders that confirmed Dr. Huggins' findings. A case series done by Sandra Sisman and Margaret Steele in 1996 on the "Use of Risperidone in Pervasive Developmental Disorders" with fourteen autistic young people age nine to seventeen years, had found that optimal doses ranged from 0.75 to 1.5mg daily in divided doses appeared to benefit thirteen of the fourteen youths. Disruptive behaviors, agitation and anxiety was remarkably reduced, with minimal side effects.

But Janssen Pharmaceutica, the manufacturer of Risperdal, nevertheless remained tardy in carrying out the necessary research to clarify the low dose use of Risperdal for autistic/PDD individuals. We could sense Dr. Huggins' frustration, which matched our own as helpless parents in this strange scenario. Despite Dr. Huggins' tireless advocacy, to date the use of low-dose Risperdal for managing Autistic/PDD/ADHD is still considered to be an off-label application of the drug.

Dr. Huggins was never one to rest. His attention was now drawn to another serious problem that he had noted for years: adverse drug effects from drug interactions not just with incompatible drugs and over-the-counter medications like Seldane, but with dietary and herbal supplements. Everyday grapefruit juice that so many people loved to consume for breakfast, was a point in case. Dr. Huggins wrote a startling article about the eclectic mix of certain drugs with grapefruit creating a potentially lethal "cocktail" – *"How safe is this cocktail?"*

From his research into the work of Dr. David Bailey of the University of Western Ontario, Canada, who first discovered that grapefruit juice can markedly augment the "oral bioavailability" of a drug, Dr. Huggins realized the potential dangers of drug interactions. It seemed that grapefruit juice acted by blocking the activity of an important cytochrome P450 3A4 isoenzyme in the intestinal wall, thereby preventing the presystemic "first pass" oxidative metabolism (breakdown) for a wide variety of drugs. In the case of the cholesterol-lowering drug lovastatin (Mevacor), there was up to a 19.7 fold increase in the plasma concentration by ingesting with grapefruit juice as compared with a glass of water.

Dr. Huggins stressed in his article:

> The ability of grapefruit juice to adversely affect the bioavailability (therapeutic concentration) of a very wide variety of drugs, is very real and must not be ignored.

Dr. Huggins continued to explore this problem, spending considerable time checking out all of Dr. Bailey's research data. One of the culprits was discovered to be the citrus bioflavinoid, naringin, present in grapefruit juice, sour Seville oranges and pomelos. The naringin is metabolized in the small intestine to naringenin, a very potent inhibitor of cytochrome P450 3A4 isoenzymes. In his new Phase V Version of *The Universal D&T Symptom Behaviour Model,* published in 2000, Dr. Huggins again drew attention to Dr. Bailey's work, quoting from his article published in *Medical Tribune, 1998,* that: *"sixty per cent of drugs that are (commonly) prescribed are metabolized to some extent by this enzyme, CYP3A4 (Cytochrome P450 3A4). Many drugs undergo first-pass metabolism by CYP3A4. Hence, the inhibition of this enzyme in the gut causes plasma concentrations of these drugs to increase markedly after oral administration. The result can be significant. For example, taking one tablet of lovastatin (Mevacor) with a glass of grapefruit juice is the same as taking 12 to 15 tablets with a glass of water."*

A mystery was now solved for us regarding this new information. We had once given Julian a dose of Seldane during a bad cold, (along with his prescribed dose of Epival). The result had been inexplicably erratic! Instead of calming Julian and giving him a good night's rest, the Seldane had seemed to rev him up; he'd spent restless hours agitated and flushed pacing the house. Perhaps he needed a higher dose? In our ignorance, we actually increased it. Worse reactions had ensued, more agitation, excitability. Something was very wrong, yet we never suspected Seldane. Perhaps we were not giving enough Epival, that the cold had roused an episodic attack. I switched from Seldane to ordinary vitamin C (luckily without additional bioflavinoids) and orange juice. Julian calmed down and got better.

With typical thoroughness and dedication, Dr. Huggins continues to this day to research all data on potentially dangerous drug interactions, and develop a new clinical management paradigm for more accurately recognizing and avoiding harmful drugs and drug-drug interactions. In 2001 he published a drug interaction handbook: "Cytochrome P-450 Isoenzyme Information for the D&T Model Applications," and continues to share his knowledge with lay and medical professionals across the country.

As he noted in Version V of the *D&T Control Model Handbook*: "the grapefruit juice-drug interaction problem really represents just the tip of the iceberg . . . "

Thirty-nine

Good evening, Dr. Huggins," said Julian. It was the year 2000; Jules going into the new millenium at twenty-three.

"How's it going, Julian?"

"I still got my jobs, Dr. Huggins. I work in the library rewinding videos, I stamp books, I push them on shelves. I work in Options counting money and I sweeps the floor. I work in Benjy's Toy-Shop in the mall. I sort the dinosaurs and pencils, I wake up the Ken dolls, I straighten them out.

"You got to have consideration for others, Dr. Huggins."

Leaving Dr. Huggins somewhat dumbfounded but beaming with pride.

Yet there were times I wept for Jules bulging out of his giant extra large jeans. I'd had to revamp his wardrobe, and found myself combing the middle-aged section of men's clothing for size XL (sometimes XXL). But the choice seemed to be between this sweet benign teddy bear everyone loved — "Oh, he's so sweet and cuddly now!" — or his former slim 147 lb but explosive self.

There was no denying that weight gain was an unwanted side effect of Risperdal, and to a varying degree of other atypical neuroleptics, the effect of the Histamine receptor blockade of the drug. It was as if Julian never felt that satisfying fullness after a meal, and needed 25% — 50% more food (in his mind) to get that full feeling, ransacking every fridge in sight to satisfy his increase in appetite. The only solution was a balanced diet low in carbohydrates, advised Dr. Huggins, to un-prime his insulin pump and to reduce the effects of reactive hypoglycaemia. Poor glycemic control will produce a marked increase in appetite with a craving for carbo-hydrates and accompanied by cycles of anxiety, agitation and sometimes rage. We steadily worked on this, though Julian's fixation on Coke and french fries was remarkably persistent! We worked out an agreement with him of one diet Coke as a special treat in McDonald's (still his favorite place) on the weekend.

Julian was now working out in the community accompanied by Jai, whom we paid out of government SSAH (Special Services At Home) funding. Though Jules worked independently on the job, rewinding videos by himself in the Port Credit Library, for instance, he yet needed an adult like Jai to watch over him, especially as he still feared gangs of teenagers and small children out on the road. Working at the library was peaceful, and I'd often tiptoe in and watch Jules absorbed in his job in the back office stamping away, seated in a shaft of sunlight. He loved the librarians and they were fond of him. He was especially thrilled with the daily calendar they gave him for Christmas – except that he refused to tear off a single page. Time forever January the first!

We soon discovered the problem facing parents of develop-mentally challenged adult children was what to do with them after graduation. As one parent put it, as long as they were in school you were lulled into a false security. Parents who had to be at work all day and were not one of the lucky ones to receive enough funding to afford a worker often had to leave their children locked up at home alone, watching TV all day and steadily eating their way through everything in the fridge. But what was the alternative?

Some parents started up a small business in Port Credit to provide some skills training and occupation. The office work included faxing, laminating, transfers on to T-shirts, etc. Jules was soon a trainee and became good at counting the money in the till, stamping envelopes and photocopying. The store survived on funding from United Way, and the proceeds of charity bingo run by aging parents (7:00 A.M. Sunday mornings), plus profit from the store itself. We had a loyal following amongst the residents of Port Credit.

Julian working in the Port Credit Library, 2002.

Jules still visited The Meadows once a week on Friday for the After-21 Programme. He met up with old buddies still students at the school. One was Alix, a PDD boy who had been in Julian's old class, and who, though non-verbal and lower functioning than Jules, was yet able to pick out notes and tunes on the piano at home, amazing his mother. Often undemonstrative, twenty-year-old Alix took a fancy to Alec when he accompanied Julian one day, and promptly plonked himself in Alec's lap and stroked his beard!

In the program Julian worked on the computer, played basket-ball, sometimes part of an ongoing gym lesson with other students, and ate lunch in the school café. He ordered and saved his monthly menus, learning them by heart. "Chicken quesadillas with garden salad and chips," he repeated dreamily. Somehow he taught himself to read the menus, reciting then trance-like by the hour.

This part of his new life was an enrichment for Julian and a reve-lation for us as he began to develop a new perspective on his school years at The Meadows, loving to meet with his old teachers, remi-niscing about past events and personalities in a detailed way that was often dumbfounding. "Remember, Ms. Bryce, in 1995 when you. . ?" He devoted special time to Mr. Collie (whom he now called "Gerald"), sitting down in a confidential way with him in his office each Friday morning.

"I knowed you a long time now, Gerald, haven't I?" he would open up conversationally with Mr. Collie, lolling in an armchair.

"Julian," smiled Mr. Collie fondly, "You have taught me so much, son, more than I ever taught you."

"Horses wear glasses."

There had been improvements to the programming over the years. Julian's last teacher in the Work Experience Programme had been one of two special education teachers along with a special education consultant in the district school board implemental in presenting the draft version of a new alternative curriculum for developmentally challenged students. As well, millions of dollars had been provided by the provincial government for early interven-tion programs – though waiting lists were still long – for autistic/PDD children, that SEAC (Special Education Advisory Committee that involved parents) and the autism society had advocated for over the years. It was too late for Jules, but a step in the right direction for the new generation.

Another surprising enterprise was Julian's enjoyment of another after-21 program in the community, called LIFE (Love, Integration, Friendship, Education). The program was similar in structure to school, with set routines for academic work, breaks, games and a walk in the park – there was also "afternoon tea." Much time was devoted to interactive card games: Old Maid, Snap, and Monopoly. Julian loved it, and he loved the director, Denice, an older woman who'd wanted to try to give challenged individuals something better than sheltered workshops after leaving school.

We came to the conclusion that LIFE provided a needed bridge between school and the world of work, for Jules.

But something was still missing. There was little offered socially for autistic adults once school life came to an end. I set about organizing a Halloween dance and it was fun. I hired a D.J. through Professional Record Players in Toronto. "Dick" who turned up with mountains of equipment turned out to be a godsend. He seemed to know exactly what music our population loved to dance to, from the Beach Boys of the '50s to the Backstreet Boys of the '90s. Mr. Collie had donated the use of the Gym in The Meadows, and it was back to old times. Everyone danced with everyone. One unforgettable evening at a Spring Hop Julian wheeled amiably round the gym for over an hour caught in the determined arms of a sweet young lady with Down's Syndrome who obviously liked him. They were dancing a slow one. Lights softened round the dancers, Julian's arms round his partner's waist; he was smiling distantly.

That was not all. In the spring, Julian began music therapy sessions in Toronto, something I'd always dreamed of for him but which had never materialized. Now I heard about the Association of Music Therapists of Ontario who recommended Paul Lauzon. Paul, with soft grey hair curling round a sensitive face, was kind, gentle, and infinitely patient. He was to prove to be therapist, friend, teacher, songwriter, poet, musician . . .

"Isn't Julian a bit old for that now?" queried a neighbor. Jules learning to sing falsetto, play Indian hand drums, the Orph zylophone, a threepenny whistle! And so much more! Surely it was never too late.

Julian in Music Therapy with Paul Lauzon, 1997–1998.

I watched each week from the sofa in the tiny front living-cum-music room as Paul kept Julian face to face, body to body, mirroring him, embraceable. "Look at me, Julian," and Julian looks and holds Paul. Paul holds him for a moment, he allows himself to be held in Paul's arms. Then — "Let's do the Cha-Cha! Jules!"

Paul puts Julian to playing the black notes on the piano, sitting side by side on the bench. Paul does not know the marvel this alone is! Humming at first, then whistling. Julian cannot whistle; I never knew that about him. Then they play together, Julian on the black notes while Paul artfully provides the melody on the white. Julian is quick: he remembers the combinations, he is enjoying this. The song Paul wrote himself ripples through the twilight beyond the confines of the dimly lit flat in the old Brownstone building on Vaughan Road, with its dusty trees and the thrum of street cars from St Clair. Paul and Julian sing together, their voices blending.

"In the cover of the forest where the hustle of my life is a long-forgotten worry, there I walk . . . "

Meanwhile, I was becoming involved with the local chapter of ASO (Autism Society of Ontario). The majority of members were young parents often with newly diagnosed children approximately four to six years of age. Most were aware of the importance of early intervention for autistic children. Many had read Catherine Maurice's book, *Let Me Hear Your Voice*, and were filled with anticipation they too might "bring their child out of autism." Maurice, like the Kaufmans two decades earlier, had cured not one but two children of autism, both in babyhood! It was a powerful testimony to the determination and skill of a mother, with the aid of two private therapists; but one that could bring pain as well as hope to these young anxious mothers.

The Autism Society of Ontario lacked the funding to provide anything practical in the way of speech and language therapists, but we older parents could help younger ones by sharing our knowledge and expertise gained over the years. A few of us, three actually, got together and formed a little group called "Experience Tells!" We started with a visit to a parent group out in the countryside where facilities were lacking. We also brought along our autistic children figuring they could demonstrate the problems of raising an autistic child more graphically than we!

I brought Julian's journals and workbooks, as well as information about The Listening Centre to give an idea of the "home program" I'd invented. And, of course, I talked about Dr. Huggins and the necessity that had arisen for a drug program in Julian's teenage years.

Julian talked and sang, and giggled. His friend, a lovely autistic young lady called Elspeth, who was high-functioning and highly verbal, sang her score from *The Wizard of Oz*. "Some day over the rainbow . . . " rang out a clear wavering soprano as the singer frolicked sideways out of the room. I noted that Julian was quite taken with her, laughing excitedly and racing out of the door whenever she veered in his direction; they spent the evening prancing in and out of doorways and round each other like young colts. Elspeth had an uncanny artistic talent that her mother had encouraged, which must have involved endless hours of patience. Elspeth drew contours round tiny toy figures, often but one inch in diameter, then colored in the outlines with pencil crayons, creating perfect miniatures. Her mother had arranged an art display of Elspeth's work in the local library, complete with wine and cheese reception. The parents were fascinated and sobered. This might possibly be their future. They listened attentively as we shared our successes and mistakes.

I realized that the anguish I had felt so many years before mirrored now in these young parents had somehow imperceptibly passed away. Julian had not been one of the ones to come out of autism, but something beautiful was unfolding nevertheless, a potential, a sweetness that was precious; who knew what he would yet "amount to"?

"Amazing!" said Dr. Mary Konstantareas. She was a well-known clinical psychologist and a professor in psychology at Guelph University, with years of experience working with autistic children. She had directed the autism clinic for young children at The Clarke Institute of Psychiatry from 1974–1991, an opportunity for Julian we had not been able to access. Now our paths were crossing. We'd invited her to clinically assess Julian's ability and potential after being on Dr. Huggins' regimen. I'd been showing her Julian's water-colors that he'd done copying my own work, doing "parallel painting." His portrait of the cat I thought remarkable, with its bright glowing orange strokes and menacing eyes so different from the old repetitive robotic self-portraits he'd always done in his journals.

She wrote in her summary: "Julian is high-functioning by all accounts, in that he can respond to almost all the items on the WISC sub-scales, which many individuals who are high-functioning in the nonverbal domain cannot manage at all, a remarkable strength."

We had just wanted to know for ourselves, *was there any improvement?* We wanted to hear a professional say it, and she did: yes, yes, yes.

Facing page: The top photo shows a drawing of Julian's before starting treatment with Dr. Huggins and being prescribed Risperdol. At the bottom, is the painting of the cat mentioned above, 1996.

My Sad Is All Gone

Forty

The real test was still how well Julian learned to cope with stress, especially the perceived threat, in his mind, from teenagers or little boys out in the community.

Amazingly he began to develop strategies.

I was driving along one day when Julian began cupping his eyes with his hands as he sat beside me.

"What are you doing, Jules?" I kept my eye on the road, but was fascinated. Julian had his head turned away from the window, still sheltering his face.

"Nothing, Mom! Nothing!" *(Don't ask.)*

I noticed the group of young, noisy high school students strolling along the sidewalk as we flashed by. Julian was hiding himself from them! He'd figured that as long as he hid his eyes they would not notice him, and he was out of danger, much like a little child. But they'd not noticed him in the first place, nor were interested in him, something he could not grasp. Yet it was ingenious what he'd figured out to do, and instinctive.

Again, walking through Port Credit one evening Julian suddenly veered off the pavement and started walking along someone's lawn to avoid a couple of children approaching down the sidewalk, some as young as six. No matter he was tramping over someone's flowerbed. This weird off-course behavior only served to draw their very attention to him, but again he could not see that. If he wasn't directly in their path then they couldn't see him!

He seemed to have a sixth sense what boys to fear. He did not mind passing calm older teenagers, seventeen year olds strolling out of high school with their sports bags. The ones he dreaded were the young pre-teenagers and small boys, perhaps because they were noisy and bickering and quarrelsome as they went their way. The exception was McDonald's. Julian always seemed to feel utterly unthreatened at the cozy prospect of a Big Mac and fries, whoever was around!

Dr. Huggins laughed as we related this. We looked again at Julian down the hall still leafing quietly through magazines, marvelling at the twist of fate in time that had brought us together that August day in 1993. Dr. Huggins had helped Julian so much over the years, but Julian had also helped Dr. Huggins as "O.J.," "Case Study #1," often enabling Dr. Huggins to refine his methodology. Of course, we knew we were just one of hundreds of cases involved, but we had been with Dr. Huggins from the beginning on this strange long journey through turbulent seas and unchartered territory of the mind and soul.

It has been ten years since we began Julian on Dr. Huggins' protocols. We would have loved not to have had to turn to medication. If only Christ could have come along as in ancient times and laid his hands on Jules, *"Thy faith hath made thee whole . . . "* But was not Dr. Huggins' formula for Julian, the essence of his approach to medication, in the end, when all was said and done, the ultimate expression of compassion — and a certain courage? Dr. Huggins had risked much. Perhaps he was not to be world-famous after all, only ever the humble dedicated human being he was. "I could not turn my back on this small, but very significant part of my medical practice," he'd once written. Risperdal was not perfect. There was no such thing as the "perfect" behavior drug — *"There ain't no such animal!"* Dr. Huggins would aver. But surely of everything out there this was the best anyone could offer for now, given human error.

For there must always needs be that "bridging" that he often spoke of, the "transition zone" existing between the obsessive driven mental states and reality; a wondrous place of great sorrow and anguish, of loneliness and regret, but also of great redemption and forgiveness, love incandescent, where our children and not least ourselves, with our many human frailties and weaknesses, do surely walk.

"Is this me as a baby, Mom?"

Julian held out a photo of himself at six months. He'd got out the family albums again that were now "his," a new obsession that showed a new emerging awareness of himself. The heavy faded albums went back to 1972, the year of Polly's birth.

With a jolt I see baby Julian in the photo in a bubbly wooly hat and jacket, nestled in my arms. His eyes are thickly lashed fringing his cheeks.

"Yes, that's you as a baby, Jules."

Julian waits expectantly, holding on to the photo. He seems to want some verification from me, some memory, perhaps some memory of him?

"You were a beautiful baby."

Had I ever told him that as a baby? I'm shocked. I realize I'd always been bent over him anxiously, my face puckered, tense, wondering what was wrong with him.

He's watching my face intently for some sign, some clue, of my love, my satisfaction with him?

"Very beautiful, Jules, the most beautiful baby in the world, and Mommy loved you very much."

I catch him often now fingering the photos on my desk. Himself at seven trying to catch guppies in the creek, at fourteen at a Halloween dance at school . . . the ones of Granpa and Granma in the garden in Willowdale, Granpa slumped in the deck chair half asleep, beer in hand . . . of himself and me, our arms stiffly entwined in the Adirondacks; he's fifteen, drawn, too thin, anxious, tensing at the camera . . . Jules looks at the snapshot a long time. How much does he remember of those broken years?

"Dad, are there roads up there?"

Jules points to the sky. Thin wispy clouds stray overhead. Seagulls soar. They careen and swoon on invisible waves over Port Credit.

"How do the seagulls know where to go, Dad?"

"Well, I guess there are sort of roads up there that only they can see," said Alec slowly.

"And Granpa's up there? Up in heaven?"

"Uh-huh, er, yes, sort of."

"Granpa has roads up there in heaven too, doesn't he, Dad? So he knows where to walk." Julian smiled contentedly.

"Rascal!" he chuckled.

Julian Orchard, 2004, age 27.

Lucky Press, LLC Order Form

Quantity	Title	Price (US)	Total
	The Bloody War, Mate: A Novel of World War II London	16.95	
	Notes from Ohio: Essays and Stories by Bryce Merlin (published with a grant from the Ohio Arts Council)	6.00	
	I was POISONED by my body . . . The Odyssey of a Doctor Who Reversed Fibromyalgia, Leaky Gut Syndrome and Multiple Chemical Sensitivity—Naturally! (in its 6th printing)	18.95	
	Pain/Inflammation Matters: Recipes for Life The first in the "Designing Health, Naturally" series	11.95	
	The Circuit: The True Story of a Policewoman's Journey from the Streets of London into the Dangerous World of Covert Operations	14.95	
	Magical Story: A Teenager's Inspiring Battle with Hodgkin's Disease	12.95	
	My Sad Is All Gone: A Family's Triumph over Violent Autism	18.00	
	The Pigeons and the Witch Doctor: Adventures of a Modern Mapmaker	16.95	
	They Called Me Beautiful: The Classic Story of a Dog's Search for Love and the Family that Rescued Him (From the true story, *Beautiful Joe,* by Marshall Saunders)	10.95	
	What Saved Me: A Dozen Ways to Embrace Life (Subject: parenting disabled child/divorce)	6.95	
	Wham! Bam! Publishing: A Strategic Marketing Plan for Authors and Publishers	10.00	
	"Will Turner's Flight Logs" Series: (historical fiction/aviation)		
	The Aviator's Apprentice (Part One)	18.95	
	Turner's Flight (Part Two)	18.95	
	The Pledge of the Three: The Z.O. Chronicles, Part One	8..95	
	With Our Own Eyes: Eyewitnesses to the Disappearance of Amelia Earhart	14.95	
	Subtotal		
	Ohio residents add 7 % sales tax		
	Shipping ($3.95 for the first book and $2.00 for each additional book)		
	TOTAL		

This order form is for shipping within the United States and Canada only.

Mail this form to and your check or money order (U.S. funds only) to: Lucky Press, LLC, 126 South Maple St., Lancaster, OH 43130

Name: _____

Street: _____

City:_____State:_____ ZIP: _____

E-mail:_____

Thank you for your order. Please allow two weeks for delivery. If you have any questions or concerns, contact books@luckypress.com. To order by credit card, visit www.luckypress.com.

7766429R0

Made in the USA
Lexington, KY
13 December 2010